SUPERWRECK

SUPERWRECK

Amoco *Cadiz:*
The Shipwreck
That Had to Happen

RUDOLPH CHELMINSKI

William Morrow and Company, Inc.   New York

Library of Congress Cataloging-in-Publication Data

Chelminski, Rudolph.
  Superwreck: Amoco Cadiz: the shipwreck that had to
happen.

  Includes index.
  1. Amoco Cadiz (Ship) 2. Shipwrecks—France—
Brittany. 3. Oil spills—France—Brittany. I. Title.
G530.A235C48 1987   944'.1   86-23831
ISBN 0-688-06954-1

Printed in the United States of America

First Edition

1 2 3 4 5 6 7 8 9 10

BOOK DESIGN BY MARY GREGORY

Dedicated to my wife, Brien. Naturally.

Contents

Acknowledgments

This book took its start from an article I wrote in 1978 for *The Reader's Digest*. First thanks, therefore, go to Dimi Panitza—scourge of writers, the Genghis Khan of EEO—who had the idea in the first place.

As the project developed, I bothered a number of lawyers for information, interviews, and documents. My primary victims were Christian Huglo, Barry Kingham, and Peter Wolrich (Côtes-du-Nord); Joseph Haller (Republic of France); Joseph C. Smith (PIL); Frank Cicero (Amoco); and Michael A. Snyder (Bugsier).

I also imposed upon my colleagues in journalism: Richard Longworth (*Chicago Tribune*); Alan Rusbridger (*The Guardian*, London); Paul Burel (*Ouest France*, Nantes); Eckard Presler (*Der Stern*, Hamburg); and especially Flora Johnson (*Chicago Lawyer*), who helped a lot more than she had to.

Among the academics who generously gave of their time and knowledge, I owe special thanks to Claude Chassé, Yveline Le Moal, and Richard Congar, Université de Bretagne Occidentale; Guy Bodenec and Laurent d'Ozouville, CNEXO; and Prof. Charles Krance, University of Chicago (CUEH).

Public servants of various categories who helped time and again were Paul K. Remias, Deputy Clerk, U.S. District Court for the Northern District of Illinois; Roger Kohn, IMO London; Messieurs Leborgne and Chaput, Radio le Conquet; Commissaire Paul Kerdiles of the Prefecture Maritime of the Second Region, Brest;

Yannick Ropers, UVLOE, Brest; Capitaine de Corvette René Martin, Aeronavale, Dax; Francois Buge, Agence Judiciare du Trésor, Paris; Senateur-Maire Alphonse Arzel, Ploudalmezeau; and above all, Jules Legendre of Portsall, the man who took the brunt of the pollution and my demanding presence.

I also owe thanks to several others: Carl Meyerdirk, director of media relations for Standard Oil, Chicago; Kenneth Sheehan, vice-president and spokesman for the American Bureau of Shipping, New York; Captain Uwe Jantzen, Bugsier, Hamburg; the several salvage specialists for Smit Tak, who received me aboard their ships in Bantry Bay; Captain David Bruce of the Liberian Bureau of Maritime Affairs, London; Captain Robert Prigent and Mme. Ginette Ravaleu, Bretons who still bear the scars of *Bételgeuse;* and finally, by far the most important of all, the formidable Mr. Gordon Victory, gentleman, poet, and technical expert, whose agreement at the outset to check my facts on the engineering side gave me the heart to start.

SUPERWRECK

1.

The Omen

Thursday, March 16, 1978. The supertanker Amoco *Cadiz,* 334 meters long and 51 wide, was battering her way northward through heavy seas, rain squalls, and force-eight winds at the upper end of the Bay of Biscay, sailing a course that would take her just to the west of the peninsula of Brittany, into the mouth of the English Channel, and then across into the shelter of Lyme Bay, on England's southern coast. Silver-gray on her flanks and bright orange on her deck, she lay as low in the water as a laden river barge—which, in many respects, is precisely what she was, although immeasurably larger and adapted for ocean navigation. Two thirds of her immense bulk was under water as she ploughed onward, but in spite of her tremendous size—upended, she would have stood higher than all but the world's five highest skyscrapers and would have considerably dominated the Eiffel Tower—she rolled and pitched heavily in the deteriorating weather, and the steeply raked flare of her bow plunged deeply into the swell, right where the red, white, and blue company logo was painted. Aft, just ahead of the red, white, and blue smokestack, also decorated with the company logo, the white accommodation block sat on the main deck like a six-story sugar cube, from which two steel wings, or walkways, split off to either side of the big ship. At the top level, inside the wheelhouse of the bridge deck, the seaman on duty was having to concentrate hard to keep her on a straight line, giving his helm a general correction of five degrees to starboard in order to counteract a pronounced and persistent yaw that was tending to drive the bow to port. Everyone agreed later that it was about as bad weather as they had ever navigated in, but not even hurricane seas could have resisted the fantastic inertia behind Amoco *Cadiz*'s graceful bow: 220,000 tons of crude oil lying in fifteen cargo compartments plus a further 45,000 or so of the deadweight of the ship alone and 4,000 tons of bunker fuel for a total of well over a quarter of a million tons, pushing inexorably forward at nine knots.

But of course the sea is not passive; it counterattacks perpetually and, in the long run, effectively. At 0600, when the first niggardly light of a decidedly inhospitable dawn was beginning to brighten the horizon, two notable things happened: Pasquale Bardari, the ship's thirty-five-year-old skipper, gave up trying to sleep after a night of insomnia; and the waves, which had been hurling themselves up against the poop deck with the encouragement of a quartering wind, wrested several forty-gallon drums of spare lubrication oil free of their lashings and sent them clattering around the rear of the ship in a viciously unpredictable dance. No sooner had Captain Bardari arrived on the bridge than he ordered engine speed reduced to 75 RPM and turned the ship to port until she was heading due west, almost directly into the teeth of the gale. Now the seas exploded and geysered against the bow, and green water coursed liberally over the main deck, but the poop deck aft of the accommodation block was relatively sheltered from the weather. Chief mate Rosario Strano and chief engineer Salvatore Melito got a work crew together and spent the next ninety minutes chasing the errant steel barrels over the slick, red deck, running a jerky obstacle course between bitts, bollards, winches, and all the other obtrusive paraphernalia common to working vessels. The chore was not without danger—the drums were teased one way by the ship's roll, another by the wind and then, as often as not, knocked off onto a third track when water washed aboard—but by 0730 they had everything lashed and secured and shipshape. Captain Bardari put the ship's nose northeast once again, signaled the engine room to increase revolutions to 87 RPM, and told quartermaster Cosmo De Nichilo to hold a course of 039 gyro. Soon they would be passing to the west of the French island of Ouessant, and then a little traffic-dodging across the Channel would bring them home to Lyme Bay. It was the last day of their six-week trip since loading in the Persian Gulf. As they changed to dry clothes in their cabins, Strano and Melito may have permitted themselves small smiles of satisfaction for a rough job over and done with, a danger overcome. They could not possibly suspect that what they took for a kind of victory was in fact only the beginning of the worst day of their lives. It was not a triumph, but an omen.

2.

Prelude:
Kharg Island to Ouessant

Pasquale Bardari was a young captain on a young man's ship. At only thirty-five, he was already the oldest command officer aboard the Amoco *Cadiz,* with the sole exception of Salvatore Catanese, a thirty-eight-year-old second-assistant engineer. The rest of his forty-man crew, all Italian like himself, averaged about age thirty, but for the most part appeared scarcely older than teenagers. The ship's Methuselah was radio officer Alfio Muscuso, positively a case for the old folks' home at forty-eight. They were typical of the computer-age's new breed of sailors, far more technicians than tars, institute-trained specialists who signed up for six months aboard ship followed by three months off, who performed utterly unromantic jobs that differed little from similar work in factory or office ashore, and who habitually said right and left instead of starboard and port, bed instead of bunk, downstairs instead of below. As servants of VLCCs (Very Large Crude Carriers), the largest moving things ever built until they, in turn, were supplanted by the monstrous ULCCs (Ultra Large Crude Carriers, which can weigh more than half a million dead weight tons or dwt), these men could expect to live in individual, private cabins, each with its toilet and shower; to enjoy three hot meals a day turned out by a professional cook and prepared according to their wishes (being an "Italian" ship, Amoco *Cadiz* had a special flour and pasta room built into her galley); to work in clean and healthy conditions, dry and warm in the winter and air conditioned in the summer, in all but rare occasions perfectly insulated from the real weather and the sea; to ride an elevator between the decks, a bit of modernism that was more sensible than luxurious aboard the Amoco *Cadiz*, since the distance from bridge to bilge was close to fifty meters; to be able to watch films and television in their free time, hear pop music on hi-fi in their lounge, play Ping-Pong or, weather and work permitting, sun themselves next to the swimming pool. So precise were the duties aboard the Amoco *Cadiz* that some men signed aboard as day workers only, and were not obliged to stand watches. Officers enjoyed the privilege of inviting their wives aboard for certain of the trips, if they so desired. There was, in fact, one woman, Franca Strano, the chief mate's wife, aboard the Amoco *Cadiz* that morning as dawn broke over the entrance to the English Channel.

This was the first time that Pasquale Bardari had sailed aboard Amoco *Cadiz* as master, although he had already commanded several other ships of the same sort, including the *Cadiz*'s "identical twins," Amoco *Milford Haven* and Amoco *Europa*. These ships, along with the Amoco *Singapore,* formed a series of four VLCCs that Standard Oil of Indiana, the Chicago-based parent company, had decided to acquire in the late sixties, after the Six-Day War closed the Suez Canal and suddenly made mastodon-sized tankers seem like an attractive economic proposition, with their ability to carry great quantities of crude oil on the 10,000-mile route from the Persian Gulf, around the southern tip of Africa, and up into the northern industrialized countries, where it was sorely needed—especially in Western Europe, which imported something like ninety-five percent of its oil. All four of the ships, identified as hulls 93, 94, 95, and 96, had been ordered, after the usual competitive bidding, from Astilleros Espanoles, S.A., Spain's most important shipbuilders, a government-controlled company with yards in Cadiz. Amoco Tankers, the subsidiary company formed for the express purpose of these acquisitions, took delivery of the ships and sold them in turn to the Amoco Transport Company, the registered owner. (At a handy paper profit, it might be added: Amoco Tankers paid $23,600,000 for *Cadiz*, for example, and sold her to Transport for $27,630,000.) Amoco *Cadiz* was officially handed over to her proud owners at 3:30 P.M. on May 11, 1974, and she had been on the Persian Gulf run ever since, on charter hire to the Shell International Petroleum Company, at a fee of $28,000 a day. As a result, the oil on top of which Pasquale Bardari and his crew members were riding that March morning belonged not to Amoco, but to Shell. Bardari was, in effect, the truck driver.

He had joined the ship on January 30, leaving his wife and two-year-old son behind in his native town of Pizzo, a little port on the Tyrrhenian Sea south of Naples. A flight to Dubai, an offshore rendezvous by supply ship, and he came aboard the empty, high-riding vessel as relief master. Loading, as usual in the Persian Gulf, was quick, efficient, and tediously businesslike, a matter for pipelines, high-pressure pumps, and automation. A comparison of this unlovely spot to an oversized superhighway filling-station complex would not be altogether inaccurate. At Ras Tanura, on the tip of a peninsula on the eastern shore of Saudi Arabia, and then across the gulf to the Iranian loading island called Kharg, a desolate patch of sand that two hundred years ago had been a pirates' repair but under the Shah became famous as the world's largest oil terminal (and later became even more renowned as an explosive bone of contention in the interminable war between Iran and Iraq), the Amoco *Cadiz* swilled her fill of crude: 98,460.32 long tons of Arabian Light at Ras Tanura, 121,157 of Iranian Light at Kharg island. As tugs inched her away from the loading point at Kharg, through an anchored flock of sister VLCCs, everything around the tanker was a persistent reminder of the modern world's apparently insatiable appetite for oil: the other ships, the iridescence of the permanent oil slick through which she moved, the sticky film of oil on her decks, the nauseating, gassy odor of oil particles suspended in a motionless, humid haze around them, the extra lube oil stashed astern, the 4,000 extra tons of bunker oil carried below decks for the greater mechanical pleasure of the giant, eight-cylinder Burmeister & Wain diesel, whose 30,400 horses afforded her a theoretical top service speed of 16.1 knots.

On February 8, the Amoco *Cadiz* "turned the corner" at the Omanese headland of Ras al Hadd, exchanging the stifling heat of the Persian Gulf for the cool turbulence of the Indian Ocean, heading southward on the long journey toward the tip of Africa at the Cape of Good Hope, where she would finally turn northward again, bound for Europe. It was the old routine, the beginning of another milk run.

Pasquale Bardari and the men he commanded were all Italians for the same reason that the American-owned boat that constituted their universe had been built in Spain and flew the red, white, and blue banner with the single star of the Republic of Liberia: It was cheaper that way. The realities of corporate economics, even in a field as awesomely profitable as the oil business, dictate cost-effectiveness at every turning, and it does not require a genius to discover (1) that a boat can be built for less money in Spain than in America, (2) that if the West African nation of Liberia is not exactly tax-free, it is a double-dandy fiscal haven compared to the developed nations of Europe and America, and (3) that almost anyone in the world will work for a lower salary than Americans. As a result of these realities, the registered owner of the Amoco *Cadiz* was the Amoco Transport Company, a Liberian Corporation with headquarters in Hamilton, Bermuda (Post Office Box 1435, to be exact), rather than its parent company, Standard Oil of Indiana, whose offices are located in the Standard Oil Building, 200 East Randolph Drive in Chicago. Further complicating an already complicated picture was the fact that the ship's operator was neither Standard Oil nor Amoco Tankers nor Amoco Transport but Amoco International Limited, a Delaware corporation with its principal place of business in Chicago. (There is even more complication available here, for you amateurs of the corporate shell game: Amoco Transport was owned on a shared basis by Amoco International Limited and Amoco International, S.A., of Switzerland, both of which were wholly owned by Amoco International Finance Corporation.) There is nothing illegal in such juridical legerdemain, any more than there is in the numbered Swiss bank accounts or the Liechtenstein or Monaco shelters that keep so many profits dry and tax-free these days, or the businesses registered on the moon, which may be coming someday in the future. But it does make for curious situations, like the fact that Liberia, with a total population of less than two million, a literacy rate of twenty-five percent, and a remarkable paucity of master mariners, boasts the world's largest merchant fleet, if you take the flag of registration at face value. Second is Japan, third Great Britain, fourth Panama (another "flag of convenience" country), and fifth the United States. It will come as no surprise to most readers to learn that America's biggest and best commercial ships are registered in Monrovia.

Italians work for less than Americans, as do the Chinese, Indians, Pakistanis, Indonesians, Koreans, and the other even more exotic personnel commonly found as crews on Liberian ships, but this does not necessarily mean that they are incompetent or that their ships are substandard. On the contrary, independent studies have proven time and again that the VLCCs and ULCCs of the Liberian fleet, especially those owned by oil companies, as the Amoco *Cadiz* was, are in general newer and better-equipped than the world's average, fully satisfy international safety standards, and have lower than average accident rates. (The same cannot be said of the smaller and older ships of Liberian registration, or of the famous and scandalous "one-ship fleets" by which many shipowners, especially Greek, commonly limit their potential liability, but that is another question.) Moreover, in this particular case, Amoco boasted a solid reputation within the industry as a quality outfit that regularly invested in the most sophisticated navigational and safety devices. Amoco spokesmen often used the figure of $1 million when enumerating the cost of the additional safety equipment that the company had voluntarily installed on *Cadiz,* without being under any obligation to do so. From that aspect, Standard Oil of Indiana can scarcely be criticized. The company fulfilled its international obligations to the letter, and even beyond.

In the wake of the disaster that befell the Amoco *Cadiz* on March 16, 1978, an enormous amount of spurious and misdirected criticism was aimed at Standard Oil, especially in France, and mostly based on denunciations of flags of convenience. All the noise made in this direction served only to obscure the deeper and truer reasons for which the company could legitimately be taken to task—reasons that are as fundamental and important as they are difficult to clearly define. They have to do with a philosophy of corporate existence that is rarely spoken in so many words but is reflected a thousand times a day in every aspect of life within the Standard Oil empire—as it is within the structure of any other huge business enterprise. The drive to strive and succeed, to work better and faster than the competition in order to offer a more attractive product, is at the very heart of the American business ethic, and millions of intelligent men and women devote the greater part of their waking hours to a passionate pursuit of this ethic. But it is all too easy, when the race to succeed becomes obsession, to cast aside good judgment in the quest for limiting expenses and increasing efficiency. A vast army of business-school graduates, each one smarter and more ambitious than the last, continually hones cost-effectiveness into a minor American art form. Within Standard Oil of Indiana, the corporate pressures resulting from this approach—the real ones as well as the imagined ones—had a lot more to do with the wrecking of the Amoco *Cadiz* than flags of convenience, as we shall see later. For the moment, though, it is enough to repeat the incongruity of the situation: a Spanish-built VLCC, owned by Americans and staffed by Italians. It is a crystalline demonstration of economic realpolitik.

Not that there is anything wrong with Italian sailors. Anyone tempted to take that line of reasoning might do well to remember the date 1492 and the nationality of the man traditionally credited with discovering America. As they set course south from the Persian Gulf that February 8, Pasquale Bardari and his fellow officers legitimately could have been described as overqualified, by the normal yardstick of the trade. All of them were graduates of internationally sanctioned nautical schools; all had passed through the normal channels of apprenticeship; and all held the requisite licenses and certificates. Requisite and even better: Of the five deck officers, three—the captain, chief mate Strano, and second mate Cosmo Vaudo—held master's tickets; of the six engineering officers, no fewer than four held chief engineer's licenses. There aren't many ships anywhere with that sort of excess of trained talent.

Qualified Italians are cheaper sailors than Americans though, and that is what interested Standard Oil of Indiana. At the time that Captain Bardari and his men were on their last voyage aboard the Amoco *Cadiz*, an all-Italian crew, with the captain the top earner at around $1,750 a month, would have cost the parent company approximately $700,000 a year, while the same number of similarly competent Americans would have fetched $1.7 million. The conclusion was obvious: for equal qualification, you choose an Italian crew. Or an Indonesian one or a Pakistani one or a Korean one or what have you. A dollar, as the old truth goes, is a dollar, especially when you've got a boardroom of expensive executives to pay for, drawing salaries upwards of a quarter of a million dollars per year per head.

The relationship between Pasquale Bardari and his American employers had not always been an easy one, or harmonious. A graduate of the Italian Nautical Institute in Pisa, he had served for a few idyllic years first as a deck cadet and then as officer on the beautiful passenger ships of the Italian Lines, learning the trade like a gentleman in his splendid white uniform. The changeover to the workaday world of tankers became inevitable when, in the mid-sixties, jetliners irretrievably replaced the great steamers. He hitched his destiny to Standard Oil in March of 1970, when he began employment as second mate aboard the Amoco *Baltimore,* a tanker of

38,714 gross registered tons. With the years he worked his way up to chief mate and finally master on a number of Amoco ships, but compared to the Italian Lines, it was a harsh and extremely demanding new environment for him. His very first performance record, signed by Captain Serra of the *Baltimore*, rated him as above average in the categories of dependability and sobriety, but only average for the rest: quality of work, leadership, personality, and experience in present position. At the end of the report, Captain Serra remarked tersely: "He needs more experience."

More experience came aboard Amoco *Brisbane* and Amoco *Cremona* before Bardari was finally promoted to master of the *Brisbane* in 1974, but he did not always leave a favorable impression with his superiors in the company. While consistently rating above average for sobriety and dependability—he was obviously a serious young man, and a hard worker—his marks in the other categories fluctuated, and his future with the company sometimes appeared dangerously compromised. In August of 1971, for example, the General Summary of Capability from his Officer Fitness Report presented him as only average in every category, ending with the recommendation: "Unsatisfactory—not to be rehired." In December of the same year, something of a personal nadir, everything was average and below average, except for the categories of initiative and ingenuity, personal advancement initiative, and departmental maintenance, where he was judged to be simply unsatisfactory.

They weren't easy years. In 1972, as chief mate of Amoco *Brisbane*, the average and below average marks continued to stalk him. A special problem was with his command of the English language and, even more telling, the classical guideposts by which commanders of ships have always been judged: leadership and handling of men. Desperately, frustratingly, his marks here continued to be below average. On December 31, 1972, the captain of Amoco *Cremona* noted that he still needed experience and improvement, adding: "Compared with his last assignment on Amoco *Brisbane*, Mr. Bardari appears to be slightly improved in capabilities, however still far from being a 'complete' officer." A handwritten note added to the report in Chicago echoed the doubt that obviously clung to the aspiring young officer in the opinion of his superiors: "Will keep on for this year. He may not have potential to go further in Amoco. This is his second time as chief mate."

In 1973, things finally began to improve. In April of that year, all categories remained average except English (below average), but the written evaluation was much better: "We noted a good improvement in Mr. Bardari's capabilities during the last months. We believe he can be taken under observation for eventual promotion." Now he was finding his way within the company. By November of 1973, as chief mate aboard Amoco *Brisbane*, his marks were all average or superior. At the beginning of the following year, he was promoted to master. Now he was the one who would be doing the grading.

At the beginning of this, his first and last voyage aboard the Amoco *Cadiz*, he had been in the employ of the Amoco Transport Company for eight years, and a captain for four. By theory and tradition, he was "sole master under God" of this gigantic vessel, bigger by far than any battleship or aircraft carrier commanded by any World War II admiral, bigger than Lord Nelson's entire fleet at Trafalgar, and in fact his enemy's fleet, and their combined size, too—but in spite of all this, Captain Bardari was little more than a cipher in the books of Standard Oil, and probably only a handful of executives in the Standard Oil Building knew him personally. Within a few weeks, though, everyone within the corporate structure of Standard Oil would know the name Pasquale Bardari and the trial that fate put him through. And many, many more people would be wondering who really was in charge of the Amoco *Cadiz*.

The trip began uneventfully, like all the others before it. The only ripple in the monotony of the ride down the East African coast was two days of fairly rough weather between Durban and Cape Town. At the Cape, the Amoco *Cadiz* stopped just long enough for a supply ship to bring fresh provisions out to her, and on February 21, she turned north for the passage up the other side of Africa. Pure routine again. And anyone searching for portents would have been hard-pressed to see the hand of malevolent destiny in the broken movie projector or the fact that the Magnavox Satellite Navigation Receiver was out of service. It mattered little: their route was as firmly established as a superhighway, and there were plenty of backup aids, radars, lorans, Deccas, and the like. After all, on an up-to-date VLCC everything was doubled or tripled, wasn't it? Redundancy of equipment meant that any breakdown was supposed to be immediately cured, or at least palliated, by a backup system. That's the way computer-age design is supposed to work: every eventuality calculated. The Amoco *Cadiz*, from all outside appearances, was a superb, modern ship, barely four years old, a good example of state-of-the-art VLCC technology, equipped as excellently as any other tanker of her size and age might be. She was officially classified Maltese Cross A1E Oil Carrier: top marks from the American Bureau of Shipping, the certification society that had watched over every detail of her construction. Astilleros Espanoles, S.A., was just as proud of her as it was of her sister ships.

Angling up toward Europe in the South Atlantic, the big tanker was averaging only 11.5 knots, a fuel-saving rate of slow steaming that was considerably off her top speed of more than sixteen knots. There was a problem with the air cooler for the main engine's supercharger, but it was hardly a cause for anyone's concern. VLCCs are so complex that there are always bound to be bugs.

When he had loaded in the Persian Gulf, Captain Bardari's orders were to deliver his cargo directly to Europoort, the modern industrial harbor built on the polders between the English Channel and old Rotterdam, and connected by canal to the Rhine. On March 9, however, as he was skirting the bulge of West Africa, he received a radio message from Amoco directing him to proceed first to Lyme Bay for lightering, and thence to Europoort. Lyme Bay is an almost perfectly circular bight in the pleasant Dorset coast of southern England, roughly between Weymouth and Torquay, and in recent years it has become a gathering place of predilection for the VLCC crowd. Offering both deep-water anchorage and protection from bad weather, as well as unbeatable proximity to several of Western Europe's most important crude discharge points, the bay has assumed the unlikely role of a kind of maritime parking lot for laden tankers whose draft is too great for their other destinations. The lightering operation, by which smaller tankers come alongside to draw off the fifty, seventy, or hundred thousand tons that will ease their keels high enough for their next stops, is now something of a local specialty at Lyme Bay.

So Lyme Bay it was. All right. No problem. Captain Bardari and his officers knew it well, as did most professional VLCC men. But first there was a little pickup to be made off the Canaries, the Spanish island group lying some sixty miles off the coast of southern Morocco. Early on the morning of March 11, a helicopter buzzed up from the airport at Las Palmas and headed out to sea for a rendez-vous with the Amoco *Cadiz*. It was a typical VLCC maneuver, again dictated by the economics of cost-efficiency. Until recent times, sailors on even the larger merchant ships would earn a break and a change of air from the constricted monotony of sea life by visits to ports, whether for cargo delivery, crew changes, or purchase of provisions. The monstrous tankers of today, though, are both too big for most ports and too expensive for dawdling. Like jet airplanes, they must be kept in virtually constant rotation to earn their keep, and loading and unloading is handled with remarkable speed and efficiency at pump terminals far from land. There was no question for Captain Bardari of coming in to Las Palmas, or even stopping his ship in the water. The helicopter landed on the Amoco *Cadiz* as she was moving, angling in past the bridge and neatly settling down on the big "H" inside a white circle traced above number two tank on the starboard bow. Three passengers emerged, toting their bags and instinctively ducking as the chopper rose up again and leaned back in toward shore.

Franca Strano, the chief mate's wife, was flanked by two men as she hurried up the deck to the white-railed walkway that led back toward the accommodation block. The first one, Antonio Assante, thirty-five, jolly, roly-poly, and voluble, was well-known to most of the *Cadiz*'s crew. Like Captain Bardari, he had been with Amoco for eight years, and was coming aboard now as relief chief engineer, under Amoco's excellent doubling-up program. Just as Captain Bardari had been relief master from Dubai to Ras Tanura and Kharg island, where he finally took over command, Assante was coming aboard at Las Palmas to work as a supernumerary alongside chief engineer Salvatore Melito during the last six days of the trip, refamiliarizing himself with the *Cadiz* and its machinery, conferring on particular problems (that air cooler would have to be taken care of), and meeting any machinists, firemen, oilers, or assistant engineers he didn't know already. Faces lit up in the engine control room in the bottom of the ship when Assante appeared. He was a knowledgeable and hard-working professional, but beyond that he was also a man of good cheer whose mere presence seemed to brighten up the atmosphere. Like most Italians, Assante was an optimist by nature. In contrast, Melito, the man whom he would relieve after Lyme Bay, was somewhat more dour, wearing the nervous smile of the chronic worrier.

The second arrival was a big, black-bearded Englishman who looked like a nineteenth-century drawing of the archetypal sailor. In fact, there was even more to the resemblance than that. It took most people a moment's thought to realize where they had seen him before, because they were sure they had, and then it came—Captain Haddock! The man looked like he had just stepped out of the pages of a *Tintin* adventure. The only thing missing was the bottle of whiskey that Hergé's master mariner always kept within close range. Lesley John Maynard, forty-one, was employed as an inspector by a London-based company called Marine Safety Services, an agency specializing in on-ship safety training. Subscribers to the MSS program, including Amoco, welcomed Mr. Maynard and his colleagues aboard their ships to conduct surveys and check the condition of fire extinguishers, rescue equipment, lifeboats, breathing and resuscitation apparatus, and all the other ancillary gear that could make the difference between life and death aboard a VLCC, should an emergency arise. Further, Mr. Maynard's duties included lecturing and drilling the crew on the care and maintenance of their equipment. With his direct, hearty manner and no-nonsense talk, Maynard, a diver and salvage expert who had worked his way up in the ranks of the Royal Navy to the grade of lieutenant before going to work for MSS, was a perfect choice for man-to-man contact with the *Cadiz*'s crew. Officers and men listened with interest and respect to his lectures. Very quickly, a bond of friendliness grew between him and Captain Bardari. Before long, it would turn into true camaraderie.

As often happens with friends, the two were quite different. Shorter than Maynard, and slighter of frame, Pasquale Bardari was as soft-spoken and reserved as the Englishman was bluff and straightforward. Physically, he bore a vague resemblance to Dustin Hoffman or Al Pacino. Like Melito, he was a worrier, constantly concerned about the million details of running a VLCC. The two men complemented each other well, and that relationship was about to be put to a test far more severe than either of them could have imagined. It was most poignantly ironic that Maynard was a safety expert, considering the ultimate fate of the Amoco *Cadiz*.

The oil that concerned them both, the sixty-eight million gallons of "black gold" in the cargo tanks below their feet, belonged to two companies of the Shell group, Shell U.K. Limited and Shell Nederland Raffianderij B.V., which affords us the chance of once more playing the game of listing the multinational permutations involved in this case: a Spanish-built and American-owned boat, crewed by Italians but flying the Liberian flag, carrying Saudi Arabian and Iranian oil on behalf of a Dutch company while an English safety expert looked on. Very soon the French would be involved, and some Germans, too.

After Las Palmas, the weather gradually deteriorated. March 12, 13, and 14 passed routinely enough, although the heavier seas were beginning to dispute the passage of the big ship, and she no longer rode with the majestic calm and smoothness of her run through the South Atlantic. The only event of any great note was Cosmo Vaudo's birthday on the thirteenth. The second mate was suitably toasted with Italian wine in the officers' dining room that evening, and was suitably ragged about being an old man now that he had turned thirty. As they sat back in their lounge enjoying tiny cups of espresso coffee after their four-course dinner, the officers may have been forgiven if they ever, even for the briefest moment, forgot that they were mariners and that they were traveling over a worsening sea. Just so, a lookout or a helmsman up on the quiet, spacious bridge on any one of those days could have succumbed to tingling intimations of invincibility after hours of gazing at the graceful bulwarks of the Amoco *Cadiz*'s bow, nearly a thousand feet in front of him, slamming through the biggest waves it could find. Just so, an engineer or an oiler, standing in the hot shadow of the Burmeister & Wain diesel that towered five stories above him, his head filled with its roar and his body shaking with vibrations from its titanic power, could be forgiven if ever he felt suffused with a kind of supernatural strength by association with all this mechanical might, as if it imparted mastery over the elements themselves.

It is normal. Human beings tend to identify with their surroundings, and today's supertankers are so huge, so comfortable, so modern in conception and equipment, so apparently impervious to outside forces that it is difficult to believe that anything could happen to them: *To imagine fragility.* Lulled into a caution-dulling sense of security by simple size, gulled by the common misapprehension that science and technology have dominated or parried the caprices of nature, VLCC crews are prime candidates for that most human and most fatal of weaknesses, so dear to authors of Greek tragedy: hubris. It is too easy to forget, when you are sipping champagne or playing cards inside a passenger jet, that there are only a few millimeters of aluminum between you and nothingness. Or that a little loose wire inside the guts of a smoothly running car can leave you helplessly stranded. Or that automatic elevators can fail. Just so, it is possible for a sailor to forget that his mighty VLCC in reality is nothing more than a bloated and underpowered oilpot, with a house on one end and a little bitty propellor behind it. For all its apparent magnificence, Amoco *Cadiz* was just a barge.

To Captain Bardari's credit, it should be said that there is very little chance that he let himself forget reality that way. Although he had never been in serious trouble, he had been at sea for enough years to understand the overpowering force of an angry sea. It worried him, and he was right. On the afternoon of March 15 the weather worsened even further, with the wind swinging erratically from west to southwest and gaining steadily in strength. At 4:00 P.M. watch officer Raimondo Salvezza noted in the log: "Heavy rolling, sea on deck." In the morning the wind had been at force five. By eight o'clock it had risen to six and by 4:00 P.M. to seven. By midnight it was force eight, and that was the cause of Captain Bardari's insomnia. He finally turned in at one o'clock in the morning and fitfully dozed as his cabin creaked and rocked and the tempest howled against his windows. Twice during the night, at 2:00 A.M. and at 3:30, he phoned the bridge for a report on the weather. Both times the reply was the same: "It is bad."

At 6:00 A.M., Captain Bardari gave up his losing battle against insomnia and came up to the bridge. He would have time for sleep later on that night, when they got to Lyme Bay. Right now, he had the loose oil drums to tend to. He altered course, and the work party went out after them.

By eight that morning, everything seemed to be in good order again, with the lube drums secured, the work crew dry and warm, and the Amoco *Cadiz* back on course for Lyme Bay. The retiring watch officer, Cosmo Vaudo, hoary with the great age of his newly acquired third decade, gave the habitual situation report to his relief, third mate Domenico Costagliola, the baby of the officers at twenty-three. Vaudo pointed out on the radarscope the other ships in their vicinity, took him to the chart room to pinpoint their position, and after a final reminder that the wind and sea had carried them slightly to starboard of their intended course, walked down to the dining room for breakfast.

The log book for 0800 Greenwich mean time, March 16, 1978, recorded a true course of thirty-seven degrees, thirty-nine degrees on the gyrocompass, with a two-degree error to the west, skies overcast with passing showers, wind southwest at force eight, sea southwest very rough, barometer 1002, air temperature seven centigrade, and the average engine RPM 87. It was the last entry ever made in the log of the Amoco *Cadiz*.

3.

The Breakdown

Also at precisely 0800 GMT (nine o'clock French time) of that same rainy morning, Captain Hartmut Weinert received a phone call from Hamburg. A powerfully built, thirty-seven-year-old German with close-cropped, curly blond hair, blue eyes, and a brusque, impatient manner, Weinert was aboard his oceangoing tug *Pacific* when the landline call came through at his berth between basins three and five in the commercial port of Brest, Brittany's most modern city (Brest gave itself the rather grand-sounding title because it was so thoroughly bashed in World War II, and rebuilt afterward) and home of France's most important naval base, including the underground submarine pens of the nuclear *force de frappe*. On the other end of the line that day was Weinert's boss, Karl Meyer, chief of overseas towing and salvage operations of Bugsier-, Reederei-und Bergungs-A.G., Germany's most important salvage company. Meyer directed him to proceed forthwith to the Straits of Dover to assist another company tug, *Wotan*, which was having problems with the tow of an America-bound oil rig in the bad weather of the Channel. As was his custom, Weinert wasted no time calling his nineteen-man crew to their stations and making ready to move. At his signal Christoph Korb, his thirty-five-year-old chief engineer, fired up the twin Deutz V-12 diesels. Captain Weinert called the harbormaster for permission to depart.

Captain Weinert had flown to Brest a week earlier to take over command of *Pacific,* a vessel he had known well ever since he began his employment with Bugsier in 1969. Shuttling between various salvage stations at Dover, Brest, the North Sea coast in Germany, and along the Baltic, he had spent his first two years with the company as mate, and then as master, alternating between *Pacific* and another Bugsier tug, *Heros*. Weinert had first gone to sea in 1956, when Pasquale Bardari was fourteen, beginning as a deckboy and plugging along through the grades of promotion—*jungmann,* ordinary seaman, able seaman, mate (1961), and finally master in 1964, aged only twenty-three. Most of his early career at sea had been aboard the small freighters known as coasters, plying the waters of the Baltic, the North Atlantic, and the Channel, until switching to tugs and salvage in 1965, after realizing that he would never be able to save enough of his pay to buy his own coaster. Bugsier had hired him away from the small Wilhelmshaven company where he had learned the tug trade, and he had been with them ever since.

It was a quantum jump for the young officer, taking him from the one-hundred-ton tugs in which he had done journeyman jobs like clearing the Elbe and Weser rivers of the wrecks of sunken World War II submarines, to some of the most formidably powerful and seaworthy workboats anywhere in the world. The oceangoing tugs of companies like Bugsier in Germany and Smit and Wijsmuller in Holland—salvage tugs for the Dutch are a national specialty, like tulips and gin—are the bulldogs of the sea, short and squat but tremendously agile and strong, capable not only of resisting the worst weather that the sea can throw at them, but of pulling a barge or a disabled ship through it at the same time. They are designed to go out and work when "normal" boats heave to or run for cover in the nearest port. Of the dozens of jobs that Weinert had handled as a Bugsier master, the majority had involved towing oil rigs to delivery in the North Sea on straight towage contracts arranged through his Hamburg headquarters, but there had also been thirty-five rescue or salvage jobs, where he and his men had gone out to get ships out of trouble. Ten of these he had brought into Brest in various states of disrepair, and others into ports in Germany and England. The weather conditions for these operations had usually been bad, and sometimes atrocious. Two years earlier he had lost a freighter named *Apollonian Wave* in a hurricane in the Bay of Biscay, when his tow spring broke—the ship eventually beached—and a year after that another towline parted in another hurricane, also in the Bay of Biscay. On this occasion it was a freighter named *Alouette,* and the parting of puller and pulled was more straightforward: the bollards ripped right out of her deck. That was par for the course, though. Every salvage tug captain loses a tow from time to time, the way emergency-room doctors lose patients when the accident has been too severe or the delays in getting the victim to the hospital too long. It is a curious life, that of a salvage tug, alternating between long periods of boringly routine work (towing a barge from Korea to California, for example) and waiting around in port, broken by sudden, unexpected, breathless sprints into danger. The captain of an oceangoing tug never knows what will be coming next. For Weinert that morning, it was to be a historical first: an attempt to salvage, in extremis, a fully laden VLCC. Never having been done before by any tug captain, the job was a completely unknown quantity.

At 0824 their lines were cast off. *Pacific* slowly zigzagged through the break in the seawall, cleared into the Roadsteads of Brest, the twenty-three-kilometer-long fjordlike arm of the Atlantic that in the seventeenth century provided a magnificently safe anchorage for the wooden fleets of Colbert and Vauban—as it does today for the surface and underwater vessels of the sprawling naval base within it—passed through the narrows known as the Bottleneck (*goulet*) of Brest, and then charged out into the open sea full speed ahead. That was Weinert's style—Popeye the sailor man!—and it suited the *Pacific*. She was already a fairly old boat by then, in comparison with many of her congeners in the salvage business, but when she had been built in 1962 she had briefly held the title of the largest and, at 8,500 horsepower, most powerful oceangoing tug in the world. Fitted with Kort nozzles—twin steel tubes that encased her propellors and ran aft—during a 1974 modification, she was upgraded to 10,000 indicated horsepower, but even with that, and her bollard pull of seventy-five tons, she was completely outclassed by more modern tugs in 1978. Some of the biggest of the more recent boats boasted twice her horsepower, but few of them could match her for speed or sturdiness. Or, for that matter, for style. Weinert felt real affection for the old-fashioned blond wood paneling in the passageways and cabins, the anachronistic brasswork, and all the other signs of the careful German workmanship that somehow made her more *wohnlich,* more homey, than the utilitarian steel-and-plastic environment prevailing aboard the newer ships.

Homey or not, though, *Pacific* was still first and foremost a workboat. On her deck and in her holds, she had the tools of her trade all set up, ready for a fast connection in the eventuality of a sudden salvage job. The main towing winch wire, 1,419 meters of six-and-a-half-inch special-strength stranded steel cable, was secured to the after arch of the long, low workdeck behind the accommodation block. Between the point where it was secured and the enormous winch drum on which its main body was wound, ninety meters of the cable lay neatly coiled in a circular well aft, known as the rope basket. Stopped down every ten meters with hemp rope, the seventeen-ton cable could thus be paid out in short, careful increments when the tow got under way, with no risk of fouling a propellor. Down along the port rail, a double-nylon towing spring, fourteen inches thick and fifty meters long, lay the entire length of the deck. Like a gargantuan rubber band, the role of the towing spring was to take advantage of nylon's capacity for stretching in order to avoid the quick jerks that might otherwise cause a line to part. In effect, it was a shock absorber. In another rope basket, starboard side this time, was coiled 110 meters of towing pennant, the steel wire that actually made the attachment to boats under tow. Also on deck was an eight-meter towing chain, attached to the after winch by a bottle screw. In theory, this chain was twice as strong as any amount of stress that the *Pacific*'s engines could possibly put on it. Theory would be proven wrong many times that day.

At 320 RPM, just a shade under the maximum, *Pacific* passed the Pointe de Saint-Mathieu, and turned northward into the Chĕnal du Four to round the tip of Brittany. The *Pacific* could hardly have been called a small boat—70.20 meters long and 11.60 wide for her 1,093 gross tons—but as she hurled her bows at 14.5 knots into the heaving hills of the sea, she acted more like a Ping-Pong ball than a heavy tug. Weinert wanted speed, so he was obliged to fight the waves rather than ride with them. *Pacific* pitched and shuddered as she sliced through whitecaps, receiving in return a boiling explosion of spray against the blunt face of the deckhouse and a stream of green water over the workdeck aft. That was all right. Neither Weinert nor *Pacific* was in the salvage business to take pleasure tours, and both of them had seen plenty of weather of that sort before. Both would hold up. By 9:40 A.M. they were entering the Chĕnal du Four, with the mainland to starboard and the island of Ouessant to port. It was tricky navigation there. At low water the shallows of the channel offered no more than seven meters of depth, and the *Pacific* drew almost five. Ten degrees off course in one direction or another would be plenty, he knew, to send his black-hulled beauty smack onto the rocks. Hartmut Weinert watched compass, radar, and landmarks very, very carefully. Soon, when he cleared the rocks of Argenton and had reached the deeper waters, he would be able to breathe easier. Of course he had no way of knowing that at that same moment the Amoco *Cadiz* was on a track very nearly parallel to his own, quite close, some seven and a half miles at sea, over on the other side of Ouessant. Or that in five more minutes that same sea that he battled for a living was going to, quite literally, strike the tanker a mortal blow.

It had been a strange morning for the Amoco *Cadiz*, according to Captain Bardari's later account. After the hazardous wrestling match at dawn with the lube oil drums, Bardari discovered that third mate Costagliola, when taking radar distances from the landmass of Ouessant and visual bearings from the white lighthouse at Pointe de Creac'h, had made several errors in plotting and charting their position, and was dutybound to give him a reprimand. At about the same time, helmsman Vincenzo Bongiardina complained that the weather and the sea were making it difficult to hold *Cadiz* on course, forcing him to angle the controls, like a pilot crabbing his plane against a flanking wind. It was nervy and bothersome, but no real physical problem, because a ship like the Amoco *Cadiz* was equipped as a matter of routine with a monstrously strong power steering system. For all their elephantine bulk, VLCCs and ULCCs are known to be "good turners."

The Amoco *Cadiz* had to use her turning capacities twice again that morning, at 0830 and 0930, according to what Bardari told investigators when it was all over. The first time, a large wave swept over the tank deck on the port side, rolling forward and smashing up against the center deckhouse. In its course over the ship, it tore two fire hoses free from their racks along the center catwalk and rolled two lube oil drums up the foredeck. The captain ordered a twenty-degree turn to starboard, giving something of a lee to the work crew that struggled out to secure the wandering equipment. Hardly had he set his bearing aright than, at 0930, he spotted a small tanker, a rogue, coming toward him off his port bow, heading the wrong way down the "up" track of the traffic separation scheme by which the Channel nations, through the good offices of institutions like the London-based International Maritime Organization, attempt to impose some order upon the world's busiest big-boat crossroads. With the tremendously crowded conditions of this busiest of all maritime crossroads—more than three hundred ships, on average, pass by

Ouessant every day—the imposition of parallel but widely separated "up" and "down" one-way lanes (just like a superhighway, with a wide, watery mall between the lanes) is only the purest of logic. But the means of policing that logic are limited; in 1978, it was still quite common for rogue ships to cut corners in carefree violation of the scheme. When Captain Bardari saw the little coastal tanker in his path he had no choice but to alter course again, for the third time that morning. He moved over to starboard. By the time the danger of collision had been safely avoided, there was too much traffic around him to get back to his original bearing of thirty-seven degrees, so he had to hold at 045 while awaiting the opportunity of edging off to port once again. The result of all this maneuvering was that he had been carried 1.1 miles closer to land than he had intended to be.

Bongiardina had been relieved at the helm at 0900 by Francesco Fede. At 0945, as the captain was scanning the shipping lanes with his binoculars, Fede noticed the ship drifting leftward at the bow and he corrected to starboard, as his fellow able-bodied seamen (ABs) had been doing all that morning, to offset the port yaw. But this time she didn't come round. Fede watched in speechless surprise as the arrow of the rudder angle indicator on the panel in front of him swung slowly over to the left until it showed hard aport. All the while, he was holding the wheel steadily at twenty degrees to starboard.

"Captain," said Fede, "we are out of control."

It could not have happened at a worse moment. At seven and a half miles off the island of Ouessant, the Amoco *Cadiz* was situated about as close to land as she ever would have come before her anticipated anchorage in Lyme Bay. And what a land: Ouessant and its surroundings, with their shoals and swift currents and landward-prevailing winds, have been a notorious ships' graveyard long beyond recorded memory. *"Oui voit Ouessant voit son sang,"* say the French mariners familiar with those waters. For the English the traditional observation may be less poetic, but it is just as much to the point: "If you can see Ushant, it means you're too damn close to land." And now, by virtue of her sidestepping maneuver to avoid the rogue tanker, the Amoco *Cadiz* was even closer than planned. The winds, always capricious by Ouessant, had been blowing from the southwest most of the morning, but were now beginning to shift around to the northwest, directly onto land. They were also gaining in intensity—forty to forty-five knots, they would be registering soon, with gusts up to sixty and seventy. It is the sort of weather that merits a tersely eloquent description in the classical Beaufort Scale of Wind Strengths: "Whole gale: very high waves with overhanging crests; sea takes white appearance as foam is blown in very dense streaks; rolling is heavy and visibility reduced."

Poor Pasquale Bardari. For so many years everything had gone smoothly aboard the mammoth oilpots he was constrained to ride since the luxury ocean liners went the way of the brontosaurus and the pterodactyl. But now everything was about to go wrong, one after the other, to make him the hapless protagonist of what was to become a textbook demonstration of the implacable mathematics of complacency, presumptuousness, stupidity, and cupidity. They added up to a terrible bill, and he was the one who got it, although plenty of others had contributed to its making.

From that moment on, everything conspired—the sea's condition and direction, the wind, the changing flow of tidal currents, bad luck, and a lot of bad judgment, past and present—to push the huge, helpless tanker toward the Breton rocks with cruelly unhurried inevitability, no matter what anybody tried to do about it. Just then, at 0945, doom was almost twelve hours away. Pasquale Bardari had plenty of time to act in any way he could, but he was already like an ant scrabbling along the down-slope of a sand well, with his own personal horror waiting darkly at the bottom of the cone.

4.

The Perfect Machine

Of all the systems aboard a modern ship, few can match the steering motor for ingenuity and apparent mechanical perfection. Basically, it is nothing more than a big, steel hand pushing a tiller back and forth, just as your hand on the tiller of a sailboat moves back and forth to change the angle of the rudder, and hence the boat's heading. But if large ships have rudders the size of barn doors, on VLCCs they are as big as the side walls of apartment buildings: 12.9 meters high and 8.17 wide for Amoco *Cadiz*, and weighing just under 160 tons. To move this enormous rectangular steel slab against turbulent sea and the inertia of more than a quarter million tons of deadweight earnestly endeavoring to go straight ahead requires a machine of quite uncommon force.

On older, smaller craft, steering strength usually came from a steam engine located amidships, obeying the helm in the wheelhouse and linked by chain to the tiller aft. Steam systems are not paragons of efficiency (lots of complicated linkages can break, go slack, or slip off leads), but they permit all kinds of jury-rigging in the event of emergency. In almost any kind of breakdown except physical loss of the rudder, a friction brake could be cranked down hard to immobilize the rudder in a neutral position while the engineers labored to make the steam engine work again, fix a broken chain or patch up whatever else had gone wrong. If the steam engine were unfixable, there was always a backup, hand-operated system that gave enough turning power for the crippled boat to creep back into port. Even better than this, many an inventive captain managed to restore steerage by running cables up onto the main deck and powering the tiller with the ship's winches.

No such friendly improvisation is possible on a VLCC. They are simply too big, and the pressure forces on the rudder too great. Someone with a taste for graphic illustrations recently reckoned, for example, that the inertia behind the *Cadiz*'s rudder in heavy weather was comparable to the weight of ten loaded railroad freight cars. To tame these forces, the only answer is hydraulics, through which tremendous power can be generated by relatively small units. Most large modern ships, as a result, are equipped with the same kind of power steering as the Amoco *Cadiz:* a four-ram, electrohydraulic servomotor. In theory, such a system is fail-safe and flawless. Theoretically, every exigency and every eventuality is covered by its maze of electric motors, pumps, valves, control rods, and high-pressure oil lines. Theoretically, it cannot break down. When you study it on a blueprint, it looks like the "perfect machine."

The "perfect machine" works by remote control. It is a closed and virtually self-sufficient system that requires scarcely any human attention beyond an input of electricity for its pump motors, a basic allotment of eight hundred liters of hydraulic oil, and the normal attentions of careful maintenance. The one installed in the Amoco *Cadiz* was of the brand Manises (the name of a subsidiary company of Astilleros Espanoles), but its conception was the same as that of the gear used in most such ships today. And in the past, too: Four-ram electrohydraulic gear has been around since before World War I, and the old *Queen Mary* and *Queen Elizabeth,* for example, steered with it, as does the beautiful Norwegian cruise ship that used to be known as the S.S. *France.* The principle is proven and classical. What changes from year to year (and from shipyard to shipyard) is the technology of design detail.

This is the way it works: When the wheel is turned on the bridge, corresponding electric contacts in the steering-gear room direct a motorized "hunting gear" lever attached to twin high-pressure pumps of the variable-delivery, reversible type; that is, they can send hydraulic oil either way without changing direction themselves. The pumps (or pump, since the system can also work with only one of them in action) force the oil through pipes into a hydraulic traffic intersection known as a distribution block, where preset valves in turn shunt it as required into the cylinders encasing four brutish rams. These rams are joined in opposed pairs, like four cannons standing with their muzzles turned against one another. Between them is the ship's tiller, a stub of forged steel just under three meters long and slightly rounded in the center where the shaft to which it is keyed drops down through the stern and maintains the rudder. The four rams—glistening rolled-steel pistons as thick as a grown man's waist—slide in and out of their cylinders in symmetrical coordination, in response to the surges of oil from the pumps, and hence from the wheel up on the bridge. When one piston is under pressure, its opposite number on the other side of the tiller stock is under suction. When the aft pair of rams moves one way, the forward pair moves the other way in mirror-image motion. On the rudder stub are universal joints and a device called a Rapson slide, which mechanically translates the rams' straight, back-and-forth movement to the rotational motion of a turning rudder. When the rams move in and out of their cylinders, they push the enormous rudder as the helmsman has ordered. When both pump sets are working on the four rams, the rudder can be swung from hard over one side to hard over on the other in less than half a minute, even if the ship is traveling at full speed. It is a formidable job, but the Manises steering engines installed in the *Cadiz* and her sister ships put out a guaranteed torque of not less than four hundred tonmeters. They had the force, then, to turn a fully laden VLCC with surprising agility.

But nothing in life is simple, and nothing is free in physics. There is always another side to consider. In this case, it is Newton's precept that for every action there is an equal and opposite reaction. The hydraulic energies that such steering systems harness in order to deliver their prodigious shoves are inevitably accompanied by a phenomenon that is fraught with great potential danger: high pressures. It is a muscular genie who is bottled up inside those oil lines, and the harder the shove of the rams against the tiller, the harder he is trying to burst out. To hold back a pressure of ten or twenty tons per square inch, shipbuilders and designers must be very, very certain that their piping, flanges, and connections are absolutely beyond reproach and that, just as an engineer designs a bridge for two or three times the weight of any traffic it can conceivably carry, they have overbuilt them with sufficient safety margins. By the same token, the ship's engineers responsible for the care and feeding of the "perfect machine" have to meticulously follow the maintenance routines laid out by the manufacturer. The "perfect machine" likes to live in conditions as antiseptically clean as a Swiss parlor. Otherwise, it gets cross.

For the first four years of its life, the steering gear of the *Cadiz* had done what was expected of it for Shell International, who paid for the rent of the oilpot, and for Standard Oil, who rented it out. Amoco *Cadiz* picked up oil where and when it was supposed to be picked up, ferried it across the drink in satisfactory condition, and dumped it where the telex machine in the radio room said it should be dumped. As far as any outsiders could have known then, the Servomotore Electrohidraulico de Cilindros Rectos Manises was perfectly problem-free. For insiders, though, those who knew the ship and lived with it from day to day, the steering gear had performed strangely from the very start—but it had gone on performing. There was that to be said for it. Everyone just assumed that it would go on doing the job. They were wrong.

The steering-gear room where the "perfect machine" lived was a spacious, steel compartment the size of a small house, located aft, above, and behind the engine control room. There was no need for permanent manning, as with the main engine. The onboard maintenance routine came to little more than a daily check by the duty engineer and a regular topping-up of the reserve oil in its overhead reservoir, or gravity tank. With its pipes and cylinders filled with eight hundred liters of Misola BH hydraulic oil, Amoco *Cadiz*'s steering machine performed its duties with discreet efficiency, talking to itself in the odd little language of the solitary domestic: whirrings of electric motors, a deeper throb of pumps delivering oil, some solidly reassuring metallic clunks of various moving parts. But, occasionally, there were also some more worrisome noises: titanic thumps and bangs as the sea hammered against the rudder on the other side of the ship's steel skin. Every time a big wave smashed against the rudder, the pumps automatically increased their delivery of oil to counteract the sea's force, to keep the rudder where the helmsman had put it. And every time that happened, the genie inside the piping network flexed his muscles, and pressures rose.

The phenomenon is known to every naval architect and engineer, and is mentioned in every marine machinery textbook. "It might be mentioned," the London-based Institute of Marine Engineers warns in *The Running and Maintenance of Marine Machinery*, "that failures have occurred due to the fracturing at the necks of the pipes which carry the oil between the ram cylinders and the pumps. . . . In one case, when the pipes fractured at the neck, the cylinders were emptied of oil and the rams were slammed from side to side by heavy seas striking the rudder. Special attention should be paid to these high pressure oil pipes after any heavy weather. It is now a requirement of the Classification Societies that a brake of some kind should be fitted to these hydraulic gears."

No one could say he wasn't warned.

5.

The Three-Hour Wave

Around the world, wherever there are beaches or comfortable vantage points for gazing out over the sea, children have maintained the pleasant folklore that the seventh wave is always the biggest one of a series. There is no scientific justification for this juvenile assurance, but it hints at some more rigorous categories and conclusions that have legitimately entered the erudite vocabulary of hydrodynamicists. Waves do vary in height and, as surfers all know, you will eventually find an extra-large one if you have the patience to wait for it. The mean height of the waves on any chosen portion of the sea depends on such variables as winds, tides, currents, and depth, but they tend to pass at periods of roughly ten seconds for about 360 waves an hour. Their average size is what hydrodynamicists term "significant wave height." But waves varying in size as they do, and the laws of probability being what they are, it is virtually certain that within the space of a thousand waves, one will be twice the height of the significant wave. This is the three-hour wave—the exception to the rule, the monster.

It is unlikely that there will ever be absolute proof of just what it was that caused the steering of the Amoco *Cadiz* to fail that fatal morning of March 16, but it is incontestable that the root cause—the first link in the chain of disaster—was an uncomfortable meeting between a rudder with an inclination for the right and a wave that wanted to go left. And, conditions being what they were that day, it might just have been a three-hour wave of extraordinarily unusual powers of persuasion. At 0945 GMT, the significant waves off Ouessant were in the vicinity of six to eight meters, but with the wind beginning to veer from southwest to northwest, they had become steeper, more jagged, and more choppy than they normally would have been under a steady wind from one direction. The three-hour wave, then, may have been as high as twenty meters—or even more. No one knows for sure, because no one was out there taking measurements at the time. When it came, though, smashing across the tanker's starboard quarter and throwing its weight against the rudder, it was copiously supplied with kinetic force. By itself, such a massive body of moving water would have been enough to create overpressures in the hydraulic piping of the Manises gear, but when the effect of the ship's yaw was added to it—the stern first mushing over to port and then back five or six degrees into the starboard sector, against the force of the onrushing wave—the overpressures quickly soared. In any modern steering system, including the Manises, relief valves are placed at strategic points along the piping network in anticipation of just such dire conditions. Sudden surges of pressure from the hammering of waves force the valve seats up against their springs, and the oil is given an escape route: It flows from the high-pressure side of the system to the low-pressure side, balancing the pressures again. The valve then drops down, restoring the sealed integrity of the machine's steel entrails, and the hunting gear can tell the pumps to put the rudder back where the helmsman wants it. That, at least, was the theory, and for four years theory and practice agreed on the rules of the game, there within the cavernous steering-gear flat of the Amoco *Cadiz*.

But what if the relief valves didn't relieve properly? And what if, somehow or other, air had worked its way into that closed network of piping? Air and hydraulic systems don't mix, as anyone knows who has had the brakes of his car purged. Air can be even more dangerous than a three-hour wave.

6.

The Drift Begins

"Captain, we are out of control."

Able seaman Fede was not in the habit of making portentous or historical announcements, and may have been as surprised at the words he found himself uttering as he was at seeing the rudder angle needle swing to the left side of the glassed-in gauge above him, all the way over to thirty-five degrees aport. Captain Bardari, who had been conferring with Mr. Maynard over a cup of coffee, strode over to the helm and stared hard at the gauge. The needle had finished its course and was stuck hard over, immobile. His first thought was the same that the captain of any other ship would have had in the English Channel: collision. The Amoco *Cadiz* was right in the middle of the world's most crowded ship traffic area, and he knew by both visual sightings and radar that there were plenty of other vessels all around him. Now, by the evidence on the control panel before his eyes, his steering system had quit on him, and like a car on a superhighway, his ship was about to veer left, out of his lane, across the mall and into the opposite lane, toward God knows what. He was also very pertinently aware of the fact that a fully laden tanker like the Amoco *Cadiz* requires plenty of space—a couple of miles under the best of circumstances—before it can come to a halt from cruising speed. Captain Bardari grasped the handle of the engine room telegraph and quickly slid it back to SLOW AHEAD and then, after a moment's reflection, to STOP. Now it was quite clear that the ship was adopting a new line, slowly bringing her head toward the north in the ponderously graceful skid that is the turning style of the VLCCs. He picked up the phone and buzzed the control room.

"We have a steering-gear failure," he said to Mr. Maynard, who had followed him to the helm. But Mr. Maynard had already guessed as much, from the gesticulations and pointings of the Italians, of whose language he understood not a word.

Eight elevator stops down within the *Cadiz*'s steely nether regions, third assistant engineer Gilberto Serventi was monitoring a broad instrument panel crammed with enough warning lights, gauges, and dials to resemble an atomic energy plant or make a plausible set for a science fiction film. His domain, the control room, was a comfortably soundproofed and air-conditioned chamber nearly twelve meters wide on the port side of the next-to-the-lowest deck of the ship, the one logically enough called Lower Platform. Behind him was the maze of instruments (including a computer printout telescriptor that could give him instant warnings and diagnoses concerning the health of his mechanical charges) and, up front, through windows thick enough to muffle the racket, an unbeatable view over the oily flanks of the Burmeister & Wain main diesel. A stylish twenty-seven-year-old with carefully trimmed hair and a droopy black mustache that gave him the appearance of an aspiring Sicilian bandit, Serventi had taken over his watch at 8:00 A.M., and was to remain on duty until noon. The oilers and wipers making their habitual rounds of attendance to the engine's perpetual need for lubrication looked up in surprise as he throttled back the big diesel and then shut her off entirely, in compliance with the signal from the bridge. The phone buzzed.

"We have trouble with the steering gear," the captain told him. "It is blocked to port. Warn the chief engineer immediately."

"Okay," replied Serventi, a young man of few words. He punched a button on his control panel six or seven times, and the engineering alarm horn blared throughout the ship.

Chief engineer Melito had changed and breakfasted after securing the drums on the poop deck, and then had joined Assante, the man who was to relieve him after Rotterdam, in the routine of the machinery inspection tour, which both of them knew by heart from the hundreds of times they had done it before. Everything had appeared normal, including the steering gear, over which they had cast cursory glances. The two friends were heading back to Melito's cabin after the inspection, but Assante stopped to chat with a crewman along the way, and Melito went on alone. He was a few steps from his cabin door when the alarm horn rang out. Without hesitating, he turned on his heel and hurried back down the steep, steel stairways toward the control room.

Michele Calise, Melito's first assistant engineer, was on an engine room platform inspecting pumps when he heard the horn and, because of his proximity, was the first officer to reach the control room, where Serventi was engaged in the fussy process of shutting the main engine down. Serventi reported the captain's message from the bridge. Motioning for a nearby fireman to come along with him, Calise hurried aft and upward to the steering flat.

Salvatore Catanese, the second assistant engineer whom Serventi had relieved at 0800, was awakened in his cabin by the alarm horn. He dressed quickly and went down. He was the last engineering officer to arrive below decks. By this time, Melito had already come to the control room and rushed away, looking more worried than ever. The amiable Assante somehow missed the sound of the alarm horn entirely—he must have been in a spot between loudspeakers—and wondered why Melito wasn't in his cabin, as he had said he was going to be. Still insouciant, he strolled on down to the chief engineer's office, saw it was empty, and was about to sit down and wait when out of professional reflex he glanced at the engine RPM gauge. It was at zero. Aha. Suddenly he wasn't insouciant anymore. He darted out the door and made for the control room but never got there. Along the way, a fireman told him the trouble was with the steering gear and not the engine. Assante went straight back to the steering flat, feeling vague foreboding. Outside of fire or explosion, loss of steering is about the worst thing that can happen to a ship. Back in the control room, Serventi noticed that the rudder angle indicator was swinging slowly back toward starboard. Did that mean it was under control again? His brief optimism died when a warning horn began blowing on the instrument panel, accompanied by a red light indicating that the oil level in the steering system's gravity feed tank had dropped dangerously low.

Calise and the fireman were the first to enter the steering flat, and what they saw at first was oil—oil everywhere. The floor was covered with it, and the steering machinery was dripping with it. Already ponds of it were forming against bulkheads when the ship rolled to one side. But most dramatically of all, a fan-shaped fountain of oil, taller than a man, was spurting up from the right-hand side of the distribution block. Treading gingerly over the slippery floor, Calise reached the chest-high work platform at the forward side of the steering machinery. It was clear that what was causing the hemorrhage was a break where the three-inch steel pipe running from the port pump joined the distribution block. It was creating havoc with the system, because the pump, like a soldier of limited intelligence but unswerving loyalty, was desperately trying to obey the helm's order to re-center the rudder by dispatching great quantities of oil forward—but it was all geysering up through the break in the line. In effect, the steering gear was bleeding itself to death. The "perfect machine" had gone mad. Calise quickly flipped the switch on the electric control panel to stop the pump. As soon as he did, though, the starboard pump cut in automatically, as it had been programmed to do by the safety interlock, a fail-safe design built in by Manises. Now it began busily churning out the fountain of oil.

Calise grabbed the railing and hauled himself up the four steps of the ladder, onto the platform. Now that he was dominating the steering machinery he could see that the four rams were still maintaining their dampening effect against the straining tiller, but their movements already had the characteristic sloppiness of a hydraulic system losing oil and getting air into its lines. He inspected the distribution block more carefully and saw that it wasn't the pipe that had burst, but rather the O-shaped flange that held it fast against the block that had come away from its seat. The flange had come away because five of the six studs that held it in place had sheared clean off. The only thing that was still holding the pipe in place, the sixth stud, down at the bottom, was bent all the way back. The wave pressure, working back against the rams, had wrenched the pipe right out of the block, treating the steel studs like sticks of balsa wood. Kneeling down and twisting his head away from the jet of oil, Calise grasped the special handwheel socket wrench provided for maneuvering valve stems in the steering flat, slipped it over the main valve that commanded the broken flange, and began turning as best he could. It was not simple: The shower of oil was coursing upward next to his ear, and the handwheel was covered with the stuff, causing his hands to slide against the friction of the valve. He yelled to Dasso, the fireman, to run back to the control room, tell Serventi what had happened, and bring back some help. It was obvious they were going to need as much as they could get.

A couple of minutes later Melito arrived, on the run, to an appalling spectacle. The oil was showering upward as strongly as ever from the separated flange, and perhaps four hundred or five hundred liters of it were blanketing the deck like a shiny, viscid carpet. The tiller was beginning to move now, swinging from side to side every fifteen seconds or so, in time with the roll of the ship. Now it was beginning to control the rams. Poor Calise was contorted on the grating next to the distribution block, trying to avoid the oil stream and make some progress with the D valve at the same time. Holding his arms out for balance, Melito slid his way across the deck to the platform, clambered up, and took over from his first assistant, working to shut down the D and C valves with an adjustable wrench he always carried in his pocket. As he kneeled over the valve, he shouted to Calise to shut down another similar pair at the stern-end of the distribution block. With their efforts joined over the next few frantic minutes, they were able to isolate the port pump and stanch the leak from the flange. In effect, they were racing the sea to save the system, but the time lost between the rupture of the flange and their arrival to do something about it—probably ten minutes— proved to be fatal. With every second that passed, more oil was drained from the system when the rams shoved one way, and more air was drawn in when they went the other way, hungrily sucking at the gap in the block where the pipe had come away. The immense pistons, designed to push the rudder, were now passively obeying it, moving in and out in response to the will of the waves. Everything had gone topsy-turvy.

By urgent groups now, the rest of the engineering personnel began arriving in the steering flat. Assante got there in time to help shut down the valves, and gradually, like a lawn sprinkler being turned off, the fountain diminished and fell back. Now it was immediately imperative to purge the enfeebled system of the air that was paralyzing it and to fill it up with oil again so that the wild rudder could be brought under control. But that was much, much easier said than done. Calise, Melito, Assante, and an engineering cadet named Matera positioned themselves at the rear of the ram cylinders and, crouching like jockeys, made ready to operate the purging cocks. It was difficult, even for professionals, not to be impressed and frightened by the noise and brute power of the tiller below them as it slammed back and forth.

As the Amoco *Cadiz* coasted leftward toward a stop, Captain Bardari ordered a signal raised that he had never had occasion to use before: two black balls superimposed on the mainmast, signifying, I am not under control. At night the balls became two bright red lights. "The Christmas Tree," mariners call it. Now, at least, officers on watch aboard other ships in the vicinity would know the reasons for his intrusion into the separation zone that divided the traffic flow within the Channel. Captain Bardari took the bridge microphone and, on channel 16 VHF, made the first of a series of "security" calls that would be continuing, off and on, for most of the rest of the day.

> *Securité, securité securité. To all ships. This is the Amoco* Cadiz. *We have steering gear failure. Please keep clear. Position approximately eight miles north of Ouessant.*

Captain Bardari asked his first mate to carry a similar message to the radio room for Morse transmission. Muscuso, slightly less fluent in English than his captain, couched it in more colorful language, first identifying himself by the ship's radio call sign, Alpha Eight Alpha November:

> *TTT. A8AN. Amoco* Cadiz *to all ships our posn eight miles north of Ouessant we have completely fallout of steering gear pse keep clear.*

The phone buzzed from the steering-gear compartment. Captain Bardari hastily picked it up, and Mr. Maynard, ever helpful, took over the mike and began repeating the security message. Standing by the port bridge wing door, he spoke the message loud and clear, in a firm baritone slightly seasoned with a bit of residual Cockney ring.

When it was all over, when the lawyers, critics, and armchair navigators of all sorts began picking apart the most minute details of the odyssey of the Amoco *Cadiz*, Pasquale Bardari was often censured for his use—or, rather, his nonuse—of the radio, and most particularly for the fact that throughout his long ordeal, as the coast of Brittany drew steadily nearer, he never sent out any message more urgent than this security call. And when he finally did, it was too late, grotesquely too late.

Of the three degrees of warning calls in international radio language, the security message, labeled TTT in Morse, is the least urgent, signifying only a danger to navigation but not requesting help of any kind. The next step on the scale is the Morse XXX message ("pan pan pan" when called by voice), suggesting an urgency aboard, and a vessel in some kind of trouble or distress. And finally, the one that everyone knows and dreads, is the SOS, "mayday" by voice, meaning: Our ship is sinking; require immediate assistance. Captain Bardari never sent out anything but the routine security messages as long as he was afloat. It was only when the Amoco

Cadiz was speared fast on the rocks—and a good deal after, in fact—that he sent out a call of distress. The logical conclusion was that either he had been unprofessionally optimistic when assessing the dangers confronting him, or that for some reason he wanted to conceal those dangers, or at least minimize them. There are grounds for accepting both hypotheses.

By 1005, twenty minutes after the main engine was shut down, the Amoco *Cadiz* had lost her momentum and was dead in the water, facing due west after having described a half a circle to port, following the path ordained by the blocked rudder. Now that the winds and currents alone were controlling her, she slowly completed the circle over the next fifty minutes, until she was heading south-southeastward. She had begun her leisurely drift toward the shore. The officers on the bridge could clearly see land during breaks in the intermittent squalls that raked the area off Ouessant all that day.

"I'm going down to have a look," Bardari told Maynard. "Are you coming?"

Already, the captain of the Amoco *Cadiz* was treating the visiting Englishman as an equal, both in status and in qualification. Throughout the rest of that day, it became apparent that Mr. Maynard's strong personality, his calm, and his apparent encyclopedic knowledge of matters nautical had deeply impressed Bardari, and as the events became tenser and more complex, he began relying on him more and more as an advisor and friend. In retrospect, his understated "Are you coming?" might well be interpreted as "Please come and give me a hand." Mr. Maynard never did refuse his hand or his friendship during the long ordeal.

Accompanied by first mate Strano, the captain and Mr. Maynard went below, leaving Costagliola and the two second mates, Vaudo and Salvezza, to keep watch, take position readings, and continue calling out the security messages. Captain Bardari and his companions took the elevator to the Upper Platform stop, walked over the bridgework of steel grating that spanned the engine-room pit, descended a ladder by the boiler, passed through a hot, narrow passageway behind it, and finally debouched by the entrance to the steering flat. Even before they came to the door, they could hear the tiller doing its destructive work on the other side of the bulkhead, bullying the rams back and forth, to the accompaniment of what Maynard remembered as "a terrifying noise."

The atmosphere inside the compartment was heavy with the thick, cloying odor of oil. On the deck plates at their feet, crewmen had strewn bags of sawdust in a vain effort to sop up oil and were now busily shoveling sand and sawdust into makeshift dams to stop the slimy stuff from sloshing back and forth with the ship's roll. The four oil-covered engineers crouched awkwardly—and perilously— at the ram cylinders, opening and closing the purging cocks in rhythm with the inward and outward movement of the rams. The point of their exertions was to open the cocks as the rams drew back into their cylinders, in the hope that they would expel the air out of the hole by the broken flange, and then to close them as they slid out, so that they could suck oil down from the gravity tank. But it was frustrating, maddeningly difficult to coordinate because the tiller wasn't just rocking regularly to and fro, but gyrating unpredictably, "weathercocking" as the seas slapped the rudder around. A few seconds too long on the purging cock as the rudder reversed direction meant more air into the system and more oil out. For a few moments near the beginning of the operation it seemed to be working, and Assante even permitted himself a brief onset of optimism when he heard the horn of the low-level alarm in the gravity tank indicating that the level had dropped. A bucket brigade of oilers and wipers hastened to pour in new oil, but soon their energies became pointless: the level had stopped dropping. The oil couldn't flow downward.

Oil—oil was everywhere, oil was everything, oil was their entire universe, surrounding them and obsessing them and utterly frustrating them. The whole bloody ship was full of oil, and now they couldn't get a few hundred liters of oil down into the gullet of the Manises, into that maze of piping that looked like a caricature of some nineteenth-century plumber's *chef d'oeuvre.*

Obeying the ancient English instinct that there must be some way he could help them muddle through, Maynard slid across the compartment and climbed up to the platform, but he quickly realized that he had no intelligent advice to give to these already harried Italians. Obviously, they knew what to do, but in this case practice was not following theory: Their efforts were having no results. Above and to his right, the oil was foaming and bubbling over the top of the gravity tank in response to wave action, and one of the firemen had rigged up a plastic sheet to keep it from slopping down on the engineers squatting on the rams. To his concern, he also noticed that it was welling out of the flange breach again. That was bad. It seemed to indicate either that the isolating valves weren't holding or that there was some damage inside the distribution block itself, somewhere along its labyrinth of drilled passageways.

Slowly, deliberately, during the eight or ten minutes that he watched, the tiller stub freed itself of the port sector and began swinging in the full seventy-degree arc from one side to the other, completely traversing its course and whanging up against the metallic stops, creating a kind of auditory exclamation point: a long, hissing scream as the rams forced oil and air out of the system, and then a great, shuddering bang as the tiller hit the stops. Maynard decided that the most helpful thing he could do was to get the hell out of the way. By the time he ducked out into the passageway behind the boiler, he could hear the clankings of metal against metal becoming even more dramatic. The rams had lost so much oil that they had become helpless against the tiller's pile-driving. He was back on the bridge by 1020. Up there, they were still confident Melito and his helpers would somehow manage to find a solution to the problem.

But how? Melito and Assante had warned them that it would take a while, and that the result wasn't certain. If only they could stop that damn rudder. Then it would be fairly simple to load up the system with oil again, keep the port pump and its two rams isolated, and steer with the starboard pump and its pair of rams. The Manises gear ran just as well with two rams as with four, only a little bit more slowly. But there was no brake, no friction stop such as the older ships used to have, to crank down onto the shaft and neutralize the rudder. There was none because the "perfect machine" theoretically didn't need one: Even with only one pump-motor set in service, its cunningly devised control system automatically made a hydraulic countermove to every undesired movement of the rudder. If the seas tried to shove it to port against the commands from the helm, the rams slid out in instant reaction to stop it. Checkmate. And if for some reason you wanted to neutralize the rudder, why, said the Manises manual, then all you had to do was to shut all the valves and hold the rudder rigid by hydraulic force, immobilized by the incompressibility of the oil. This solution fully satisfied the Classification Societies' requirement mentioned in the textbooks that "a brake of some kind should be fitted to these hydraulic gears."

But everything had gone awry. Everything was reversed, the opposite of what it was supposed to be. The clever Spanish design was no longer following its logic: Each time the rams were forced backward, they pumped more oil out of the system, and each time they extended, they sucked more air in. The engineers on the rams struggled desperately with the machine's suicidal behavior, but they were getting nowhere. The most fatal sign of all came when it began to heat up. The mixture of oil and air was being churned up into a steamy froth, which, pressurized by the system, heated and expanded, taking up the spaces that otherwise should have been filled with oil. Melito and his friends soon smelled the acrid odor of burning oil from the rams' seals. He mentally cast about for some way—some other way, any way—of stopping the tiller. The only solution he could think of was a set of chain blocks, of the sort they used for hefting machinery and machine parts around the engine room. It struck him as thoroughly improbable, but it was worth a try: Hook one end up on a structural beam and then try to get the other end around the tiller somewhere. But the best and heaviest chain fall they had in the machine shop was rated at five tons. Considering that the rams, when healthy, had to deliver four hundred ton-meters to move the rudder, that didn't look too hopeful. What else could they do—throw chairs and mattresses and wooden boards down against it? Jam it with something? Hell, the tiller stock could chew up steel beams, the way it was behaving now.

The ironies were piling up, down there in the bowels of the Amoco *Cadiz*. Naturally, as everyone knew, all the Classification Societies' rules, all the international conventions governing tankers, specified that any steering system had to be backed up by an auxiliary system, in case of failure of the primary one. Naturally. But this was a four-ram set with two entirely independent pump-motor sets. In theory, it was a double machine, perfectly redundant and covering the eventuality of a breakdown. It was all covered in the 1971 American Bureau of Shipping rulebook under which the *Cadiz* had been built:

5.13.5 AUXILIARY MEANS OF STEERING

a. When not required. An auxiliary means of steering will not be required where power operated steering-gear units and connections are fitted in duplicate, or where the main gear is of the dual-power hydraulic type, having two independent pumps and separate leads to the pump prime movers from the source of power, provided the attachment to the rudder stock is designed for strength in excess of the requirement of the Rules.

Everything was doubled, just as the rules specified. Everything, that is, but the gravity tank and the distribution block. And it was precisely with the distribution block and the gravity tank that they were having trouble. The first was making the machine bleed to death, and the second was unable to feed in new blood. Find a way around that dilemma.

Over the next three quarters of an hour, Captain Bardari phoned down three or four times to the steering flat, and each time Melito could tell him only that they were working on it. No prognosis, no commitment, but things were obviously bad, and getting no better. The officers silently looked at one another as the rudder continued its uproarious rampage, sending its terrifying noise and vibrations right through the ship with every vengeful crash against the stops. When second mate Salvezza went down at around half past ten, he was amazed to see metal—bolts from the crosshead, pieces of the universal coupling—flying around the compartment. It was clear that the steering engine was breaking up, and that it was unhealthy to be in the same room with it.

Meanwhile, Amoco *Cadiz* continued to creep slowly landward, heading 160. The weather was getting worse and the seas were roughening, but if any casual visitor had been helicoptered aboard the big oilpot at that fate-charged moment, he would have been hard-put to notice anything amiss. The electricity and heating and plumbing and navigational equipment were all working perfectly, and the main engine could be started up on a few minutes' notice. Everyone aboard was comfortable and warm and well dressed, with the exception of the oil-splattered engineers below. But they were out of sight; what could be seen looked fine. The huge ship rolled in the heavy seas, certainly, but it would have been difficult for our hypothetical visitor not to have felt the greatest security up there on the lofty bridge, and even harder to perceive any danger in the cabins or lounges, or in the kitchen, where lunch was already being prepared—a good Italian lunch with pasta, salad, meat, and wine. The Amoco *Cadiz* had all the outward appearances and appointments of a self-sufficient and well-appointed seagoing city.

Shortly after eleven o'clock Captain Bardari walked down to the radio room, one flight of stairs under his bridge, on the port side of the accommodation block. He directed Muscuso to place three radiotelephone calls. All three recipients were former mariners who had retired from the sea to take office jobs with the company, just as he was planning to do some day: captains Scarel and Milanesi in

Genoa, both crew supervisors for Amoco; and Captain William Riddell, Amoco's deputy manager of marine operations in Chicago. Captain Bardari badly needed to confer with his bosses. The popular, romantic tradition of the ship's captain being sole master under God was born before the invention of the radiotelephone and international corporate lines of authority.

Bad luck: There was no answer at Captain Scarel's number, and at Captain Milanesi's house only his wife was home. Bardari returned to the bridge and rejoined Maynard, waiting for the Chicago call to come through. At a quarter past eleven, an ashen-faced Assante appeared, personally carrying the news that there was no longer any chance of fixing the steering gear. He and his engineers had been hoping to somehow get it purged and working again, but now a second line had blown out: The pipe leading from valve X to the distribution block had exploded, lifting right off the block and sending a gusher of oil all the way to the ceiling. That had finished it. Now the steering system was empty of oil. Nothing more could be done. The tiller was smashing away the bushings that connected it to the rams. The best they could hope for was to hold the tiller with a chain block. Melito was working on that.

"We'd better get some tugs out here, and quick," Bardari told Maynard. He went down to the radio room to call Brest Radio.

What seamen call Brest Radio is known along the Breton coast as Radio le Conquet, a modern, well-equipped listening post of the French postal and communications ministry, built specifically to service ships by passing messages, booking radiotelephone calls, and maintaining a permanent alert for distress signals on the three standard international distress frequencies: 2182 kilocycles, 500 megacycles, and channel 16 on VHF. Le Conquet is a pleasant Breton village of white stucco houses on a point of land that juts into the Atlantic twenty-five kilometers west of Brest, at the southern end of the Chenal du Four, where the *Pacific* had passed earlier that morning. Henry Chaput, the gray-haired, avuncular station director who with professional whimsy had decorated the walls of his clifftop office with news photographs of shipwrecks, knew something was amiss out there on the other side of Ouessant, because at 1020 one of his operators had caught a snatch of an unidentified TTT message: ". . . keep wide berth steering failure."

There was no reason for alarm, though. It was not a distress call, and it was meant only for the information of other ships. Now, quite suddenly, there was this Captain Bardari of the Amoco *Cadiz* who was asking about tugs after trying his two calls to Italy and waiting for the one to America to come through. At 1120 Radio le Conquet received the official tug request by Morse in the 500-kilohertz band:

> A8AN. Need a tug assistance position ten miles north of Ouessant steering gear failure. Full cargo.

Chaput knew that the only large, oceangoing tug in the vicinity was the *Pacific*. Although no French salvage company had deemed it worthwhile to station a ship there, Bugsier had shrewdly chosen Brest as a good central location for normal towing operations (such as helping the *Wotan* through the Straits of Dover with her oil rig) and a likely spot for ad hoc salvaging, since traffic was heavy the year round at the entrance to the Channel, and the weather generally bad. Indeed, the *Pacific* had built an enviable record—and good profits—for herself and Bugsier working from that post. With Weinert in command, *Pacific* had already pulled ten disabled ships into the safety of the Brest Roads.

The French navy had three tugs based in Brest, but they were small (4,000 to 4,500 horsepower) and limited strictly to navy business—nuclear subs, mostly. Even if the navy had wanted to help, it couldn't: One of the tugs was laid up for repairs, a second, the *Malabar,* was on mission by Belle Ile on the other side of the Breton peninsula, and the third, the *Tenace,* was with the French fishing fleets off Newfoundland. As for the various harbor tugs servicing ships in the *port de commerce,* there was no need to think twice about them. Harbor tugs can't even leave port in such weather. They would swamp. So it was *Pacific* or nothing, but it appeared that for once fate was going to be kind to sailors in distress: The German tug was not only available and healthy, but, at the point where she was navigating, a good deal closer—by a couple of hours, probably—to the casualty than she would have been at her anchorage in Brest.

Chaput paged her, in English as with all international radio traffic, on channel 16 VHF:

> *Pacific Pacific Pacific. We have call from tanker Amoco* Cadiz *position ten miles north of Ouessant. Requests tug.*

Chaput informed *Cadiz* that the *Pacific,* call sign DNCH, had acknowledged the tug request. In fact, the tug's radio operator, Winfried Vogel, had already picked up the call on his own. He listened in on the emergency frequencies with just as much assiduity as

the employees of Radio le Conquet. Having done his part as inter-
mediary, Chaput left the rest to the captains of the two ships to work
out between them. The contact had been made. That was what
counted. Aboard the *Cadiz,* Captain Bardari felt conflicting emo-
tions of relief and anxiety. The tug was on its way, apparently, but
he also knew that his problems weren't over with yet. He hung on in
the radio shack with Muscuso, waiting for his Chicago call to come
through.

Aboard the *Pacific,* Captain Weinert was having a bumpy
lunch with chief mate Gerhard Brandt and chief engineer Christoph
Korb when a voice on the intercom requested him to come to the
bridge. There was Vogel with news of the disabled tanker. Weinert
told him to make contact immediately and offer assistance under
Lloyd's Open Form. Without further thought he turned the tug
around, into the wind, back toward Ouessant, course 207 degrees.
He figured he had an hour to go before reaching the casualty, which
Brandt was already looking up in *Lloyd's Register,* a fat, regularly
updated compendium listing the particulars of all the world's commercial shipping: two hundred and thirty thousand deadweight
tons. He gave a little whistle. That was quite a piece of iron, this
Amoco *Cadiz.* He and *Pacific* had never towed anything that big before, not laden, anyway—nor had anyone else, for that matter.
However, it was not Hartmut Weinert's style to doubt. They would
work it out. He signaled the engine room to increase the revolutions
to 340, the absolute top. *Pacific* charged directly into the wind and
weather, which by then had risen to force ten. Fighting the waves,
she slammed up and down now, pitching heavily and receiving solid
blocks of water against her deckhouse where there had been only
spray before. As they completed their turn and began heading westward, they were just off the buoy marking the rocky shallows of a
place called Portsall.

7.

Succor on the High Seas: Antagonism and Incomprehension

At 1130, the bridge phoned down to the radio room to tell Captain Bardari that Mr. Maynard had made direct VHF contact with the tug. It was German, its name was *Pacific,* and she was rated at 10,000 horsepower. She would be arriving in about an hour. It was the first good news Bardari had heard all morning. Offsetting that were the noises from the steering flat, growing more alarming by the minute. Now the rudder and tiller were chewing up the machinery with such enthusiasm that they could clearly hear it up on the bridge, clanking and bonking, sending reverberations throughout the ship with each Herculean thrust of the rudder. Pieces of metal were flying around the steering flat like shrapnel. When Melito and his work crew tried to arrest the tiller with their five-ton chain block, the sea dashed their pretensions with contemptuous ease, snapping the chain like a piece of yarn. A chunk of the universal joint to which they had tried to attach the chain's hook flew free, clubbing able seaman Nicolo Giampaolo on the forehead above the left eye. Second mate Salvezza spent the best part of the afternoon tending to him, first in the ship's infirmary and then in his cabin.

The call to Captain Riddell finally came through. Roused out of bed at 5:32 A.M., Riddell rapidly grew wide awake as Bardari related in long, gloomy detail the steering-gear breakdown. At least the tug was on its way, though, so it looked like their immediate problem had been taken care of. Riddell agreed that the best destination for the tow would be Lyme Bay and advised Captain Bardari to call him back at his office in the Standard Oil Building in a couple of hours. Riddell, whose title in the Amoco *nomenklatura* was manager of vessel operations, tried in his turn to call his superior, Captain Claude D. Phillips, vice-president of Amoco Transport Company and superintendent of marine operations for Amoco International Oil Company, but Phillips, a man of matutinal habits, had already left home to catch the early commuter train to Chicago. Well, all right, then. Riddell would be seeing him in the office a little later.

Captain Bardari returned to the bridge for a situation report. The weather, he could see, was no better. Radar readings indicated that they had drifted almost two miles closer to land since the *Cadiz* had completed her involuntary circle in the middle of the traffic separation lane. Now they were already approaching the landside limit of the northbound lane, but, luckily, traffic was not heavy that morning: Only two other ships had passed in their vicinity, and rather distant, at that. It was at this point that Captain Bardari asked Maynard to start writing an account of the morning's events, a chronological narration that would be equivalent to an informal log. Why? It could be that as a supernumerary, Maynard had no duties just then (it was scarcely the right occasion for lectures or audiovisual presentations), and hence had the time to follow the captain around and keep track of what was happening when. More likely, though, he intended to use Maynard's notes as a basis for later writing up a properly finished version of the ship's log, which his numerous bosses at Amoco would surely be waiting to see. Ditto for the safety and insurance investigators, once the tanker had been pulled to its destination. Later investigations showed that it had been customary among Bardari's crew to write up their logs ex post facto, rather than minute by minute. It was easier to bring it all together that way, and made it look neater. As fate would have it, Maynard's three pages of penciled notes turned out to be the only on-board chronology that the *Cadiz* could offer to history in regard to her own shipwreck. These perfunctory little scribblings proved to be the source of a great deal of legal dispute in the years that followed, and they suffered in the comparison with the impressively massive, neat, and professional documentation presented by the officers of *Pacific*. The Maynard account did not argue the most convincing case for the Amoco Transport Company.

Shortly before noon, the captain took Maynard and Strano down to the steering flat for one final look. No one had any more illusions about coming up with an eleventh-hour solution. Their visit was more like a formal gesture, a certification, a ceremonial witnessing of death. The racket inside the compartment was horrifying, more like a boiler factory than a ship. The tiller had destroyed the linkages to the ram pistons, and was now crashing against steel stops in front of the ram cylinders. Impossible to tell how much further the damage could go; for all they knew, the whole thing would keep on thrashing and flailing until the rudder wrenched itself free and fell into the sea.

The possibility of the rudder falling off became something of an *idée fixe* aboard Amoco *Cadiz*. Even earlier than this trip to the steering flat and then throughout the rest of the day, the fear of a massive ablation under the stern of the ship was a constant source of anxiety for the captain and Maynard. It explains in large part why Bardari did not use his perfectly operative main engine more than he did and sooner than he did. With the wind and swell coming over his starboard beam, his ship had taken a natural position of drift facing more or less toward land. This was contrary to theory, which had long assumed that tankers, being low in the water, would offer their prominent accommodation block as a kind of rudimentary sail, and hence would eventually turn bow to the wind. It turned out that theory was wrong: Unpredictable animals that they are, VLCCs have demonstrated a preference for immobilizing themselves abeam to the wind and wallowing in the trough of the swell. This being the case, many wondered why Bardari did not run his engine in reverse, to try to back away from the coast. Later, when he was much closer to land, this is precisely what he did—it worked somewhat, although not as well as they had hoped—but there was no question of going astern while his engineers were down in the compartment trying to fix the gear. That could only have increased the force of the rudder slams, rendering the repairs even more difficult and more dangerous. Even after the engineers had given up, though, he still could not bring himself to call the engine room for reverse power. Wouldn't that make the slamming worse? And couldn't that in turn make the rudder fall away, to come crashing down against the screw? And then where would they be, with no rudder and no screw? No: Bardari decided to stand pat at that early hour of the game. The tug was on its way. Better not to take chances. Or was it? Many were the armchair admirals who insisted (safely, after the whole drama had been played out) that he could have gained an hour or so of surcease by beating in reverse from the moment of the breakdown.

On this, their final visit to the steering flat, Bardari and his officers stayed only a few minutes; there was no point in risking injuries from flying metal. Much to their credit, Melito and Assante tried again with another chain block in spite of the danger, but the second attempt proved as useless as the first. After that, they had no more tricks. There was nothing aboard the Amoco *Cadiz* that could stop the tiller. From that moment on, they closed the door to the oil-filled compartment and abandoned the steering gear, like an old friend committed to bedlam. For the rest of that day, and into the night, they could hear it raging and knocking within its steel box.

Twelve o'clock. Speaking directly from the bridge into his VHF microphone, Captain Bardari called the *Pacific* for the first time himself. Above all, he wanted to know the tug's position and estimated time of arrival. A few seconds later, Weinert's voice crackled back over the bridge loudspeaker, answering in cool, businesslike English. "You can see me," he said, and, indeed, after carefully scanning the horizon to port, Bardari could make out a bobbing pinpoint of white—*Pacific*'s superstructure—with the sea bursting around it.

At 1208, *Pacific* called back, "I take it this is Lloyd's Open Form," Weinert said.

"No," replied Captain Bardari. "I want a towage rate to Lyme Bay."

That didn't sit well with Hartmut Weinert. Not at all. Bardari's unexpected refusal was the first manifestation of disagreement, the first grain of sand of a destructive friction that grew steadily worse throughout that day, quickly turning to irritation, then anger, and finally into a kind of war, a battle of nerves and useless recrimination that had the two captains totally at cross-purposes when they arrived at the supreme moment of crisis. That battle was not the cause of the grounding of the Amoco *Cadiz*, of course, but it may have been a contributing factor. It is not impossible to imagine that the oilpot might have been saved if the two masters had been able to work together in an atmosphere of serene cooperation. That they could not do so must be laid squarely at the door of Captain Pasquale Bardari and, by extension, of the Standard Oil Company of Indiana.

Weinert was furious. If ever there was a classic case of salvage, this was it: a fully laden tanker helpless in the water, a few miles from the coast, drifting at the whim of an onshore wind. What was this business about a towage rate? Didn't they know what danger they were in? Weren't they able to see land? And didn't they know that masters of salvage tugs work only on Lloyd's Open Form (and, in the case of *Pacific*, its German equivalent, DSG, for certain specific categories of work), that even if Weinert had wanted to work on a straight towage rate, he didn't have the right to do so, deals of that sort being the exclusive domain of the front offices? What did Bardari take him for—a sausage merchant or something? Didn't he understand the realities of life?

Adamant, Captain Bardari continued to insist upon the towage rate to Lyme Bay. It is clear that he did understand the realities of life, but his realities were a good deal different from those of Captain Weinert. He had learned them during his eight-year apprenticeship with the American multinational corporation that employed him and in whose murky waters his career had very nearly foundered back in those harsh early days when his masters were consistently rating him average or below average, and when Chicago was wondering out loud whether he had a future with Amoco. Pasquale Bardari's realities had to do with deadlines and performance ratings and cost-effectiveness, and all of their spoken and unspoken exigencies were summed up in the *Tanker Operations Manual,* the Bible of every captain of the Amoco fleet. The paragraph covering towing and salvage assistance begins bravely enough:

> In any case where human life is in peril or where the vessel or cargo is threatened with damage or loss, the Master shall immediately take all precautions for the safety of his vessel and all on board, and to that end he shall exercise his own best judgment without restraint.

So far so good, although the very fact of outlining such obvious and traditional verities to the master of one of the biggest ships in the world smacks of patronizing legalistic pedantry. But there is a good deal worse. The manual continues with a caveat direct from the heavy hand of the Standard Oil *nomenklatura:*

> So far as is consistent with the foregoing, the Master should endeavor to notify the Marine Manager's office by the quickest possible means when outside assistance is required, and when the circumstances of the case permit, utilize the assistance of available Company vessels. Before accepting assistance from a non-Company vessel, the Master shall, if practicable, advise the Marine Manager of the terms of the agreement to assist, i.e. whether salvage or towage.

A few months after the accident, the Liberian board of inquiry in London, staffed by some unusually qualified English and American experts, read this paragraph with stupor, then commented with typical Liberian understatement:

> In the view of the Board these last two sentences are capable of being construed so as to limit the over-all authority and responsibility of the Master for the safety of his vessel, as expressed in paragraphs 1-2-5 and 1-2-6 of the same document. This strikes the Board as most undesirable and such as is only too likely to lead to divided responsibility. The time spent by Captain Bardari in the present case in seeking to obtain instructions from his Owners, when his vessel was in a situation of grave peril, suggests that there was indeed in his mind some degree of confusion as to the extent of his own responsibility.

The Liberians were being polite. There is not the slightest doubt—he demonstrated it time and time again during the crucial hours that followed this first radiophonic meeting with Captain Weinert—that Captain Bardari felt a good deal more than "some degree of confusion" as to how much authority he had for making decisions that might cost his employers a lot of money. He may have been scared by a Lloyd's Open Form because he was sure that it would mean a big bill to Standard Oil. Anyone who has spent even a little time in or around a large corporation knows the paralyzing pusillanimity that can be engendered by the big-company mentality, and the rigidity of the lines of command. Pasquale Bardari was right in the middle of the corporate dilemma, and it turned him into a maritime Hamlet, unable to make the big decisions on his own.

Thus began a melancholy subplot to the story of the last day of the Amoco *Cadiz*, a sad and perhaps crucial breakdown of communications between two men who between them held the key—however tenuous and chancy it may have been—to what was shaping up as the biggest single loss in maritime history. Captains Weinert and Bardari, as they shouted "no, no, no" to each other over their VHF sets, were all that stood between the rocky, fish-rich Breton coast and 219,617.32 long tons of poison. The spilling of that poison assured them both of a place in future history books, and once and for all supplanted another name as the world's symbol of ecological horror: *Torrey Canyon*.

The background to the feud between the two captains requires some explaining, not only because the truth is difficult to discern when two parties are at odds, but also because this most critical aspect of the Amoco *Cadiz* drama was scandalously—and often viciously—misinterpreted and misreported in the world's press, and especially in the French press. It is time to set a few things right.

The Lloyd's Open Form (LOF) is a standard legal document for a proposed salvage operation, a four-page contract emitted by the famous multipartite English insurance corporation popularly known as Lloyd's of London. It is called "open" because it is literally open, with no amount of money being stipulated for the salvage job: The sum to be paid is determined later in London by a professional arbiter. At the top of page one, beneath the title "Salvage Agreement," is a statement of the contract's fundamental premise, in eloquently stark English: NO CURE—NO PAY.

Every salvage company has reams of the LOF on hand, and of course makes sure that every one of its tugs also has an ample supply. They are the standard paper of the trade, like order forms for salesmen or accident declaration sheets for insurance people. Under normal weather conditions, the salvager and the master of the ship in distress fill in the blanks, sign the forms, and exchange copies, but of course this is not always possible. When the sea is too rough to actually pass from one ship to another—as it was on March 16—a simple radio statement from the captain of the casualty is often enough. Or the statement may be formalized by radiotelegram confirmation. Once the acceptance has been stated, the work of getting the crippled ship to safety gets under way. There is never any talk about fees or money. The rationale behind the LOF, the whole reason for its existence, is to avoid the possible loss of time, property, or life through haggling.

Much is misunderstood about salvage at sea. It is neither legally possible nor practically feasible for a tug to demand exorbitant rewards such as half the value of a VLCC in danger, as the press often suggested in the heat of the Amoco *Cadiz* affair. In fact, contrary to persistent popular legend, even if you come upon an abandoned ship on the high seas, it is not necessarily yours. The owner may reclaim his property, but he will have to indemnify the salvager before he can get it back. And if in the bad old days ruthless captains may have driven cruelly harsh bargains to save a ship in distress, such situations today fall under the infinitely more civilized realm of the Lloyd's Open Form. The LOF binds the signatory parties, if they cannot agree on a settlement among themselves, to accept the later findings of a Lloyd's arbiter in London. Neutral, objective, and knowledgeable, he weighs several elements in fixing the amount of the award for any salvage job: the extent of the efforts required, the skill and energy displayed by the salvagers, the value of the salvaged vessel and its cargo, the risks incurred by the salvagers, and the degree of danger from which the casualty was saved. The amounts awarded by arbiters, if based on a percentage of value of ship and cargo, vary considerably, which is only logical: A salvager who spent a week trying to pull a small yacht off a reef might be awarded eighty percent of its value and still lose money. But if it is an immense prize like the Amoco *Cadiz*, where the total value of ship and cargo might be in the vicinity of $40 million or so, an award of only a couple of percentage points brings the salvager's earnings well over $1 million. Everything depends, then—but one constant is that the party of the casualty will always tend to minimize the gravity of his damage and the extent of the dangers from which his ship was saved. Keeping this in mind will help in understanding much of what went on that afternoon and evening.

One more fact of marine life needs explaining: the role of salvage companies and their tugs. Without doubt, this question is the one that was the most wildly distorted in the lamentable affair of the Amoco *Cadiz*. Salvage and towing is a highly organized, highly competitive, but entirely honorable profession that had its birth in the nineteenth century, when steam power made it possible to "tug" boats against winds and currents. The Dutch (Smit International, the Netherlands' biggest, is also the biggest in the world) are particularly masterful at the trade, but the English, Germans, and Americans also dispatch their overpowered oceangoing tractors to virtually any point on the globe where a pull is needed. By far the greatest part of such a company's business consists of the normal drudgery of delivering oil rigs, barges, caissons, ships sold for scrap, etc., from one place to another—at a price agreed to before the job is undertaken and sealed by normal contract.

Daredevil salvaging plays a relatively small role in the trade, but wherever there are ships crossing bodies of water, there are bound to be shipwrecks, or at least ships in distress. It is only natural, then, for the salvage firms to station their tugs at the points of greatest intensity of traffic and most capricious weather conditions. When there is trouble, these companies' tugs are generally the only succor available—and the navigators in trouble are delighted and grateful when they see their businesslike snouts bashing in over the horizon. Oceangoing tugs such as the *Pacific* and her more modern sisters are equipped not only to tow, but also to pump leaking ships dry, fight fires, and send divers to work underwater. They are a very expensive investment (today's big new ones cost in the vicinity of $20 million, not counting crew), and when they are sitting idle in port they eat up lots of company money. It is reasonable, then, that when they go out for rescue work—almost invariably in hideous weather conditions—they should expect to earn large sums. Red Adair doesn't risk his neck for charity when he puts out oil well fires around the world, and yet no one has ever pointed an accusing finger at him as an unconscionable bandit; it is well established in folklore that dentists are highway robbers, but we're happy to have them around when we have a toothache. Same thing with sailors and tugs.

Withal, a grossly unfair legend concerning the intervention of *Pacific* quickly arose in the aftermath of the shipwreck, largely developed and spread by the more irresponsible and sensation-seeking elements of the French press. The story they invented was that Captain Weinert sadistically withheld his aid to the Amoco *Cadiz* until Captain Bardari agreed to his piratical demands. The time lost in haggling was, therefore, what made the grounding and subsequent pollution inevitable. The legend began one day after the grounding, when French television interviewed a crew member of the Amoco *Cadiz* who never gave his name or his position aboard the ship. But he was not lacking in easy accusations.

"It's a question of money," he insisted. "Even at sea. We sailors call the rescue tugs sharks. I call them jackals. With tugs it's always a question of money. If there's a boat in difficulty, it's a hunt. It's a question of billions. The first tug that gets there has a chance of earning enormous sums. There are tugs that demand up to half the value of the cargo and half the value of the boat."

For a man who called himself a sailor, he clearly understood nothing about the workings of the Lloyd's Open Form. His misapprehensions, unfortunately, are all too common in the trade. Experienced observers of the maritime scene know that few crew members understand the LOF. Worse, there is no lacking of ships' masters who share their ignorance. Bardari, apparently, was one of them.

Now that *Pacific* was in sight, first mate Strano and his three-man work detail donned rubber boots, yellow slickers, and the Day-Glo-orange life vests issued to sailors of the Amoco fleet and made their way to the bow. This was not easy: A powerless ship, even a VLCC, rolls heavily when it is dead in the sea, and with each fifteen-degree list to one side or another, green water streamed across the deck. On the *Cadiz*, twin railings ran down the center of the deck, but there was no raised platform, as there is on many other modern tankers.

Strano and his men slogged laboriously forward, heads tilted against the wind and rain that pelted them from the right, gripping the rails with both hands, occasionally clambering up on them like monkeys when a sea came rolling over the deck. Already, they discovered, a long length of railing amidships had been torn away by the storm. Having come directly from the warm coziness of the accommodation block, they were shocked and stunned by the cold. The temperature was hardly above freezing; within minutes the rain and wind-driven spray had numbed their fingers dead. The mere idea of being swept overboard into that chaos of gray-green water was enough to terrify a man. It's going to be a hard day's work, thought Strano, and he was right.

At length they reached the meager shelter of the sharply raked forecastle that gave their big oilpot a surprisingly graceful silhouette up front. Stepping cautiously, handhold to handhold—one hand for yourself, one hand for the work—drenched by the showers of icy spray being flung back over the lip of the coaming, they set safety ropes around the area of the bow: They would have to be working in dangerously exposed conditions there when the tug arrived. One final job finished off their preparations, but it wasn't an easy one: making ready the heaving line.

The heaving line is always step one in any towing operation. Usually it is a nylon cord, perhaps a centimeter in diameter and capable of holding a weight of a few hundred kilos. It is what you start pulling everything aboard with, the classical story of starting with a small line to a bigger one and a bigger one, until you are dealing with the full mass of the main towing wire itself. While one of his men struggled up to the platform at the very tip of the bow, Strano lay on the deck beneath the platform, a long grappling hook in his hand. Directly in front of him was an egg-shaped opening in the ship's steel skin, about as wide as his shoulders, called the Panama fairlead. All ships have fairleads spaced around their bows and sterns, because all ships eventually have to pass mooring ropes out to docks and jetties—or to the "mules," electric tractors that pull ships through the Panama canal, which of course is where the name comes from. Roughly speaking, fairleads are only ropeholes, but they come in many designs, shapes, and thicknesses, depending on who made up the specifications. There is no set rule. On the Amoco *Cadiz*, it was a solid iron casting, like an eye, set into the bowplates. As he lay on the deck peering through the gaping orifice, Strano had a chilling close-up view of the sea, but what interested him was the nylon cord thrown out from above, over the top of the forecastle. After a few unsuccessful stabs, he managed to catch it on his grappling hook and drag it back in through the fairlead. He tied it securely around a bitt, and the AB at the bow above him brought his end back down as well. Now the *Cadiz* had a heaving line through her fairlead; she was rigged to pull in the rest of the towing gear. Strano picked up his walkie-talkie and reported to the captain that they were ready.

It was almost half past twelve by then, and *Pacific* had just arrived. Strano and his men watched her with satisfaction as she churned stolidly through the huge seas off their starboard beam. On the bridge, Maynard recalled, everyone was overjoyed to see her, and their spirits rose accordingly. Carefully, methodically, Captain Weinert took his tug around the casualty, looking her over, mentally balancing tide, wind, and swell, and figuring out the best way to make the hookup. *Pacific* was tremendously reassuring, with her sturdy black hull, twin A-frame masts, and powerfully growling diesels. No one doubted for a minute that she would be able to get them to Lyme Bay, least of all Hartmut Weinert. Their problem was as good as over.

Captain Weinert took *Pacific* around the stern again, cut the engines, and stood off, letting her drift with the weather. Now, riding on the water like a cork instead of ploughing into it while under power, the tug shipped less green water over the workdeck, and the crew was able to go out to prepare the tow. Taking a second look, Weinert may have felt his optimism wane. Up close, this floating, horizontal skyscraper with the sea coursing in over it looked like a pretty formidable challenge to take on. He knew that *Simson*, farther up the Channel by the Casquets, off Cherbourg, was on her way, having been ordered by their Hamburg office to turn around and assist *Pacific*. But that was 150 miles, and that meant ten to twelve hours in this weather. Until then, he would just have to do what he could.

He didn't like the looks of this barge. She was a recent ship, but she already looked crummy, run-down, and unkempt, streaked with vertical orange lines of rust along the entire length of her hull. She didn't look well-maintained or shipshape. You wouldn't find unpainted rust lines like that on *Pacific*.

And he didn't like what he had been hearing on the radio, either, over the VHF contact with the Amoco *Cadiz*'s bridge. Once again he proposed his normal salvage conditions of the Lloyd's Open Form. And once again the Italian captain—he was already thinking of him as "the Italian," just as those aboard the tanker soon were referring not to *Pacific*, but "the German tug"—said, "No, no, no," and insisted on a straight towing rate to Lyme Bay. It was stupid and maddening. He didn't even mention any figure, and just kept repeating the insistence on a towing rate, whatever that was supposed to be, and telling him he should contact AMOCOSHIP, Chicago, by telegram or telex. He seemed completely spooked by the LOF. What sort of a captain was he, anyway? And another thing: Who was the captain? It wasn't always clear who he was talking with, and who was the voice of authority. Sometimes it was the Italian, but then, even more often, it was another man, who spoke very good English. Captain Weinert had no way of knowing about Mr. Maynard, but the change in voices confused him and put him on edge. It was just another chip in the growing pile of misunderstanding and incompatibility between the two ships.

8.

The First Tow

At a quarter past one, a sharpshooting crew member of the tug—chief mate Brandt in this case—braced on the platform outside the bridge, hit the tanker's foredeck perfectly with his first shot of the Kongsberg rifle. The Kongsberg is a nifty little Norwegian invention, a rifle that looks like most others, with the exception that at the end of its muzzle protrudes a comically large "bullet," a hollow, orange projectile about the size of a hefty man's forearm. Inside the projectile are a couple of hundred meters of neatly coiled nylon shooting line of 325-pound breaking strength. The marksman on the tug fires his carbine, the projectile flies over the gap between the two ships, uncoiling nylon as it goes, and then clatters down onto the casualty's deck: A line has been established, and it is tied to the heaving line already run out through the Panama fairlead. With the two ships thus connected, everything after that goes according to the routine of pulling across heavier and heavier lines until the full, final towing rig of seventeen tons has been made fast. So *Pacific* got its first line across rapidly—but under what terms?

A thousand times since that day Weinert has retold the story of the tow, and the details never change. Continuing to affirm over VHF that he worked only by Lloyd's Open Form, he received in return the endless litany about the "towage rate," repeated over and again. You contact your owners and I'll contact mine. We'll let them work it out. In other words: Let's pass the buck on up to the bosses. It was a radiantly classical illustration of the big-company mentality. Just as fervently, Weinert continued to refuse the straight rate, until Bardari finally buckled later that afternoon. His version of events is far more convincing than that of Captain Bardari's, and everything that transpired that day, all the evidence adduced in the investigations since, tends to corroborate it.

What Captain Bardari told the members of the Marine Board of Investigation convened after the wreck by Liberia's Commissioner of Maritime Affairs was quite different from Weinert's version. After initially refusing his proposal of a flat rate, Captain Weinert at length said, "Okay, okay," and put the line aboard. In Bardari's mind, then, that meant that he had won the argument and extracted the verbal contract from Weinert at 1314. The exact amount, he figured, could somehow be worked out later, between his front office and the Germans. He was off the hook. Or so he may have thought. But it is clear that the pressures of the moment were leading him toward delusion. The fact is that no tug master in the world would have accepted a straight towage rate under the conditions that prevailed then. Bardari should have known it.

Contract or not, Weinert put a line across to the Amoco *Cadiz*—which, in fact, was contrary to his company's standing instructions. But he was not entirely naive in this. As an experienced tug master, he knew that acceptance of a line by the captain of a casualty could later be construed in arbitration court as tacit acceptance of the LOF. Meanwhile, he was damn well going to wring a formal commitment to LOF from the Italian.

Captain Bardari was spooked by the LOF because he was afraid it was going to cost Amoco a lot of money. He was in radio-telephone communication with Chicago throughout that day and evening, talking with his bosses and asking for instructions. Even so, Amoco insisted afterward that Bardari was at all times complete master of his ship, free to make any decision that he deemed best, without any constraint whatsoever. But in the age of instant satellite communication, and with respect to a huge company like Amoco, whose lines of authority are so rigid as to have given birth to the kind of *Tanker Operations Manual* which we have already seen, such a contention is simply not believable.

Captain Bardari was a competent and well-trained sailor, but he was working for Amoco because he was cheaper than an American. This fact alone placed him in a position of psychological inferiority in relation to his bosses in Monrovia, Liberia; Hamilton, Bermuda; Baltimore, Maryland; or Chicago, Illinois (depending on which part of the corporate shell game it pleases you to choose). He was earning the approximate salary of a low-level executive drone or a high-level secretary within Standard Oil's corporate structure. In spite of his awesome ship—or ships, because he was shifted from one to another like a utility infielder—he was small beans within the company, a minor bureaucrat. Now, then: Even if the company assured him that he was the absolute pasha of the *Cadiz* or the *Europa* or the *Milford Haven,* it is improbable that he would make ad hoc million-dollar decisions like the chairman of the board. He would phone up his bosses to check first. Bardari knew very well that the entire universe of the VLCC is built around cost-effectiveness: its size, its automation, reduced crews, its nearly perpetual movement, the ideal, fuel-conserving RPM of its engine, the business-school whizzes who determine where it will go and when. Life isn't so simple anymore: Pasquale Bardari could have had a diploma framed in genuine walnut veneer attesting to his title as absolute master of the Amoco *Cadiz*, but he was still going to worry like hell about spending a million dollars or so of company cash.

And rightly so—any loyal employee of any company should be. Nor is there anything wrong or immoral with the principle of cost-effectiveness. It is altogether praiseworthy for corporations large and small to labor to give consumers better products at lower prices. But every system has its drawbacks: If distant boardrooms decide to build gargantuan tankers and set them afloat on the world's oceans, they may lower company expenses, but they increase the likelihood of terrifyingly vast pollutions. And if cost analysts can save money on the oilpots (a couple of million dollars apiece) by building them with only one rudder and one screw instead of two, then they raise the statistical likelihood of irreparable breakdowns, because no machine is perfect, neither a tanker nor a spaceship. If a company views its boats as transportation units, and their crews as dispensable and mutually replaceable domestics, then there is always the chance that they will behave like domestics, rather than commanders, when the moments of difficulty arise.

"Just imagine the man," speculated an American observer who was familiar with the case, "flying to Chicago to meet his employers for the first time. There he is, a little Italian mate on one of their ships, and he gets in the elevator to go to Captain Phillips's office on the fiftieth floor of the Standard Oil Building. Look at it: eighty floors of Carrara marble—pure Carrara marble!—the fourth highest building in the world, and he's going up to the office on the southeast corner of the fiftieth floor. Can you imagine the impression that makes? That's not Standard Oil, that place—that's heaven!"

Could Captain Bardari have made the decision to accept the Lloyd's Open Form without checking with Chicago? The answer is no, not really, everything considered—and he didn't. There was endless discussion of this point after the grounding, and although Bardari insisted that the decisions during that day were all his, the fact is that as he drifted agonizingly toward the Breton coast, Amoco Chicago was calling around Europe, over the skipper's head, speaking as the voice of authority, seeking a flat towage rate for him wherever they could find it.

Thanks to twentieth-century technology the communications with Chicago were superb, but some ancient atavisms were at work to make them inoperable over the few yards of sea separating Amoco *Cadiz* and *Pacific*. The climate of mistrust and scorn between the two ships and their masters would go from uncomfortable to poisonous before the day was over. A painful early example arose almost immediately, when the first tow was being made fast. Before Brandt fired the Kongsberg rifle, Captain Weinert stood off the stern of the *Cadiz* and radioed the tanker detailed instructions on how to secure the connection:

"We are coming on your starboard bow. We are shooting a line over your bow. Then you bring this line between your Panama fairlead . . ."

At this point, Weinert maintains, the *Cadiz* interrupted him to inquire: "What is a Panama fairlead?"

Again, it may or may not have happened exactly like that. It could be that Weinert misunderstood the query, or it may be that his Teutonic manner of enunciation confused a native speaker of a Latin language, but it clearly underlines the animosity that was already there, and that grew steadily throughout the day. For Weinert, it was worth an ironic laugh with his mate, Brandt. Of course he wouldn't know what a Panama fairlead was. He had to ask what "bollard pull" meant, too. *Natürlich.* He was an Italian sailor. Time and again, Weinert would rage against what he called "the bad seamanship of the Italians." Just as, time and again, Captain Bardari and his officers were to rage against Weinert for what they perceived as guile, ruthlessness, dishonesty, and, finally, bad seamanship. The climate was unhealthy from the start, even before the first line was across. As *Pacific* stood off readying her gear, Mr. Maynard had already begun listening in on channel 28 while Weinert spoke to headquarters in Hamburg, "eavesdropping," as he himself later admitted. He was stymied by the high-speed German, but even if he had learned something, it hardly could have helped to develop the serene concentration and cooperation both ships would need if they were to succeed with the rescue. Already, they were adversaries.

The tow connection started well. Strano and his men tied the Kongsberg line to the one they had passed through the fairlead, tossed it over the bow, and then pulled it back in through the fairlead. The Kongsberg line brought up a thirty-meter length of heavy rope: the heaving line. It was cumbersome and wet, but that was nothing compared to what followed: the five-inch-thick 220-meter messenger line, much too heavy for human muscle. Strano and his men secured it around the drum of the *Cadiz*'s forward winch, and steam power brought the rest aboard. Hanging onto the safety ropes that they had rigged earlier, they made the steel cable of the towing pennant fast to two bitts, one forward and one starboard. Ten turns on one and six on the other, as Weinert had instructed, and it was ready for the tow. At the end of the pennant was a steel eye, and through it was "threaded" a seven-meter length chain, painted white (for better visibility against the hulls of casualties), as thick as a man's wrist. Strano winched in until the chain was half in and half out of the Panama fairlead. This was the crucial point of the tow, the only part of the complicated operation where any serious chafing could occur, and it was precisely for this reason that Weinert chose to span it with the sixty-five-millimeter chain, the strongest element of his tow rig. Weinert had inspected the fairlead through his binoculars, but from his vantage point it was difficult to judge its quality. All he could tell for sure was that it was of the classical Panama type, rather than the "bull nose" or other current designs. That could be good or bad. It depended on how it was made.

After the chain came the spring, a fifty-meter length of supple nylon hawser rope, doubled over, each side fourteen inches around, which lay half in and half out of the water. With one end attached to the chain, the other was shackled to the main tow wire, which disappeared under the surface in a long, submarine sag and reemerged only where it came up to ride on the towing bows, the stout steel arches that protected the tug's aft workdeck. The dynamics of large-ship towing are such that the main wire is hardly ever visible, being so heavy that the sag, or catenary, drops deeply down in the gap between the tower and the towed, exactly in the manner of the main cables of a suspension bridge. The rougher the weather, the longer the line has to be, and the deeper the catenary. This simple law of physics was apparently ignored by those aboard the Amoco *Cadiz*, because it, too, added to the confusion and recrimination of the day.

Everything was made fast by 1330. *Pacific* began moving off to starboard, paying out the towing wire from the drum winch aft of the smokestack, where the open workdeck began. "Towing easy," inching forward as the drum unrolled the cable, Captain Weinert was once again facing almost directly into the wind, but at the slower speed the encounter between the sea and his bow was much less dramatic. The situation was hardly ideal, but it seemed about under control. The *Cadiz*, rolling and pitching awkwardly in the swell, was heading almost due south—just a few degrees off to the southeast—and had the weather on her starboard beam; dead ahead lay Ouessant and then, farther to port, directly downwind, the Breton mainland itself. Weinert had decided from the start to tow to starboard, into the wind. For him, this was an obvious choice, hardly worth a second thought: The island lay straight ahead and the mainland to the left. Therefore, he should go right. Elementary. If he could turn the tanker, break her free of the trough of the swell, all the rest would be relatively easy. Lined up together, bows into the storm, he could pull forward, the way boats are meant to go, all the way to Lyme Bay. When eight hundred meters of wire had been paid out, he called for more engine power but quickly realized that the line was still too short: The wire became dangerously taut, whipping and snapping against the tow arches, the curved steel rails that held the wire above the workdeck and over which it rode as the winch paid it out. He lowered the engine RPM and winched out two hundred meters more of line, "driving" the tug from the little command bridge aft, where the controls of the main bridge were duplicated. Tug skippers learn to work looking backward, their eyes on the cable and the casualty. The mate can always keep a lookout up forward.

Two o'clock passed. The tanker seemed to be moving a little, maybe ten or fifteen degrees, but it was hard going. Harder than Weinert had expected. She was hardly budging at eighty percent power, and Weinert didn't dare apply any more, for fear his line would break. Now *Pacific* began falling off to starboard, skidding sideways under the enormous burden of the wallowing deadweight behind her. Weinert wound up his starboard engine 20 RPM more, steering with his propellors. The tug steadied, but still didn't advance. They were five and a half nautical miles north-northeast of Ouessant.

Aboard the *Cadiz* the atmosphere, if not exactly jubilant, was one of relief and optimism. From the bridge Captain Bardari, Maynard, and the mates could clearly see the bow slowly swinging to starboard in the direction of *Pacific*, heaving and bucking into the sea at ninety degrees to them, off toward the right. Bardari radioed Strano to come back from the bow, where they had been working for more than two hours under exhausting and dangerous conditions. At 1416 he asked Maynard to note that the men were safely back inside, and the Englishman duly wrote it in his chronology. It was one more example (and there would be others before long) of the extraordinary solicitude of Pasquale Bardari for his crew. Throughout their mutually shared ordeal, he displayed an almost fatherly concern for their health and safety, and they responded with a loyalty and warmth that is rare on any ship, and all the more so on the modern, frigid, officelike VLCCs. Things were looking better. Bardari and his friend permitted themselves a can of beer apiece with lunch.

Over the radiotelephone Captain Bardari was pleased to inform Riddell that he had a towing contract to Lyme Bay, and that the job was under way. Did he really believe it was as simple as that? Perhaps. That was what he said at the Liberian hearing, at any rate. Within a few minutes after hanging up, though, his easy optimism was to suffer a crushing blow: LOF began rearing its ugly head again.

When he walked up the stairs from the radio room, the bridge personnel were buzzing with indignation over what appeared to be a new situation, a new twist in the game of the Lloyd's Open Form: The Germans had stopped pulling. Or had they? Strano remembers returning to the bridge at around 1430 to hear his captain repeatedly asking *Pacific* why they were not towing. Now the Amoco *Cadiz* had slipped back to her original heading of almost due south. And once again, Weinert came across on VHF to demand the Lloyd's Open Form. "We already have a contract for Lyme Bay," Captain Bardari insisted.

Aboard *Pacific*, Captain Weinert was growing more and more aggravated. "They don't realize what a bad position they're in," he said with an oath to Brandt. And then he had a surge of real anger. Here they were, trying to keep the Italians from going onto the rocks, being thrown around by the sea—two of his men would be injured before the day was out—doing their damndest to get the job done, while up there in the cozy bridge of their goddam oilpot the Italians were drinking coffee and amusing themselves by bargaining with him. Well, to hell with them.

"Either you give me a Lloyd's Open Form," he shouted into the radio, "or I cut the tow!"

Or did he?

The last few lines are entirely my invention. They are a synthesis, a summing-up of the events that occurred at around 1435, as they were reported by Mr. Maynard and the others aboard the *Cadiz*. Their version is that Captain Weinert, unable to make Captain Bardari accept the LOF at the start, first agreed to a regular mileage tow, put the line aboard, pulled a bit to show he could do it, and then throttled back his engines and began his blackmail. According to this version, Captain Bardari retaliated with a counterthreat of his own: "You cut the line and I'll call the coast guard."

It was, at best, a hollow menace. Did he know that France did not even possess a coast guard? Perhaps not. Certainly he could have sent out a general distress call, but there were some real, practical reasons and some intangible, psychological ones for him not doing it. For one thing, he had understood from Radio le Conquet that *Pacific* was the only tug available and his understanding was entirely correct. The only other one within even approximate striking distance was the *Simson*, also of Bugsier, *Pacific*'s 16,000-horsepower cousin. Even then, she was hammering her way back toward them at full speed, passing a couple of laboring (and probably surprised) container ships on the way, and making a spectacular show of her head-on battle with the elements. When brutes like *Simson* take on the ocean, the result of the match is generally a draw, which is as good as anyone can hope for. As things turned out, she arrived just a bit too late.

One of the most tantalizing speculations about the unhappy Amoco *Cadiz* concerns *Simson*'s arrival time. When Captain Bardari lost his steering, *Simson*'s skipper, Martin Winter, was returning from Punta Arenas to Hamburg, and he had his tug on an up-Channel course off the coast of Brittany. When, at 1153, he received the radio call from Captain Meyer directing him to go and help Weinert with the disabled VLCC, he had already spent more than two hours steaming away from the Amoco *Cadiz*'s position since the steering breakdown. And this is what brings on the speculation: If Captain Bardari had sent out a precautionary "pan" message right away, instead of the security call, if he had asked all available tugs to stand by, since their assistance might be needed, *Simson*—which would have come running, as any salvage tug would in those circumstances—might have arrived on the scene up to four hours earlier than she finally did. Those extra two hours lost while she steamed away from the tanker meant a loss of four hours in all—two hours down, two hours back. As a result, Weinert and *Pacific* were condemned to handling the chore all by themselves.

Should Bardari have made a general distress SOS call at that point, when he was arguing with Weinert? Many observers thought so afterward, but Bardari must have concluded that it would make him look downright silly: a general distress while he was actually tied up to a salvage tug. And pointless, too, because he already knew from Le Conquet that *Pacific* was the only tug available in the vicinity. And anyway, what if he did it, what if he got on the radio to scream for help, alerting patrol planes and passing ships and lifeboats and ministers of the interior and newspapermen and boy scouts and sharks, how would he look in the eyes of the world and before his superiors in that great alabaster-colored phallus in Chicago called the Standard Oil Building when he tried to explain that he wasn't getting on with the master of *Pacific*? In the macho world of seamen, would this not be judged as a sign of panic? Of whimpering instead of calmly getting his ship to safety? An *Italian* ship. Like the *Torrey Canyon* . . .

But there is a final explanation for his failure to issue anything more alarming than the famous TTT call that day, one that holds more weight than all the others: money. Once again, the Lloyd's Open Form must be considered. Unquestionably, Captain Bardari was thinking ahead to the Lloyd's arbitration in those early hours. He knew that one of the prime elements taken into account by the arbiter in fixing the amount of the award was the degree of danger from which the casualty was rescued. It was in the interest of Standard Oil for him to minimize the appearance of these dangers, and thus help lower the amount that would have to be paid to Bugsier. By crying to the world that he was in distress, he would be giving Weinert and Bugsier a valuable trump card to present to the arbitration board. Very likely, this same reasoning explains why he consistently refused to give *Pacific* information about his rudder, in spite of repeated requests from Weinert and Brandt. He would have preferred for them not even to know that he was entirely without steering. He didn't want to appear helpless. He was thinking of the good of the company.

Naturally, Captain Weinert denied that he ever stopped pulling, and he was able to produce an impressive batch of documentary evidence to buttress his assertion: his fair deck log, his bridge notebook, his radio log, his engine room log, and his engine maneuvering book, all of them meticulously updated minute by minute, in apple-pie order. Everything shows that he was pulling all the while, as hard as he dared, but that *Pacific* was simply not strong enough to overcome wind and weather and the immense bulk of Amoco *Cadiz*. She came around some, but never more than a few degrees, and then she slipped back. It was a new and troubling experience for him. Never before in his career with tugs had he failed to turn a casualty—but then, of course, no one before him had ever taken on a laden VLCC in weather like that. Now, with his tow wire—and his nerves—dangerously taut, Weinert realized that the best he could do was to hold her until *Simson* arrived on the scene. One thing was good, though: The angle of drift had changed; even though he was making no progress against the wind, it was apparent that *Pacific* had considerably slowed the tanker's progress toward the rocks.

Did Captain Weinert ever make a threat to force Captain Bardari's hand on the LOF? He denied it energetically, but given the extraordinary circumstances of that Thursday afternoon, it would seem entirely plausible that he may have, at one time or another, out of pure vexation if nothing else. *Pacific* was the only straw Captain Bardari could clutch at in the hope of avoiding disaster, and here he was, jabbering on about mileage rates. Tug and casualty captains have never gotten along famously, but there were limits. Who was doing whom the favor here? He had a good mind to let them stew in their own juices. He picked up the microphone and . . . well, it could well have happened that way. Captain Weinert was in the position of strength, and Captain Bardari in one of utter weakness. It was silly of him to think he could whipsaw the German into a bargain towing job.

Even if Captain Weinert had made the threat, any experienced sailor would have known it was pure bluff. In one furious gesture, he would have been throwing away a thousand meters or so of towing gear, any hope of getting salvage money (his personal share of the salvage award would have been two percent), and his reputation as a serious master. He would have owed the world an explanation for the worst oil spill in history, and possibly had some deaths on his conscience as well. Not even to mention owing Bugsier Reederei thousands of dollars for the gear he had chucked overboard into the drink. No, it is not serious to think that Captain Weinert would have cut his line. But it is not to be excluded that he may have talked a little bit about it on VHF, to pass the time of day. If the Italians felt like flea-market bargaining, well, then, the Germans could show their skill at it, too.

Captain Bardari was in great agitation now. "I went back to the bridge," he recalled. "I called the tug. At times I got no answer. I always repeated, asking him to tow, to start towing the ship."

It was a pathetic situation. His fine firmness dissolved, and his optimism of only a few moments earlier evaporated into shock. It was at that moment, at 1435, that he maintains he assented to LOF and told Weinert he was going to call Chicago and inform them of the change.

Inform them of the change, or ask their permission? As far as Weinert was concerned, he had no LOF at 1435, in spite of the fact that he was pulling. (If the Italian couldn't understand that, too bad for him.) What really happened at 1435, according to Weinert, is that instead of granting the LOF, Bardari abdicated his responsibility and told him to contact AMOCOSHIP Chicago and work it out with them. That is, if it really was Captain Bardari he was speaking with: Half the time, it seemed to be the other one, the one who spoke English so well. He clearly remembers the voice telling him, "The captain's very busy talking with Chicago." It was maddening and impossible to try to deal with these people. Who was in charge? What was going on?

At a quarter past three, Captain Weinert called the bridge of the Amoco *Cadiz* once again, and once again met with frustration. The communication between the two ships had become a dialogue of the deaf. "Are you the captain?" he asked.

"No," replied the English voice. At length a man who identified himself as the master of the ship did come onto the air.

"Captain," said Weinert with slow deliberation, "you are in a very bad position. You have a very big ship. The weather condition is the same, very bad. And I must have a Lloyd's Open Form. You accept it. Please, you accept it."

"No, no, no."

The same old story, all over again.

"I remember, I think, for my next forty years," Weinert recalled later with a rueful grimace. "No, no, maybe four noes."

It hardly could have made any difference in the long run, because Weinert was already doing what he could, but Bardari's credibility is further damaged by the fact that Maynard's handwritten account of events gives reason to the captain of the *Pacific*, in the matter of when the LOF was agreed. His entry for 1435 reads:

> It was observed that the tug had stopped pulling. Tug requested Lloyd's open agreement. Agreement refused. Tug told to contact Chicago. Tug threatened to release tow.

The denouement was slowly coming around. It was clearly impossible for the stalemate to continue while the pretty little white houses of the Breton coast were coming into view and the onshore wind was blowing harder than ever.

Abandoning his radio, Weinert put his demands in writing, by sending a telegram. It came through via Radio le Conquet, over VHF on channel 26, at exactly 1530: *"Tug Pacific requests Lloyd's Open Form no cure no pay, to be confirmed by telegram through Radio Brest."*

At 1536, Muscuso received a second radiotelegram, addressed to Master, Amoco *Cadiz*/A8AN, and officially registered via Brest Radio: *"I confirm that services being rendered on basis Lloyd's Open Form salvage agreement no cure no pay.—Master Pacific"*

At 1555, Captain Bardari had a five-minute radiotelephone conversation with Captain Riddell's boss in Chicago, Captain Phillips, and at 1615, Muscuso sent the following radiotelegram to Le Conquet (call sign FFU). Captain Bardari had written it himself on a slip of paper:

> *Capt. German tug DNCH FFU—*
> *We accept Lloyd's Open Form salvage agreement no cure no pay.—*
> *AMOCO CADIZ/A8AN*

At last. By the time the message went to Le Conquet and back to *Pacific*, it was 1625. Four hours had passed since the arrival of the tug.

In Chicago, there was unusual turbulence within the august confines of the Standard Oil Building. It had started just after Captain Phillips had arrived in his southeast corner office on the fiftieth floor, to be greeted with word from Riddell that the *Cadiz* was in trouble. Confirming the news was a telex from Bugsier's agent in London. Here came the LOF again:

> We are the London agents of West German towage and salvage company "Bugsier Reederei und Bergungs A.G." of Hamburg. Their salvage tug "Pacific" 10,000 IHP, twinscrew/Kort nozzles reported to Bugsier, Hamburg at 11:35 GMT today, intercepted message from "Amoco Cadiz" stating position 8 miles north of Ushant Island (lat.48.48 north long.05.08 west) with rudder damage. Tug "Pacific" in ballast proceeding on speculation and E.T.A. alongside "Amoco Cadiz" around 12.00 hours GMT today and has offered her services to master "Amoco Cadiz" on basis Lloyd's Open Form "no cure no pay." Weather in area at the moment is west north west force 9 to 10.
>
> Bugsier's salvage tug "Simson" 16,000 IHP, twin screw, presently off Cherbourg and proceeding to assistance on speculation, E.T.A. 22.00 hours today.
>
> At the moment we have no further information and are awaiting further advice from Bugsier. If you have received advice from master of "Amoco Cadiz" that assistance of tug required kindly confirm if Lloyd's Open Form "no cure no pay" terms and conditions are acceptable.
>
> We will keep you advised.

Phillips, portly, white-haired, and rubicund, had the intense blue-eyed gaze and brusque manner traditionally associated with men of the sea, and, indeed, he had been something of a merchant marine wunderkind, having been ship's master at only age twenty-four. He had left the sea shortly after the war to begin a remarkably successful career in Amoco's Marine Operations Division. Then fifty-five years old, he was approaching the top of the ladder. He put down the telex and picked up his phone.

Southeast corner office to northeast corner office: view over Lake Michigan and the Chicago Yacht Club and view over the Navy Pier and Lakeshore Drive. Such were the differences between the office geography of Claude Phillips and his boss, Harry Rinkema, president of Amoco Marine Transportation Company. Phillips's elder by one year, Rinkema had the strong chin and mouth of the ambitious and the glasses and conservative business suits of the classical, old-style executive. He took the call from Phillips in his office at a quarter past eight in the morning, told him to keep him informed of developments, and in turn notified his superior, Leland C. Adams, president of Amoco International Oil Company. For the moment, the news stopped there: There was no point in alerting the president or the chairman of the board until they heard how matters were developing.

For the rest of that day, and then on into the night, Captain Phillips's office became the nerve center for dealing with the tanker's problems, and Rinkema was in and out all day long. As were many, many others. Early on, someone decided it would be a good idea to have some expert counsel on hand, so Randall T. Clair, chief of Amoco's legal department, was brought in to join the group. When the first ship-to-shore call from Captain Bardari came through, Phillips listened to the details, asked a few questions, and then passed the phone to a group of technicians from the engineering department, whom he had summoned for this express purpose. Among them was an Italian ship's engineer who happened to be passing through Chicago. Navigating between Italian and English, he and his colleagues aboard *Cadiz* discussed the problem at such length that Captain Phillips finally had the call transferred down to the engineering department in order to free his phone. Questions and advice flew back and forth with ease over the 6,500 kilometers that separated them, but there were no magical solutions, no better ideas for what to do.

Captain Phillips called Hamburg and Rotterdam, seeking the straight towage rate that his seagoing experience must have told him would not be available, and then, after yet another anguished call from Captain Bardari, resigned himself to the inevitable and accepted the LOF.

"The captain of the ship was instructed to so inform the captain of the *Pacific*," Rinkema noted afterward, in his handwritten reconstruction of the affair. At noon, after a rushed meeting with Adams in Phillips's office, Rinkema suggested to Phillips that they lunch together at the Mid-America Club upstairs, leaving Riddell to maintain the phone watch. Now that the tug was attached, the general mood was optimistic.

Mr. Maynard went down to the radio room to find Captain Bardari just replacing the radio headset. "That's it, then," he said. "Chicago now agrees."

"Okay," said Maynard. "I'll inform the tug."

"Yes, please."

Maynard got back on the bridge VHF, reconfirmed the acceptance of LOF, and again asked *Pacific* to begin towing. Captain Weinert was either too busy or too angry to talk with him. He didn't answer, and nothing seemed to change: Amoco *Cadiz* was heading a bit to the west of south, around 200 degrees; almost perfectly at right angles to starboard, *Pacific* was heading 280, facing into the wind but having no success in bringing the tanker with her. Her Kort nozzles, running all the way back to the stern, disguised the foam and froth that would be churned up by conventional screws. All that Maynard could discern of any towing activity was the white chain at right angles to the bow and a bit of the perlon spring as it dropped into the foaming waters. Six or seven hundred meters away to the right, swaying and bobbing, occasionally disappearing entirely from view in the trough of the waves, *Pacific* continued with her inscrutable, silent, solitary labors. Scrutinizing her through his binoculars, looking for but not finding her telltale wake, Maynard concluded that she was not pulling.

But he was wrong. Just how wrong, he learned at precisely 1616. *Pacific* had been pulling all along. Hard enough for the tow connection to break.

9.

The Second Tow

At 1616, Weinert was in the radio shack having a cup of coffee with Vogel, after having dictated his telegrams; chief engineer Korb was down in the engine room baby-sitting with his beloved diesels; and Mr. Maynard was, as usual, on the bridge of Amoco *Cadiz* with Captain Bardari.

For Weinert, it was the sudden surge forward that told him what had happened, a very perceptible jolt accompanied by an instantaneous drop in the level of vibration. He put down his cup and ran back to the aft wheelhouse, muttering Germanic oaths. In the engine room, Korb, too, felt the tug jerk ahead, and saw the RPM gauge swing upward. Now the boat was lying differently in the water. Korb made his way back to the winch room, where he knew he would be needed to oversee the job of hauling the line back in. For Captain Bardari, who had just returned to the bridge after sending his telegram accepting LOF, the signal was a sound that he could describe only as "a wrenching" that immediately directed his attention to the bow. But it was the ever-observant Mr. Maynard who described the moment the best.

"We were all standing on the starboard side of the bridge," he remembered, "and our ship gave a violent roll to port on an enormous sea. The tug in its turn disappeared over a crest of a wave into a large trough heading away from us. The catenary of the tow came right up to the surface. You could see the line going out from the bow about fifteen, twenty degrees from the horizontal, and the next thing, we saw it drop away in the water."

On the bridge of the Amoco *Cadiz* there was a long, shocked silence, followed by cries of dismay. In the space of those few seconds, the situation had changed from bothersome (the LOF business, the intransigence of the German) to desperate. *Pacific* was all they could possibly hope for, and if she wasn't up to the job, what was going to keep them off the rocks? What indeed. Captain Bardari picked up the VHF microphone.

"The line has parted," he said dully.

"Yes," answered Captain Weinert. "I agree."

"We'll have to attempt to maneuver astern," Captain Bardari said. He buzzed Melito and asked him and Assante to come up to the bridge. The three of them conferred in Italian as Mr. Maynard looked on. After five minutes or so the engineers returned below, and Bardari told Maynard that they were going to try the engine in reverse, starting slow and winding her up. The hope was that the flow of water provoked by their maneuver would force the rudder to one side and prevent it from whanging back and forth. Still and always, the thought that obsessed them was the idea of the rudder falling away and damaging the screw. No one knew what direction the ship would take, either. If the rudder did stick to one side, would she start turning a circle? Impossible to say, but they had to give it a try. Until *Pacific* retrieved her gear and rerigged, that was all they had.

Within minutes the Burmeister & Wain was faithfully throbbing again. Nothing happened. Or rather, what happened was so slow that it was difficult to perceive any difference in their position at all. What was noticeable, after Melito had wound the engine up to 80 RPM, was that the rudder not only did continue to swing back and forth, but was doing so harder than ever, shaking the deck under their feet with each blow against the stops and the rams. That was too much. The captain instructed Melito to lay back on the RPMs. For the next two hours and nine minutes—far longer than they had imagined would be necessary—Amoco *Cadiz* ran at slow astern.

With agonizing slowness, her position changed in response to the screw. She was so heavy, and the dumb mass of her inertia so great, that it took fully an hour before the engine could break her free of the drift line and show any effect. During that hour the officers on the bridge were offered an object lesson in the difficulties that *Pacific* had been facing in her attempt to bring the tanker around, with less than one-third of the horsepower of their Burmeister & Wain.

Ponderously, sluggishly, the huge ship readjusted her position, beginning to back into the wind, as theory said she ought to. After more than an hour had passed, her bow came about slightly to port, until it was pointing south-southeast. Now her line of drift became more lateral than forward, more toward the east than the south. They were above the gap that separated Ouessant from the mainland, crabbing awkwardly sideways. They didn't seem to be coming closer to the landline, but the problem was that the Breton peninsula in that area also reaches northward into the sea. With their eastward drift, unless something stopped them, they were bound to intersect the landmass sooner or later. They were on a collision course.

The Mid-America Club occupies the entire eightieth floor—the top—of the Standard Oil Building on the lakefront in Chicago. It is, in the proud description of a Standard Oil public-relations man, "the best luncheon and dining club in the region," and everything about its appointments reflects the power and opulence that mark the building itself, with its 1,136-foot facade of pure, white Carrara marble—8,000 tons of it. ("Michelangelo molded his famous sculptures from the same Carrara marble," a Standard Oil brochure reminds visitors.) The carpeting is gold, fittingly enough, at the eightieth-floor elevator stop, the walls are black marble, and the paneling is burnished walnut. At the reservations desk, a distinguished lady confirms your table or, if you are not a member, politely but firmly turns you away. The ceiling is lofty, as they all are in the Standard Oil Building—Edward Durell Stone, the architect, indulged in the luxury of space, placing only eighty floors where ten or twenty more would have fitted—and the view over the Chicago skyline is absolutely spectacular. It would be hard to beat the lounge, with its easy chairs upholstered in red velvet, its indirect lighting, and its profusion of green plants, for reassuring comfort.

The stroll into the main dining room, occupying the building's north face, takes the lucky member past a picture window, behind which fine Bordeaux and Burgundies doze in the temperature- and humidity-controlled atmosphere of the *cave à vin.* In the dining room the gold carpeting motif continues, but the chairs at the widely spaced tables are either rust-colored or green and mahogany. A bank of green plants separates one dining area from the next, and a soft flow of Muzak from discreet loudspeakers provides diners with a harmonious audio carpet. The Mid-America Club is definitely a big-league place, an executive place, fit for the highest levels of the Chicago business community who form its membership. It was here, at a quarter past one, that Harry Rinkema and Captain Phillips had their lunch interrupted by a phone call from William Riddell. Riddell's message was that he had just finished a radiotelephone conversation with Captain Bardari: The towline had parted. This news put an early end to what had started out as a pleasant lunch. Rinkema and Phillips descended to the fiftieth floor.

Aboard *Pacific*, Captain Weinert let his tug drift as his crew winched in the towing rig, leaving the bridge to contact his superiors in Hamburg. This time, they agreed, he would have to try to pull Amoco *Cadiz* by the stern. Her bow was facing in toward land, and they certainly didn't want to go that way. It had proven impossible to turn her into the wind. So the best they could hope for was to tie up to the stern, pull with the help of *Cadiz*'s own engine in reverse, and hold her off the coast until *Simson* arrived. Then the two of them would be able to tow her together. In retrospect, there were some criticisms of this decision, but it was probably as good a plan as any. It is not at all certain that all the combined minds of all the greatest admirals in history could have saved Amoco *Cadiz* that afternoon.

Captain Weinert had another reason for wanting to avoid the bow of his cumbersome casualty this time: He didn't like her Panama fairlead. Not one bit. In fact, he was convinced that it was responsible for the breaking of his chain. Above all, as far as salvage is concerned, a fairlead should be fair, as in one of the many definitions of that most versatile word: "Without sudden or angular deviation, as in line or surface; smooth-flowing; as, a ship's fair curves." This vulgar, ordinary piece of equipment, a simple casting, an eye set into the ship's skin, hardly appears to be of much intrinsic importance when compared to such glamorous components as engines, steering gear, or navigational instruments, but there can be moments when it is not only important, but crucial. Aboard *Pacific* a few days after the disaster, Weinert explained for me, with drawings and diagrams, what was wrong with the tanker's fairlead. Apparently designed for nothing more than mooring, in his opinion it was too shallow, too angular, too sharp. When he was pulling at ninety degrees to the bow, he said, the fairlead did the opposite of what it should have been designed for: Rather than alleviating the chafing effect by presenting a softly rounded surface over which the chain could safely lie, the fairlead actually bent links as they clanked through during the initial tensioning. When the big waves came along to hurl the two ships apart, he theorized, a bent, weakened link gave way.

At five minutes past five, as the thin winter light was already beginning to fail, Captain Bardari sent Strano and his men forward again, to unwind the towing pennant from the bitts, pull the chain out of the fairlead, and make ready to set up the second tow, which, as far as he knew, would also be from the bow. The long slog down to the length of the deck was no easier than it had been at noon, and the weather, if anything, had turned even worse. Working in painful slow motion, Strano and his men spent well over an hour freeing cable and chain and stowing them in a locker under the forecastle. When they had finally finished, the captain came in over the walkie-talkie to order them all the way back to the other end of the ship: The tug had decided to tow from the stern this time.

Aboard *Pacific*, Weinert's deck crew was making things ready on their side. But if the freeboard of the Amoco *Cadiz*, even fully laden, was seven meters, aboard *Pacific* it was less than two. Weinert's men worked with the sea as a constant companion: next to it when they were riding a crest, below it when they were in a trough, and, a good deal more often than they would have liked, inside it when the tug got in its way. As they drifted closer to shore and into shallower water, the waves became steeper and higher, swarming repeatedly over the deck. By dusk the waves were eight to ten meters tall, and thoroughly uncooperative: Weinert lost twenty percent of his deck labor force when able seamen Johann Horwath and Manfried Gross were picked up and thrown around by two separate waves. One man ended his free ride against the main winch and the other against the towing wire. No bones were broken, but both men were cut and bruised badly enough to be put out of action. They would have to wait more than thirty hours before they could be hospitalized, but they could count themselves lucky at that, since security is a somewhat approximate notion on the rear deck of a salvage tug. Aboard *Pacific*, crewmen worked with neither safety lines (they get in the way) nor life vests, which, because *Pacific*'s inflated automatically on contact with water, would actually increase the risk of being swept away by a passing wave. Horwath and Gross, like the rest of their mates, possessed extremely developed instincts for holding onto passing pieces of tugboat when the seas levitated them.

With the foul weather, the job of putting the new tow rig together became frustratingly slow and difficult. Weinert increased his labor force by pressing chief officer Brandt into service, and the steward, the cook, and two assistant engineers along with him, but even so, an operation that usually took no more than half an hour or forty-five minutes dragged on under the floodlights for almost two and a half hours, and it wasn't until close to 7:00 P.M.—well past nightfall—that *Pacific* was finally ready for the second try. And everyone knew it would be the last one.

The hours passed in these anguishing thirty-minute segments as the officers of Amoco *Cadiz* paced nervously around their palatial bridge, impotent to do anything but watch the tug recede farther and farther from them on its independent drift line and listen to the rudder's plangent complaint below. By dusk, *Pacific* was more than three miles off, imperturbably bobbing up and down, silent and sibylline. It was a nerve-wracking, desperate situation. Captain Bardari swallowed his pride and asked Weinert if he knew any other way to raise more tugs. "*Simson* is forty nautical miles away" was Weinert's only reply. Then silence again, and empty static over the VHF speaker.

Shortly after 1800, Captain Weinert called Captain Bardari to inform him that this time he would be towing from the stern. It was the first anyone aboard Amoco *Cadiz* had heard of a change in plans. By the stern? Captain Bardari didn't agree at all—he had been planning to continue as before, with *Pacific* turning his heading from the bow, so that he could steam smartly away from the coast once he was in position. Then they could go on to Lyme Bay together, with his own screw acting as the driving force and *Pacific* steering for him. There was no doubt in Captain Bardari's mind: The tow from the stern was all wrong.

Captain Bardari protested, but he was quickly learning some hard facts about the salvage business. The cruelest of all was that the decision was not his to make. *Pacific* was going to come up by the stern, and there was nothing he could do but acquiesce.

"He submitted to *Pacific*'s powerful persuasion," was the way Mr. Maynard described it later.

Back in his northeast corner office, Rinkema decided with Phillips to put Amoco's Oil Spill Contingency Plan into action, just in case. The chances of a grounding were looking more likely. At least they could try to anticipate it. Phillips returned to his office, still accompanied by Clair, the lawyer, and began making phone calls. Most of that day he would be either phoning or waiting for calls to come in.

"If everything else fails, we will have to send out a general distress call," Captain Bardari had warned. That sounded very ominous. Rinkema and Phillips decided to plan for the worst.

The Oil Spill Contingency Plan included a number of legal and insurance measures, preparation of emergency cleanup equipment, contacts for the purchase or rental of equipment and the like, but also, and of especially great importance, laid emphasis on public relations. Carl Meyerdirk, a low-key, relaxed Jimmy Stewart type who bore the mellifluous title Director of Corporate Media Relations, would soon be called on to play a front-line role in dealing with a press that was almost unanimously hostile.

As Clair stuck to him like a shadow, taking notes, Captain Phillips continued with his calls until one came in from Hamburg: Captain Meyer of Bugsier informed him of the plan to tow from astern, and added that the changing tidal currents in the evening ought to help the boat stay away from the rocks. Phillips was surprised by the new tow plan, but declined to contest it, figuring that second-guessing could help no one. Rinkema went off to apprise Adams of the latest developments.

At 3:45 P.M., Rinkema walked down to Phillips's office again to see if there had been any later word from Europe. There was none—no reports, nothing. Phillips had fallen into a somberly pensive mood, wondering whether the silence indicated good news or bad news.

Captain Weinert was not acting on caprice, of course, with his decision to tow from aft. He was far more experienced in towing than anyone aboard Amoco *Cadiz*, and he also knew the waters of Brittany a hundred times better. He was damned if he was going to try to pull straight ahead when the rocks were looking him in the face just a few miles ahead, clearly visible already before nightfall. He was also determined to avoid another fiasco with that sharp fairlead. No—he would pull straight back and wait for *Simson*. And if the Italian had some complaints about his behavior, he had plenty about his, too. He still didn't know the exact state of the tanker's rudder. What was he trying to hide?

By a quarter to seven, *Pacific*'s tow gear was pieced together and ready to go again. In all, the job had eaten up two hours and twenty-two minutes. Captain Weinert brought his tug back at full speed to the position of the *Cadiz:* twenty-six more minutes. Since the rupture of the first line, Amoco *Cadiz* had drifted some four and a half miles east by northeast, inching her path sideways toward the coast. When the veil of rain squalls lifted, the lights along the shore-line stood out with dramatic and disheartening clarity. She was approximately three miles to the west of the shallows marked on navigation maps as ROCHES DE PORTSALL: the Rocks of Portsall, where Weinert had turned around, more than seven hours earlier. Now, as *Pacific* approached, Captain Bardari was just finishing up a six-minute conversation with Chicago. He gave his position, described the weather conditions and, once more, the plan of towing from astern, adding the obvious: This was surely their last chance. If the two didn't work this time, they would go on the rocks.

At five minutes past seven, Maynard noted in his account: "Tug making final approach." She was slewing around with considerable agility but often at mad angles, two 1,500-watt searchlights blazing from the mast above the bridge and another one of 3,000 watts from the aft A-frame. It was this piercing Cyclopean gaze that remained for most of that night trained on the casualty. Aft of the *Cadiz*, all the work lights were on, too. Up on the signal mast, the two black "not under control" balls had been replaced by the red lights of the Christmas tree. The last act was ready to be played out.

It was clear that the situation was truly desperate. The needle on *Cadiz*'s depth recorder traced a neat, steadily declining clearance under their keel. With the shallower water the waves grew steeper and more unstable. Maneuvering was tricky, in spite of *Pacific*'s twin screws and triple rudders. Captain Weinert had to bring his tug as close as possible to get within range for the Kongsberg rifle, but he knew that the wrong sequence of wave patterns could slide him down a hill of water and slam him into the tanker's opulent gray flanks. He ordered Captain Bardari to stop his engine, lest the screw foul the towline, but it was like asking a drowning man to let go of a rope. His screw in reverse had been Bardari's only protection from the rocks, the only gesture of self-defense remaining at his command. Now, as he signaled Melito to cut the Burmeister & Wain off, he felt suffused with regret and anguish.

Waiting for the Kongsberg projectile, Strano and his men huddled on the stern and watched as *Pacific* churned up below them, turned smartly on itself, and presented its starboard side to the tanker's stern. Braced against the railing outside of the aft wheelhouse, Brandt brought the Kongsberg to his shoulder, took aim, and fired.

Everything went wrong. And as usual, those who acted out the drama disagree passionately about what happened and whose fault it was. Whatever the truth of detail, the end result was this: at least five and perhaps as many as six or seven Kongsberg lines were shot from *Pacific* until one could be made fast aboard Amoco *Cadiz*. Nearly an hour more was lost in the process. By the time the heaving line was finally caught and the towing rig hooked up—hastily and sloppily, everyone agrees, because by then they were on the edge of the precipice—the tanker was only nine minutes from grounding. She pulled the tug with her like a child dragging a toy on a string.

Captain Bardari and his mates later complained that the tug placed itself improperly by coming up to their port side and having to shoot the Kongsberg into a force ten wind, which carried the projectile away before it could reach their deck. Half the time, the *Cadiz* crew couldn't even see it. In short: bad seamanship by the Germans. Such after-the-fact criticism angered Weinert, who was quick to point out that in those abominable weather conditions, on a moonless night, maneuvering in close to fire a little nylon line across an enraged, Götterdämmerung caldron of a sea, the notion of ideal positioning is rather academic. He placed *Pacific*—playing the commands for throttle, rudder, and screw like a maestro of applied mechanics—as best he could, and if at times that didn't appear perfect to the Italians, he had a thing or two to say about the way they fetched the lines, too. All of the Kongsberg shots, he insisted, reached the tanker's deck. The crew just couldn't—or wouldn't—go get them.

Much later, when it was all over, Weinert described that Wagnerian night to investigators of the French Senate, who were working on one of the innumerable reports to which the grounding of Amoco *Cadiz* gave birth. His account, backed, as usual, with meticulous on-board documentation, was far more precise and detailed than anything offered by the Amoco parties, but its end result was easily as damning for the adversary as anything offered by Captain Bardari or his officers. And "adversary" is the right word. That is what things had come to. The Senate report gives a chilling picture of how impossible the relationship between the tug and the casualty had become by then. This is the tale of that crucial hour, as Weinert outlined it.

1910: First Kongsberg shot. Falls on starboard side of superstructure. Remains on the starboard bulwark. VHF call to casualty on channel 6: "The line is on the starboard side aft." Amoco *Cadiz* crew unable to find the line. Being light, it soon breaks. Captain Weinert sees "eight to ten crewmen of Amoco *Cadiz* sheltering in the lee of the superstructure to the right of the smokestack on the port side of the main deck." Decides to maneuver the tug to get closer to crew of Amoco *Cadiz*.

1915: Second Kongsberg shot. Falls on the deck. "The men could have grabbed the line if they had run toward the stern. But the crew didn't act quickly, keeping sheltered for too long. The line breaks again."

1920: Third Kongsberg shot. The projectile went to windward of the smokestack and then fell between the smokestack and the superstructure. Although the crew of the Amoco *Cadiz* could have grabbed the line again this time if they had hurried, they did not do it.

1926: Fourth Kongsberg shot. Falls between the smokestack and the superstructure to port. Crew grabs it. Crew takes the Kongsberg line aboard the tanker along with twenty-five meters of half-inch heaving line. Also winches in the 110-meter messenger line with the little eye at the end of it. Eye passes through starboard fairlead.

1936: "I was surprised to see the messenger line fall away from the casualty. My crew brought it aboard the tug, where we saw that there were about five meters of heaving line attached to the little eye of the messenger line. The outside edge of the heaving line looked like it had been cut with a knife. I cannot avoid thinking that the crew of the Amoco *Cadiz* must have made some mistake."

1937: Sea: Heavy with high swells and sometimes breaking waves which land on our aft deck. Motors stopped. *Pacific* drifts forward under port side of Amoco *Cadiz*. Impossible to maneuver while crew brings messenger line aboard. Call the Amoco *Cadiz:* "The messenger line was brought aboard and you let it drop. Why?" No answer. "I'm going to come around again to the starboard side. Watch carefully when we shoot again." No answer.

1950: *Pacific* has described a circle and is now close in to the starboard side of the Amoco *Cadiz*'s stern.

1955: Under the stern of the Amoco *Cadiz*. Open up the starboard engine to send our stern toward the casualty. VHF call from Amoco *Cadiz*: "We're dropping anchor." No more information. No comment from *Pacific*.

1957: *Pacific* under stern of Amoco *Cadiz*. The fifth Kongsberg shot fired. Falls to starboard of smokestack. Grabbed by crew. Tug stopped.

20 hours to 2005: Captain observes that the anchor does not seem to have had an effect on the drift of the boat.

2016: Sees that the tow cable is through the fairlead. Begins maneuvering forward.

Captain Weinert seems unfairly harsh in his judgment of Strano and his men. His images of terrified Italians huddling against bulkheads while doom stalks them are too easy, too caricatural. It is altogether possible, for instance, that most of the Kongsberg lines were lost not through cowardice or incompetence but through simple inability to spot them as they sailed over the black void between the tug and the tanker and then landed somewhere in the ragged shadows of a storm-swept, tungsten-lit deck. Nor was it possible for them, once they had located the lines, to saunter over and pick them up, as if it were a garden path—not in that weather. It is certain, though, that the crew of the Amoco *Cadiz*, being VLCC sailors, were no match for the experienced deckhands of *Pacific*, who doubtless would have been able to grasp the lines and set up the tow right away, from the very first Kongsberg shot. Sending men like Strano and his crew out to do that job under those conditions was approximately like dispatching librarians into a boxing ring. The result of their inexperience, the weather, and the night was that the hookup of the second towline was egregiously clumsy and took too long: nearly an hour to get the gun line aboard, and then fifty more minutes to secure the tow rig in a hurry-up, makeshift manner. The time lost proved to be fatal to Amoco *Cadiz*.

A few minutes after 1930 by his watch, after Strano had informed him by walkie-talkie that they had pulled a line in but then lost it again, Captain Bardari made a decision that many felt he should have made a good dealer earlier: to drop anchor. This time it was second mate Cosmo Vaudo he delegated to go forward, with a work crew of one boatswain and two ABs. Vaudo remembers it as the worst weather he had ever encountered on the deck of a ship: Beam onto the sea, *Cadiz* was broaching to pitiless ranks of white-caps that entirely submerged the starboard side, briefly freed it in a furious seething of foam as the tanker rolled to port, then blanketed it again on the return roll. It took Vaudo and his men a quarter of an hour to make it to the bow. He had been up since 3:30 A.M. for his early morning watch, but it wasn't fatigue that was bothering Vaudo just then.

His orders were to drop the port anchor only. Captain Bardari had not even mentioned the starboard anchor when he had given him the assignment. This raises a few troubling points. First of all, it is most unlikely that even both anchors could have stopped the Amoco *Cadiz* where she found herself then, with the buoy of la Grande Basse de Portsall looming up on her port bow. It is an exaggeration to say that anchors are useless on a VLCC (they go down and perform their function in the quietude of the Persian Gulf), but at any speed over one knot they are little more than symbolic. With the inertia of a hard drift behind it, the astronomic weight of a laden supertanker would require an anchor the size of a house to arrest it, and a chain of such enormous girth as to be virtually unmaneuverable. Just then, *Cadiz* was drifting at about two knots and rolling and pitching heavily as well. Dropping the port anchor alone was little more than a gesture and everyone knew it—including Vaudo as he struggled to free the wire lashings that held the anchor chain where it passed over the high, iron wheel maintaining it above the deck level.

Why only the port anchor? The absolute truth has not been established, but there have been plenty of theories. The most often repeated rumor is that the starboard anchor windlass had been broken for several days or even several weeks, and that Amoco and Captain Bardari elected to continue the trip with this faulty equipment. No one has offered any proof of this insinuation, but in the marathon legal proceedings that followed the grounding, Amoco's adversaries did manage to unearth vexing evidence of a corporate attitude toward the safety-profit equation that was at times singularly cavalier—and in which the anchor windlass was the least of sins. Captain Bardari and his officers maintained that the starboard windlass was in perfect working order at all times right to the end, but that it was impossible to use it because they couldn't get to it. With the ship presenting her starboard beam, and therefore all the equipment on the starboard side to the sea, the winch was under water. It was night, the temperature was only a degree or two above freezing, they were out of control in a full storm. Pasquale Bardari would not allow his men even to try to swim into the maelstrom to struggle with the starboard anchor. That is their version at any rate, and until proof to the contrary it is as good as any other.

Why, then, did not Captain Bardari think about the anchors many hours earlier, and prepare both port and starboard for dropping when he had daylight, slightly less hideous weather, and better position in the water? Why not, indeed? Even if it could be argued that dropping anchors would have made no difference, it would have been a sign of prudent seamanship to at least get them prepared.

At 2003 Vaudo radioed to the bridge that he was ready to drop, and a minute later Captain Bardari instructed him to let go eight shackles of chain, or two hundred meters. He followed their progress intently through his binoculars, sweeping the area of the bow for the foamy white outlines of oncoming waves and shouting a warning at their approach. Vaudo and his men took shelter until the danger had passed, then continued with their chore, winding down the anchor chain link by link with the anchor windlass motor. When the eight lengths of chain were out, they closed the steam valve of the windlass and hammered down the brake until it could go no farther. The chain came taut, and Amoco *Cadiz* briefly altered her position once again, pivoting on the chain until the bow was pointing almost due west. The seas attacked the helpless ship with redoubled violence against the small resistance from the dragging anchor. Vaudo opened up the steam valve a crack and the windlass ground back enough to hold the chain. It was a straight face-off: the mechanical force of the steam winch against Mother Nature. The mechanical side wasn't doing very well that March 16. At first, the windlass seemed to hold, tensioning backward in a tug-of-war for possession of the anchor, holding the chain rock steady. But with the seas washing in on them, the flat, exposed bow of an oilpot was no place for watching a tug-of-war. Vaudo led his men through a little access door into a storage hutch under the forecastle, a damp repository for cables and other miscellaneous gear needed at the stem of a VLCC. As they squatted against the damp bulkhead they felt like small adventuresome insects that had managed to stray inside a large drum. The sea hammered at the bow behind them and the deck above them, accompanied now and then by a riffle of clankings as the anchor chain pulled out in short bursts. The noise meant the windlass wasn't holding, after all.

Underwater all hell was breaking loose. The nyctalopic submarine creatures inhabiting Roches de Portsall were the only witnesses, though, as twenty-two tons of high-grade Spanish iron plowed across the sand and rubble of the French continental plateau, looking for the right rock to do battle with. It didn't take long before the anchor caught a fluke against a piece of solid granite and came off second best, shearing off at the base as if it had been made of putty. *Olé!* Soon the fluke on the other side met the same fate, and *Cadiz* was left dragging only two hundred and fifty meters of chain and a formless stump of iron. The remains of the anchor, dredged up later by the French navy, are eloquent testimony to the inadvisability of man or machine doing direct battle with the sea when it is angry.

By five minutes to nine, Strano and his work crew had made eight turns of the cable around a set of bitts by the central fairlead. The rigging was hasty and slack, but at least they were attached to the tug again. Captain Bardari ordered him and his men to leave the deck and get inside: They were only minutes from grounding, and he wanted them in a safer place. Strano protested into his walkie-talkie, but couldn't hear the answer over the roar of the wind. He ran to a telephone inside and requested five more minutes at the stern.

"No," said Captain Bardari with finality. "Clear the stern immediately. No one should stay there any longer. We are too close to the rocks."

Tethered together once again, Amoco *Cadiz* and *Pacific* drifted past the buoy marking the Portsall shallows, la Grande Basse de Portsall. Amoco *Cadiz* wallowed in toward the rocks sideways, pulling the tug with her. Captain Weinert vividly recalls seeing the buoy's beacon move idly past abeam his wheelhouse, making a mockery of his churning propellors. Time had been too short to run out one thousand meters of towing wire, or even eight hundred. The best he could do under the circumstances was to pull easy, his engines at slow ahead. He had only four hundred meters of wire behind him and feared that any higher speed, any greater torque, would break the connection again. He pulled northward, not quite at right angles as before, but still angling considerably off *Cadiz*'s starboard quarter. Once again, everything was going wrong. He had told Bardari to put his engine full astern to help him with the pull—but nothing was happening.

What was happening was that the captain of the tanker was now at complete cross-purposes with him, and was simply refusing to do as he asked. It was the final and perfectly logical expression of the bitter quarrel that had driven them for more than nine hours and would continue right to the end. Feverishly inspecting charts, the depth sounder, and the seething white chaos of spray everywhere around him, Captain Bardari had become convinced that the closest rocks lay astern, only meters away. In anguished response to Weinert's order to put his engines astern, he tentatively pushed the engine telegraph to SLOW ASTERN, looked at it for a moment, then slipped it back to STOP. He couldn't bring himself to do it. The crunch could come any second.

"No!" he cried into the handset. "The rocks are astern. We cannot go astern. We have to go ahead. You must pull our stern to port."

The imperturbable Mr. Maynard's notes show an entry for 2100: "Tug advised to pull our stern to port."

Weinert, just then, was doing his damndest to pull her stern to starboard, and getting nowhere. If there was one thing that he was not going to do, it was to turn around, go the other way and drive his tug right onto the rocks, because that is what it would have meant. Towing her to port would be madness—that was toward the shore!

By then it was all academic, anyway. At 2104, the Englishman's voice came into Weinert's wheelhouse over VHF, grave and strangely ceremonial: "Sir, we are grounded."

10.

The Grounding

Throughout that day of March 16, various shore points kept a desultory watch on the movements of the Amoco *Cadiz,* but for the most part they did so entirely without alarm and without perceiving any danger. With the curious dovetailing and overlapping that characterize the French administration, at least four different ministries can be involved in watching maritime traffic in the vicinity of the coast, and each has a natural bureaucratic tendency to crouch carefully within the shell of its own function, which does not necessarily involve its neighbors from the other ministries. Complicating matters even more is the fact that these functions are not always clearly defined for every eventuality. But worst of all, in 1978 there was no organization specializing specifically in the safeguarding of the country's coastal waters—there was no French coast guard. Nor is there today, for that matter, but the navy, chastised by its disastrous performance in dealing with—or, rather, failing to deal with—the wandering oilpot, has considerably improved its alertness to Channel problems, its training, and its equipment. Today, the policing of the Channel is handled with impressive efficiency. But it wasn't in 1978.

On that March day, as Amoco *Cadiz* lumbered heavily toward the rocks with her load of crude oil, all of the following were official spectators: Radio le Conquet (Post and Communications Ministry); CROSS, or the Regional Operations Center for Surveillance and Rescue (Merchant Marine Secretariat); the lookout posts, called semaphores, manned by navy personnel; the Navy Operational Center of the Marine Prefecture, known as COM (Ministry of Defense); and the manned lighthouses of the area (Ministry of Equipment). As that day went by, and as later investigations made clear, all of them were about as effective in preventing the disaster as an audience in a theater. One and severally, they watched the drama unfold, some with occasional concern, most with indifference, and all of them with blissful ignorance of the full import of terrible reality that was right there, before their eyes. None of them could or would take any effective steps. When the wreck finally happened, the most they could do to show their disapproval was to refuse to applaud.

The Second Maritime Region, responsible for French coastal waters from the Spanish frontier to the Mont-Saint-Michel, is the naval bureaucracy whose command post—the COM—is located in the gray-stone medieval fortress, called Le Château, that looms above the entrance to the port of Brest. At the head of the Second Maritime Region—there are two others, one in Cherbourg for the northern area and another in Toulon for the Mediterranean—is an admiral who bears the title of *préfet maritime,* and who commands the French naval forces in the Atlantic. He is a big and important man. In addition to the warships, support craft, and airplanes under his command, twenty-three semaphores, staffed by navy personnel and directly tied by telephone to the operations room in the fortress, are neatly spaced along the coastline of the admiral's region. Five of them watched the disabled Amoco *Cadiz* as she set into her fatal drift line that day, but such was the weight of habit, routine, and complacency that no one thought twice about it until it was far too late. They never realized what was happening right under their noses and neither, apparently, did COM.

At a quarter past one, just about the time that Strano and his men were grasping the first heaving line, the semaphore at Stiff sighted the two boats. The semaphore asked *Pacific* for a report, and she replied that she was towing Amoco *Cadiz,* a Liberian tanker. The duty man reported the information to COM, and transmitted the bearing. COM rogered the message, but took no further action. No one had said anything about an emergency. Throughout the rest of that afternoon, Stiff continued to follow the convoy and record its position by radar, apparently without alarm. That same afternoon, two more semaphores, one on the little island of Molène, between Ouessant and the mainland, and the other at Aber Wrac'h, on the north shore above Brest, picked up the movements of the two ships. Molène took the trouble to call Creac'h and wonder about what was going on, but worried no more when they were reassured that it was just a tanker under tow. Throughout that day, the semaphores bounced mutually reassuring messages back and forth, reinforcing the easy conclusion that everything was okay and under control. Both COM and CROSS joined in the same ritualistic delusion. It was a commonly held characteristic of that day that many individuals in several different places saw only a small piece of the entire picture, and that each one assumed that someone else had the entire event in view—but no one did. And at 1830 on the dot, as regulations said they should, the semaphores of Stiff, Creac'h, Molène, and Aber Wrac'h closed down for the night, just like grocery stores. As astonishing as it may seem, these stations were manned during daylight hours only. Rules are rules.

Throughout the day, Radio le Conquet continued to put radio-telephone calls through to Hamburg and Chicago as requested, neither listening in nor recording them, in compliance with democratic principles and the oath taken by postal communications employees. Le Conquet also passed the ship-to-shore telegrams back and forth, setting up the LOF. As far as Chaput knew or cared, it was a simple commercial affair between ships. No one had told him otherwise. No one gave him any indication of trouble. He remained in this pleasant state of ignorance until exactly four minutes to eight that evening, when he got a telephone call from the town of Portsall.

Portsall, some thirty kilometers northeast of Brest on the upper end of the peninsula, is a little fishing port picturesque enough to support an entire picture-postcard industry. With its nearly perfectly circular harbor and its blue and white fishing boats bobbing on their moorings at high tide or lying down to rest on the mud when the tide is out, it is the quintessential image of Brittany. It is so small (permanent population 1,200) that it is not even a town, really, but a subtown, an adjunct to the larger, neighboring community of Ploudalmezeau. There are the odd tradesmen and shopkeepers, of course, and a couple of hotel-restaurants for the summer tourist crowd, but the real business of the population is the sea: fishermen, shellfish-hunters, and harvesters of a particularly useful seaweed called goemon. Portsall's harbor is drawn well back from the sea, protected by a rise of sandy land on the left and white stucco houses of the village itself on the right. Straight ahead, through the estuary, is open water and the shallows: Roches de Portsall.

Jean Gouzien was a fifty-eight-year-old fisherman with a house near Portsall harbor who, as part of his civic duties, was second in command of the Portsall lifeboat, which is occasionally called out to render assistance to fishermen or vacationers in trouble at sea. The lifeboat had had its moment of glory fifteen years earlier when it helped save the crew of a Greek freighter that grounded on the rocks two kilometers away. Prompted by the rough weather that had kept him ashore, Gouzien had taken a postprandial stroll up to a promontory overlooking the sea slightly east of town. Peering into the night, he saw something a hell of a lot more impressive than the Greek tub had been, and he didn't like it at all: the lights of two ships, moving erratically, out beyond the Grande Basse de Portsall buoy. One of them, he noticed, was showing a Christmas tree. He hurried home and rang Radio le Conquet. Nine minutes later, Le Conquet telexed an advisory to CROSS, adding that both vessels appeared to be quite close to the rocks. Several messages went back and forth until the right answer was found, the one that allowed everyone concerned to shrug his bureaucratic shoulders: It was only Amoco *Cadiz* being towed by *Pacific*. Officially, then, all was well. But no one had bothered to query either boat.

At 2035, an off-duty sailor at the Molène semaphore did what Gouzien had done three quarters of an hour earlier, saw what he did, and became even more thoroughly alarmed: two sets of lights, seven nautical miles to the northeast. He went into the workroom, checked his compass and his charts, and came up with the conclusion that many others before him should have reached: Something was very wrong up by Roches de Portsall. He immediately contacted Brest. Only then, when grounding was twenty-four minutes away, did COM begin to put two and two together: The big picture had finally dawned on someone. Stiff and Aber Wrac'h were called back to duty, and the operations personnel who had gone home were brought back to Le Château. But by then, of course, it was much too late for anyone to do anything.

There wasn't really anything that anyone could have done in any case, but if the big picture had appeared several hours earlier, at least the navy could have saved some face by trying energetically to stave off the inevitable. As it was, they were caught with their pants down. And as an added fillip, just to insure that decision making would be well-nigh impossible that day, fate decreed that Vice-Admiral Jacques Coulondres, *préfet maritime,* the man who owned the Atlantic, should be away when it all happened, taking part in an official ceremony in Paris. Fate played a pretty good game of cards that day.

At around nine o'clock, Jean Gouzien and anyone else who for any strange reason may have taken it into his head to venture into the tempest blowing onto the shore by Portsall would have had one of those horror visions that are so rare as to come once in several lifetimes, like the farmer in a field who happens to look up just a few seconds before two planes collide, or the unconcerned pedestrian who happens to witness a murder. The vision was that of a big ship about to go aground. Just above and to the right of the harbor, past a dirt road and then across an open field of scrub grass, there is a particularly good place for watching the sea, called Pointe Scoune. At the edge of the field, flat tablelike rocks quickly drop off and give way to the water, but then reappear several hundred yards farther out in the form of jagged, teethlike pillars of granite. As the water deepens, the pillars disappear from view, but they are out there nonetheless, a few meters under water, marked by the buoy of Corn Carhai and Grande Basse de Portsall.

Any hypothetical nocturnal strollers would have looked down from Pointe Scoune at a panoply of bright and strangely displaced lights and known something was wrong, even if they were not sea people. Not even the little fishing boats venture that close to the rocks at Portsall. Amoco *Cadiz* would have been clearly defined by the soft, effulgent illumination of her white accommodation block, standing in striking contrast to her garishly lit deck astern, with the two red signal lamps of the Christmas tree above. Of *Pacific,* they probably would have seen little more than running lights and the brilliant beam of the 3,000-watt rear searchlight, off to the right, sweeping shoreward over the tanker. Ever so slowly, with a kind of placid dignity, the lights crept closer and closer to shore, until the searchlight's beam was stabbing strongly enough through the rain to reach the coast and cast its rays against the white stucco of the houses. Aboard the *Cadiz* at that moment, all the systems and conveniences for the comfort of the population of this self-contained little modern city were still functioning to perfection: elevators, hi-fi, reading lamps, heating, showers, refrigerators, ovens. For all we know, the pasta in the stainless-steel galley may still have been hot and buttery and *al dente.* Then, piece by piece, the big boat began disappearing into the night as her lights winked out. Within a few seconds, all that remained was the searchlight on the right, the call of the twin Deutz diesels, and the two lamps of the Christmas tree, disembodied red points arcing back and forth in the rain. Then the little city was dead and useless and beginning to grind itself to bits.

In the last few minutes of his ship's life, Captain Bardari took advantage of Amoco *Cadiz*'s splendid internal communications system to ring around the different departments that were still manned. A tanker laden with oil quickly frees enormous quantities of hydrocarbon gases when it is punctured, so an obvious imperative is to suppress all possible sources of sparks. The captain ordered the officers to make ready to throw the electrical master switches at his signal. One final time, he repeated the instructions for mustering by the bridge. Then there was nothing more to do but wait for the crunch.

She touched first aft, at the level of the pump room, which lies directly under the front of the superstructure. It wasn't just a tentative scrape, that first grounding: Amoco *Cadiz* rode a high wave over a spire of rock and then came down to impale herself upon it. The rock cut cleanly through the plating of her bottom, thrust deep into the complex network of piping and machinery of the pump room, and ruptured the rear wall of number-four cargo tank. The result was spectacular and immediately perceptible on the bridge.

"There was a great, grinding crunch," Mr. Maynard remembered. "The ship lurched violently. There was a terrific roaring noise from the pump room and a rush of air from the pump room fans and the pump room itself. The doors were blown open, and in about eight seconds the front of the bridge was covered in crude oil, where the water-and-oil mixture coming up from the pump room flew straight up the front of the bridge."

The gash was so huge and deep that the pump room flooded instantly. Like a piston invading a cylinder, the sea roared in and compressed air, oil, and water into an energy-charged mass that sought the only way out—through doors, fan heads, and air outlets. Captain Bardari ordered the engineers up from the engine room and gave the signal for all power to be cut off. He mustered the crew on the bridge, repeatedly warning them not to panic. Within a quarter of an hour everyone was accounted for, including an ashen-faced Franca Strano, lost inside her Day-Glo-orange life vest. The vacation trip she had signed on for was giving her plenty of material to tell the girls back in Genoa about.

After impaling herself, Amoco *Cadiz* rolled and grinded on her rocky sword for about five minutes, immobilized as the seas battered her the length of her starboard side. Then another huge wave lifted her free and she continued her course landward in a southwesterly direction, still pulling *Pacific* with her. There could be no more bridge-to-bridge VHF talk from that point on, since the radio had gone dead when the electricity was shut down. Now, with his command post dimly lit by spark-proof emergency lamps, Captain Bardari was reduced to walkie-talkies. With them he was still able to reach *Pacific,* and indeed did speak with her several times after grounding. But—was it because of pride, absentmindedness, or what?—he never did ask the tug to send an SOS for him. That final distress call was going to be a big problem for Captain Bardari.

He was on the horns of a dilemma: He needed to communicate, but he was afraid to use the equipment for it. He had at his disposal a big, battery-powered emergency transmitter down in the radio room, as well as a smaller portable set intended for use in a lifeboat at sea. But they might send off sparks, he thought, and God only knew what a spark could have done to them—send them to their rewards, a Nagasaki-sized fireball, maybe.

The best alternative seemed to be a flare. In spite of the legendary phlegmatic poise said to characterize the English, and in spite of the admirable calm he displayed throughout the entire saga of the Amoco *Cadiz*, it is easy to imagine that Mr. Maynard, who was by now something like the co-captain of the ship, had his heart in his throat as he made his way along the railing to the end of the bridge wing, whence he could look straight down into the seething turmoil of the sea. Leaning into the wind, as far away as possible from the hydrocarbon vapors, he prepared his first flare. It was a moment fraught with anguish. The ship was reeking of gas, and images of spark plugs and fuses and detonation caps sprang inescapably to mind as he made ready to let it go. Mr. Maynard fired straight up. The flare darted into the sky, a brilliant red star that lit the area around them as it descended on its parachute, carried away toward land by the wind. Amoco *Cadiz* rolled and stank and chuffed snorts of crude oil up the front of her superstructure, but she didn't explode. For good measure, Maynard fired a couple of more flares. Now, at least, they had sent out the visual equivalent of an SOS.

Spurting oil from top and bottom, Amoco *Cadiz* lurched oafishly shoreward, trapped inside the rocky maze of the reef line, bonking and nudging against lesser protuberances, in effect finding the path for an ingenious channel that carried her far closer to land than anyone around Portsall would have thought possible. She had an appointment with a rock designated as Men Goulven on marine charts of the Portsall area. It took her twenty-six minutes to get there after the first grounding. They were long minutes.

"There was a bit of panic," a crewman admitted as he remembered that first encounter with the rocks. "We were all ready with our life vests, and we went out to see what was happening. We saw that the sea was really terrible. And at the same time we started to smell the gas coming out of the broken hold. While we were trying to put the life rafts into the sea, the captain was on the bridge sending up rockets, and because there was a lot of gas we were afraid. That was logical: You start the radio or a little bit of light or a little bit of electricity, that could cause an explosion. The first thing we did was to switch off all the lights—the boat completely turned off. The machinery, that didn't exist anymore."

Everything conspired to make the wreck of the Amoco *Cadiz* as bad as possible. She rode in for her act of hara-kiri on a spring flood tide, and the unusually high water enabled her to pass over many of the rocks that would have stopped her farther out, to finally plant herself so deep within les Roches de Portsall that lightering operations by smaller tankers in the days that were to follow would have been utterly impossible, even if the weather had been willing.

Throughout the tanker's drunken wanderings, *Pacific* held on stubbornly, pointing her nose northward and increasing her engine RPMs as she paid out more towing wire. By 2115 she had seven hundred meters out and was close to full power. Once again, she began falling off to starboard, even as she was being dragged back toward the shoals. Captain Weinert put the starboard engine to full. The tug straightened up, but the tow wire became dangerously taut. Now all he was able to do was to keep his face into the weather. It was the casualty that was doing the pulling. At 2130, he sent a crewman aft with the "flex," an electric grinding wheel strong enough to cut right through the main tow wire in an emergency. If he came up against the rocks he wanted to be able to free himself of the tanker.

Also at 2130, Amoco *Cadiz* ended her wanderings, 2,000 meters from the shore. She slammed into the reef stern first, opening up her bottom under the engine room. This time, there could be no wave high enough to lift her off Men Goulven rock. Her last movement was to pivot around to port, dragging her useless anchor chain across the bulb of her bow from left to right. Now she sat with her bow pointing in toward land. Seen from above in the days that followed, her last position looked exactly like a ship that someone had driven deliberately ashore, straight ahead, and parked there.

The site that fate had chosen for Amoco *Cadiz*'s final resting place left her with her stern impaled on a rock twelve meters or so under water and her bow on another one, six or seven meters under. Between, the length of her crude oil holds, the depth of the water was twenty-five to thirty meters: perfect conditions for breaking a ship in half. Once she had finally stopped moving in toward shore, the conditions became even more atrocious. On the boat deck and bridge, everyone held his breath for a few seconds and waited: would she explode or wouldn't she?

At first it seemed certain that she would. Pressurized air came screaming out of the engine room fan heads, followed by an internal thump and a sound like a stick of dynamite going off under the deck, as a jet of flame shot up from the top of the funnel. Then, amazingly, miraculously, the ship held together, unexploded. During those few terrifying seconds, the cavernous engine room had been smashed and carved open by the rock, and the mixture of air, water, and bunker fuel had ignited on contact with the still-hot boiler, or perhaps the exhaust manifold of the Burmeister & Wain. But there was only enough time for a single flash explosion before the Atlantic Ocean crowded in and claimed dominion. Then everything was flooded below decks that could be flooded, and the ship was held stationary, pinned to the rocks fore and aft. The sea began to go to work on the rest of her.

The change was immediate. The waves on which she had been riding earlier now came rolling in to break against her in an endless repetition of hammer blows, swarming over the main deck and cascading high up against the superstructure. It had been a natural reflex action for the captain to order the crew to the boat deck, but it quickly became apparent that any classical attempt at abandoning ship would be pure suicide. The port lifeboat hung out on its davits, ready to go, and that was the way it stayed until the sea destroyed it. Captain Bardari brought his men back inside the superstructure. By pure animal instinct to get as far from danger as possible, they made their way up the stairs to bridge level. Their cozy little microenvironment, which until half an hour before had offered every modern comfort, had been transformed into a stinking, cold, wet iron hulk. They would have been better off on an old wooden sailing ship. At least wood floated. Sheltering inside what was left of their oilpot, the crew of Amoco *Cadiz* was acutely aware that nothing about her would float anymore. Except the oil, of course.

It was the beginning of a frightening, miserable two-and-a-half-hour wait for a rescue that seemed more and more problematical as time passed. Without some kind of intervention, they had no hope whatsoever. Captain Bardari ordered the lifeboat emergency transmitter brought to the bridge. Its hand-cranked generator emitted an automatic signal of twelve dashes followed by a double SOS and the call sign A8AN. Theoretically, Muscuso knew, it had a range of fifty nautical miles, but he was getting no answer at all in response to his furious crankings, not even from *Pacific.* They had to face a reality that was as obvious as it was depressing. The goddam thing was broken. It just didn't work. They would have to count on *Pacific* to call for help for them. Which is exactly what happened.

Aboard the big tug, Captain Weinert had not given up pulling, even at the second grounding. For all he knew, Amoco *Cadiz* might still free herself and ride favorable currents outward, especially with the help of *Simson.* As the odor of crude oil spread over the entire area, he ordered no smoking and signaled down to Korb for full speed ahead on both motors. At 2150 he called Radio le Conquet on VHF channel 28:

> *To Coast Guard—We are need a helicopter for the tanker Amoco* Cadiz, *he is grounded and fired red rockets and he lost crude oil.*

The English phrasing was a bit Hamburg-style, but the import of the message was starkly clear. It set into action the forces that eventually plucked Captain Bardari and the others to safety. The eloquence of his message also reflected Captain Weinert's realization that he was going to have to take some exceptional measures, even at the risk of damaging his machinery. He was already at the normal full towing speed of 250 RPM (a burdened tug can support far fewer revs than when in free motion), but he brought them up to 270. After a minute had passed, he phoned down to Korb and requested an emergency 300 RPM. Warily, one eye on the pressure and the other on the temperature—he really didn't approve of this—Korb gave it to him. Shuddering under the extreme effort, vibrating so heavily that she burst thirty light bulbs in the process, *Pacific* labored for seventeen minutes, then suddenly surged forward and smoothed out: The second tow had parted. This time, it turned out to be the shackle between the towing pennant and the chain, but the meaning would have been the same whichever part it was that broke:

"Und that was the end of the story," Weinert recalled a few days afterward with a fatalistic shrug.

In the Standard Oil Building, Captain Phillips and Harry Rinkema got the news at about 4:00 P.M. Chicago time, when Captain Rutkowsky, Bugsier's night watch officer who had replaced Captain Meyer, came through to repeat what they had just heard from Weinert by radio: Amoco *Cadiz* was aground, "absolutely dead," showing no lights and sending no radio signals. There were distress flares. The area where she had grounded was very, very bad, and so was the weather.

Captain Rutkowsky was about to go on with the conversation when Captain Phillips interrupted him and said he would have to sign off. There seemed to be a call coming in for him on another line, direct from the scene. Phillips picked up the phone, but nothing was there. After waiting in vain for six minutes he gave up. Using his other line, he called the French embassy in Washington to give official notification of the grounding and the pollution that possibly could follow.

A quarter of an hour after *Pacific*'s second tow broke, *Simson* arrived. By some brave and extremely temerarious sailing at full speed, navigating solely with radar and his Decca Navigator because visibility was approximately nil, Captain Martin Winter had managed to cut more than an hour from his ETA, but he was too late nonetheless. If only he had been called a little earlier. . . . There was no doubt about it: if Amoco *Cadiz* had emitted a standby call for tugs within half an hour of the breakdown, *Simson* could have been on the scene four hours earlier, and even *Pacific* would have been there an hour or so quicker. Now helpless and useless except for relaying radio messages, the two tugs spent the rest of that night circling to windward of the wreck, staying on the sea side of the buoys and keeping a careful watch on their depth recorders.

After the warning from the Molène lookout at 2035, the navy had tardily sprung to life and manned its semaphores in the vicinity with exceptional night watches. Soon a steady flow of information was marching in to the Commande Opérationnelle Maritime, including positions and sightings of Mr. Maynard's distress flares. At

2200, Radio le Conquet relayed *Pacific*'s notification of the tanker's grounding to CROSS headquarters on the tip of the Normandy peninsula, in the hamlet called Jobourg.

"Okay," Jobourg replied. "Operational headquarters in Brest notified and will send planes and helicopters."

Around this time occurred a curious and little-known incident, a footnote to the Amoco *Cadiz* story that might be taken as a technical exploit by some or an appalling demonstration of slavish fidelity by others: Captain Bardari had one last conversation with his boss. This was the call that Captain Phillips had been waiting for, and finally it came in—but in this case, it was a weird, roundabout communication rather than a true phone call. Bardari had managed to raise *Pacific* by walkie-talkie, and asked Vogel, the radio operator, to place a ship-to-shore call for him to Chicago. When the line was established at 2155 GMT, he was able to check in with his superiors by proxy from his battered, oil-spattered bridge. For the next twenty-five minutes an electronic ballet saw Captain Bardari's report go via walkie-talkie to the *Pacific*'s radio room, where Vogel took notes. Vogel then repeated the message into his microphone, whence it flew out to Le Conquet, whence Chaput and his men satellite-bounced it via the regular telephone channels to Chicago. The same chain worked back from Phillips in reverse, and the conversation, if you can call it that, got the basic information across. We know nothing of the detail of this conversation beyond a garbled note, hastily (and ungrammatically) jotted by one of the operators at Le Conquet:

Loosing crude oil—tug *Simson* to near also indistress position.

The call was a nice display of the marvels made possible by twentieth-century communications, as well as proof of the first effective cooperation between *Pacific* and *Cadiz.* But it also had a grotesque side to it, as an illustration of the company spirit that apparently pervades VLCC captains: In his very hour of agony, with his boat a cold and dirty wreck twisting under his feet and, for all he knew, about to blow him sky-high, Captain Bardari felt compelled to check in with his boss. As if he could do anything about their plight.

What the boss was able to do was to go on with his phone calls: to the U.S. Coast Guard, who might have some advice; to the underwriters who insured the hull; to Shell, owners of the cargo; to the

French naval attaché; to Bugsier and other salvage specialists; and to the American companies that had powerful emergency pumping equipment available. There was nothing more he could do for his boat; what counted now was the Oil Spill Contingency Plan.

At 7:30 in the evening, Rinkema left the office and returned home, leaving Captain Phillips, still dogged by the ever-attentive legal counsel Clair with his legal pads, to carry on into the night with his crisis team. When he phoned in for an update at 8:30, Phillips told him that he had heard that all the crew except the captain and the English safety inspector had been removed to safety. That was good news, but neither one of them could understand why Amoco *Cadiz* had never used her diesel-powered emergency generator or the big battery-powered radio to send messages. Quite obviously, neither one of these executive sailors could imagine the frightful conditions aboard their oilpot or the visceral fear of sparks and detonations.

Phillips and Clair maintained their vigil throughout the night, observed with curiosity by the crews of cleaning ladies who carried on with their nocturnal chores of vacuuming and emptying waste baskets. At home, Rinkema dozed fitfully. At 4:30 in the morning he rang Phillips, to learn that Bardari and Maynard were safe, and that the weather was apparently moderating.

Rinkema heaved himself out of bed and got himself ready to come into the office. On the radio, WBBM had already broken the news. Worse, they were saying that the ship had already broken in two! How could that be, in such a short amount of time? Both he and Phillips continued to wonder about that when he arrived on the fiftieth floor at ten minutes to eight. Diagrams of the steering motor were strewn around Phillips's office. In company with Leland Adams, president of Amoco International, Rinkema went to break the news to the bosses at the top. Their first stop was the office of George Myers, president of Standard Oil. Myers warned them against speculating to outsiders about the accident and went off to brief his own boss, John E. Swearingen, chairman of the board, the man at the top of the heap.

Down at the bottom of the heap, in Portsall, Jules Legendre was warm and comfortable inside his pretty retirement cottage at the end of a cul-de-sac a stone's throw from the beach when he first heard the news that something was amiss out by Men Goulven. It was around 2130 when he received a phone call from the Molène semaphore and, yes, come to think of it, he could already smell oil. That night and next morning, tens of thousands of Breton house-holders caught the smell and reacted with exactly the same thought: the oil-burner tank was leaking. It was only after going outside and checking that they realized that the smell was not just in their house, but everywhere.

The semaphore called Legendre because he was mayor of Port-sall and a man who was well known and respected in all the nearby hamlets around the coast. A man of the sea himself, he had fled France with the German invasion, joined the Free French forces in England, and spent the rest of the war in service with the sub-marines, graduating from them to the merchant marine after the liberation. For twenty-three years he had plied his trade as officer-electrician aboard BP tankers, ending his career aboard VLCCs, which he knew well and detested thoroughly.

Shorebound by an early retirement at age fifty-seven—he had refused, by principle, to continue his career aboard ships flying flags of convenience—he had found himself with enough time on his hands to stand for municipal council in the local election for which Portsall was administratively attached to the neighboring metropolis (population 4,297) of Ploudalmezeau. Elected, he was named dep-uty mayor of Ploudalmezeau, with special responsibility for Portsall. With his soft voice and grave, understated manner, Legendre com-manded respect among the fishermen and *petits commerçants* of Portsall. Later, when the press discovered him, reporters appre-ciated him for his frankness and willingness to speak while everyone else was blathering, and photographers delighted in his gray-eyed gaze and white beard: He was the perfect image of the old sea-wolf who had come back to land.

Telling his wife not to wait up, Legendre climbed into his car and drove over the dunes until he was opposite Men Goulven. Until four in the morning he watched *Pacific* and *Simson* playing their searchlights on the unlit wreck, watched the helicopters swoop in and do their incredible aerial ballet, and finally drove back home to catch a few hours of sleep. He would be needing them.

In his little house directly on the port in Portsall, Jean Qui-voron and his wife, Rosa, had turned in early that night, but not be-fore she had remarked on the bizarre smell of rotten onion that seemed to be around them. They were awakened between 10:30 and 11:00, when Jean Gouzien and two friends came banging on their door. They needed a boat.

Quivoron, a fifty-four-year-old fisherman, was an imposingly large and powerful man whose natural stature and two-packs-a-day chain-smoking habit had endowed him with a braying, stentorian voice that was in itself as good as any fishing boat's foghorn. He was also a man who had the reputation of fearing nothing, and the owner of *Le Mouez Ar Mor,* an eight-meter wooden fishing smack powered by a sturdy seventy-five-horsepower Volvo diesel.

"There's a boat on fire," explained Victor Louedoc, one of the men accompanying Gouzien. A fisherman like the others, Louedoc was the chief of the Portsall lifeboat, the man who had the responsibility of trying to save shipwrecked crews. If he had the wrong information in detail, he was right on the basic fact of the wreck. COM in Brest had contacted him and the Aber Wrac'h lifeboat to see what they could do. But, as the continuing ironies of fate would have it, Portsall was bereft of its municipal lifeboat at that time because it had been sent away on loan to the island of Sein, south of Brest. Sein's own boat had been damaged in January while coming to the aid of the navy's brand-new escort vessel *Dupérré,* which an inexperienced helmsman had driven straight onto the rocks during high-speed trials at night. So Louedoc needed Quivoron and his boat. Without further questions, Quivoron slipped into his boots and his slicker.

"Tu ne vas pas sortir par ce temps-là?" ("You're not going out in this weather, are you?) demanded Rosa, and Quivoron shrugged. *"T'inquiete pas"* (Don't worry"), he said, and went out into the storm with his three friends.

"I told them I'd go with them," Quivoron recalled later, "but I knew that was a very bad sector out there. I wouldn't go there in good weather, and this time it was night, pitch black. And in that weather . . ."

Bent low against the rain and hail, the four men rowed out to Quivoron's boat, fired up the Volvo, and clattered out toward the breakwater. Plowing straight ahead into the heaving black mass of the seas and then bearing right, they managed to position themselves approximately between the coast and the wreck, but in spite of the mere 1.10-meter draft of his boat, Quivoron could find no passage to approach closer than one kilometer. Everywhere they turned, explosions of white foam, breaking through the covering layer of crude oil, indicated an unseen reef, and between the wind, the currents, and the roller-coaster ride that the waves were giving him, Quivoron had to call on all his experience at the wheel and knowledge of the coast to avoid disaster for himself and his friends. The best they could do was to hang around where they were, on the off chance that they might be able to help anybody who took it into his head to abandon ship. But for once, there was a positive side to things: Quivoron was so impressed by the overpowering presence of hydrocarbon gas all around him that he did not dare light up a cigarette. His health could only have benefitted.

By 2:00 A.M., after watching the arrival and departure of three helicopters, Quivoron and his friends turned *Le Mouez Ar Mor* around and chugged back into harbor. Later they learned that the lifeboat from Aber Wrac'h had done exactly as they did, but on the other side of the reefs, where they were hidden from view. They, too, had returned to port after the helicopters had done their work.

"Ca y est" ("That's it then"), said Quivoron. *"Il n'y a pas de pétard"* ("No firecrackers tonight"). At least there was that—she hadn't blown up.

In the port, Legendre was waiting for them on the quayside with a colonel of the Gendarmerie, anxiously awaiting any information they could give. Quivoron could offer little encouragement: "That boat will be finished in two or three days," he predicted, gratefully lighting up a Gauloise.

Aboard the tanker, just about the time that Quivoron was preparing to go out into the storm, the sea took a decision for Bardari and his crew when a tremendous wave flung itself over the deck and across the superstructure, picked up the port lifeboat where it hung on its davits, and smashed it into three pieces. The center section dropped into the water, and the two end sections remained dangling in shattered shards from the cables. The starboard boat was facing into the weather and could not be swung out, so that ended any debate about leaving the wreck by boat. Now the avenues of escape had been narrowed down to two: helicopters or swimming.

They were a pathetic lot: wretched, cold, and half-gassed from breathing hydrocarbon vapors; frightened that an explosion could come at any minute; not even sure that their messages had been heard or their flares sighted. Captain Bardari waited half an hour longer and then decided that he would have to take the big risk. He asked Muscuso to go down to his radio room and fire up the battery-powered emergency transmitter. Once again, there was a collective holding of breath as Muscuso disappeared below. The set came to life, and he touched the Morse key. Once again, there was no explosion. Working by torchlight, woozy from gas fumes, Mus-

cuso sent out his first SOS and was relieved when an immediate ac-
knowledgment came back from Radio le Conquet. The story of the
next forty minutes aboard Amoco *Cadiz* can hardly be told better
than by the radio messages themselves.

2318, to all stations from Amoco *Cadiz*:

*SOS from A8AN. Tanker aground need immediate assistance pls. AS
AS* [stand by]. *SOS. from A8AN. QTH QTH* [Here's my position]:
*48,36.2 N 04,45.9 W. Tanker aground need immediate assistance if
possible helicopter. We have only channel 6 VHF.*

2337, to all stations from Amoco *Cadiz*:

SOS from A8AN. Amoco Cadiz *grounded. Full loading with pollution. Require immediate assistance and crew rescue by helicopter. Pls
advise helicopter that we have VHF contact channel 6 only.*

2345, Le Conquet to all stations, after repeating the SOS:

Tanker has only chl 6 VHF stop tug Pacific */DNCH and tug* Simson
*/DAIC standing by stop laberwracs lifeboat proceeding stop ships in
area pse keep sharp lookout and report to FFU.*

Midnight, Amoco *Cadiz* to Le Conquet:

*Now helicopter here thank you. Helicopter effecting crew rescue now.
Here closing and going up to bridge standing by to abandon vessel.*

0121, Le Conquet to all stations:

SOS reference Amoco Cadiz/*A8AN stop now crew abandoning ship
by helicopter stop distress traffic ended resume normal working.*

11.

The Rescue

It wasn't as simple as all that.

The sequential reproduction of these radio calls is misleading in that they make it appear that Amoco *Cadiz* had only to send out her personal SOS and—presto!—the rescue helicopters magically materialized a mere forty-two minutes later. In fact, the delay was closer to two hours (one hour and fifty-four minutes, to be precise) rather than forty-two minutes. The French naval authorities had "officially" known that something was very wrong since the alarm from the Molène semaphore came in at 2035. Likewise, another telephone call from the Aber Wrac'h semaphore to navy headquarters in Brest reported the tanker's red flares at 2142. Finally, after *Pacific*'s helicopter request, the naval airbase at Lanvéoc-Poulmic had been aware of the SOS since five minutes to ten GMT. But, bureaucratic time lags being what they are, and preparation of sophisticated equipment being what it is, something over an hour and a half passed before the first chopper could get off the ground.

But once it did, it performed magnificently. In fact, the helicopter crews of Flotilla 32F of the Groupe des Porte-Avions et de l'Aviation Embarquée Aéronautique Navale are the only true heroes of the lamentable Amoco *Cadiz* affair—especially a diabolically skillful little man named René Martin.

It was not your ideal night to go out flying. But then again, it wasn't particularly pleasant for open-air promenades on ship decks, either. After the first couple of hours in the dead hulk of their leaking oilpot, the crew of Amoco *Cadiz* was in physical and spiritual misery. The sea pounded so insistently at the base of the superstructure that it eventually managed to smash all the windows and blow open latched doors. When intrepid crewmen staggered down and jammed them closed, the sea responded by ripping the door frames right out of the bulkheads. After that, water columns shot up the stairwells every time a new wave arrived, then fell away with monstrously reverberating gurgles and sucking noises that echoed all the way up to the bridge. The cylinder and piston analogy held good there, too: Every wave pushed a wind blast into the superstructure, and then reversed it when it receded, with a violent, sucking roar of water. At the top level, inside the bridge, there was shelter from the weather but a tremendous profusion of gas, enough to force the crew out onto the bridge wing and back behind the port side of the accommodation block, where there was something of a lee. There, the temperature was one degree above zero, but it felt incalculably colder with the impact of the wind and spray. And, of course, the zephyrs brought precipitation with them that evening—sometimes rain, sometimes soggy snow, sometimes even a rattle of sleet. It was awful. On top of all that, there was the ever present fear that comes from sitting on a time bomb. Amoco *Cadiz* was heaving and creaking under their feet. Would she fall apart? Would she subside into the sea? Would she explode? No one, not even the most qualified officers, had any idea. In their spanking new yellow slickers and Day-Glo life vests, they waited numbly for something to happen. Luckily for them, René Martin was just then changing into his Superman suit.

Lanvéoc-Poulmic is an unprepossessing little military installation on a hillside above the cove of Poulmic, a dozen miles across the roadstead from Brest. At the bottom of the hill, near the water, are the mess halls and some of the living quarters and administrative offices; at the top, a short, wind-swept airstrip, a control tower, a prefabricated office block, and a huge hangar, home for the ten SA 321 Super-Frelon helicopters of Flotilla 32F and the one hundred and seventy men who work in, on, and around them. In 1978, the flotilla was basically an antisubmarine outfit, and most of its six-bladed Super-Frelons (Super Hornets) were equipped with an impressive array of electronic tracking and killing gear that is as heavy as it is space-consuming, leaving only corridors and crannies for any passengers to crowd themselves between the consoles. They are big helicopters, as spacious as they are husky: With their three Turbo-meca jet turbines of 1,500 horsepower each, they can lift seven and a half tons, and are rated for twenty-seven passengers beyond their normal five-man crews. Being so close to the ocean—Lanvéoc-Poul-mic is the westernmost airbase in France—the helicopters were in-evitably called for the double duty of lifesaving at sea, in addition to their sub-killing mission. The Amoco *Cadiz* gave them a chance to see how good they were at it.

René Martin didn't look much like Superman. Scarcely taller than the average jockey, with rapidly thinning gray hair and the face of a ten-year-old boy who somehow had turned forty, Martin would have been chosen for roles of dentists and accountants if he had been an actor. It was only in his lively brown eyes and the rapid, economical way he moved his hands and body that an outsider might have been able to discern anything out of the ordinary about this odd little man. A Breton himself, he had been born into the Aeronavale in the pretty port of Morlaix, where papa held the rank of petty officer and worked as a radio officer. He had enlisted at age eighteen, qualified as a pilot of fixed-wing aircraft at age twenty-one, and three years later moved over to the helicopters, where he had remained ever since. He proved to be something of a genius at making these airborne eggbeaters do his will, and was one of the few pilots at Lanvéoc qualified for both night flying and winch rescue missions. By his fortieth year he had attained the not-so-exalted rank of lieutenant de vaisseau. Apparently the powers-that-be in the navy didn't know how to appreciate quality.

Superman and his wife, Annie, lived with their four teenage children in a little house four kilometers from the base, over on the other side of the town of Lanvéoc. They had retired for the night at 10:30 P.M. French time (0930 GMT), and an hour later the phone began ringing. Martin stumbled across the bedroom and into the kitchen, figuring that it must be for him. Logical: He was the only pilot qualified for night winching who lived so close to the base. He was right, as usual, and off he drove into the night, happily breaking the speed limit as he drove through Lanvéoc. By then, Captain Bar-dari, Mr. Maynard, and their forty-two fellow castaways had been waiting for about an hour and three quarters. They had slightly less than one more hour to go.

Martin changed into his Superman suit at the base: aviator's olive-drab overalls, Mae West, and the big white helmet with the microphone coming down across his mouth. After making the ritualistic checks of his machine—the flight mechanic had already been going over it for more than half an hour—Martin hefted himself up into the *poste de pilotage* of the commander, on the right-hand side, while his co-pilot, principal maître Dagorn, took the left-hand seat. Between and slightly aft of them sat the flight engineer. In the rear, behind the flimsy bulkhead at their backs, the winch man-navigator and the diver strapped themselves in. They had plenty of room: *Bravo Alpha,* as their chopper was designated, was in its troop-carrying configuration, that is to say empty of the antisubmarine electronics that encumbered the other ships. Their flying machine looked like a great big rowboat with a cover over the top, a boom on the back, and a rotor on the top. The shape was not an accident: Super-Frelons in fact *are* boats, in the sense that when they put down into the water they float. Maybe that could come in handy tonight. You never know.

Bravo Alpha lifted off, Dagorn at the controls and Martin handling the radio, with the peculiar forward-leaning running start characteristic of the big freight helicopters, which lack the dragonfly agility of their smaller brethren. All Martin and his crew knew about their mission was that there was a boat in trouble in the vicinity of Aber Wrac'h, probably a tanker. There was no detail about the kind of trouble, the size of the boat, or the number of persons involved. Their orders were as precise as they could be under the circumstances: "Go take a look, and report back by radio."

Bravo Alpha set off toward the coordinates they had been given, flying a curved, left-to-right course shaped like a parenthesis in order to avoid the overflight of Brest. After the roadstead, leaving the lights of Brest below and to their right, they clattered over the darkened farmland of the Breton peninsula toward Portsall. From take-off to arrival, flying with the wind at ninety degrees to their left, they made the forty-kilometer trip in less than fifteen minutes. At three hundred meters over the mainland, they smelled oil. When they came to the coastline, where the lights below gave way to blackness, Martin took over the controls.

"Il faisait un temps dégueulasse," he recalled. Filthy weather. When they had climbed to avoid the big radio antennas at Pointe du Petit Minou, the rain that had been splattering against the windshield turned into a fierce rattle of sleet. The flight mechanic turned his torch on the outside thermometer: zero degrees, exactly freezing. That was not good. According to regulations, the Super-Frelon was not supposed to fly at all at temperatures less than two degrees cen-

tigrade above zero (thirty-five degrees Fahrenheit), since it was not equipped with de-icing gear. Dagorn gave the commander an inquisitive look, and Martin unhesitatingly directed him to plough on. Sure, they could turn around and go back home if they really wanted to stick with the regulations. They could also wait for the month of July. What the hell. That would not be the only time Martin broke rules that night.

Now, as they passed the coastline, it was a matter of finding the casualty. That was not so easy. Principal maître Legall, the winch man, was at his automatic doppler navigator's table, making corrections with the two arrows in front of him, guiding them to the theoretical point in the sea where the wreck was supposed to be lying. But they needed a little less theory and a little more practical help to actually find it, now that they were there. Martin flew straight on, holding the course that normally ought to make them intersect the point of the distress call. Nothing. No visual, and no radio response from the casualty or the tugs that were supposed to be there, in spite of *Bravo Alpha*'s repeated calls—nothing. The big flying boat lumbered straight on into the wet, black void, shouldering aside the wind, its two red navigation lights blinking bravely.

Three hundred feet below, heaving up and down on the Atlantic, Martin Winter, who was spelling Weinert as *Pacific* retrieved and tidied up her tow gear, saw the blinking lights and quickly put two and two together. The captain of *Simson* headed his tug directly toward land and switched the twin beams of his forward 3,000-watt searchlights onto the Amoco *Cadiz*. That proved to be just what Martin needed, and he understood Captain Winter's gesture perfectly: That searchlight beam was a finger pointing in the night. Good. Now practice could take over from theory. Martin whirled *Bravo Alpha* into a U-turn and "walked" down the length of the searchlight beam, turning on his own front light when he reached the end of the range of *Simson*'s beam. He flew straight on, groping in the night at 180 kilometers an hour. Only when he was almost on top of the accommodation block was he able to see anything, and not until then did he realize that he had a VLCC on his hands. He had to make a few decisions very quickly.

Theoretically, Martin's assignment had only been to reconnoiter the job, report the situation back to base, and then determine what course of action should be taken. Now, though, as he swept past the enormous ship, it was clear that he would have to do something right away. It looked like regulations were going to suffer once again.

Going strictly by the book, he had no right to be there in the first place, given the temperature. Further, there was no question of attempting a rescue in those conditions. Armies everywhere have rules for everything, and the French, being a literature-loving people, have probably more than most. In this case, Martin knew very well that the rules forbade him from carrying out night winching operations except on certain French and allied warships whose positions were correctly marked and whose crews were versed in the codes and signals of standard operating procedure. In short: no SOP, no rescue. But, as everyone knows, Superman doesn't bother himself with the rules of ordinary mortals. Martin spoke into his microphone.

"Dagorn, je vais virer à trente degrees d'inclinaison en descente vers trente mètres. Tu mets la main sur le collectif et si je passe en-dessous de trente mètres, tu réagis immédiatement. Lis-moi le badin. . . . Crassin, surveille la méchanique. Annonce-moi les pleins et les tours turbines si j'arrive près des limitations. . . . Legall, ouvre la porte et prépare-toi à me guider en finale."

("Dagorn, I'm going to turn on a thirty-degree angle, down to thirty meters. Keep your hand on the pitch and if I go below thirty meters, take immediate action. Read me the air-speed indicator. . . . Crassin, keep an eye on the machine. Let me know the fuel levels and the turbine RPMs if I get near the limits. . . . Legall, open the door and prepare to guide me on the final approach.")

Martin made a tight turn and came back on his tracks, into the wind at seventy kilometers an hour, angling downward to an altitude of one hundred feet, his front light ablaze. A minute later, the sullied white superstructure of the tanker came looming up at them. He slowed his forward progress, stabilized his position, and finally held firm above the bridge's port wing. Staring fixedly right, at the reference point he had chosen—a portion of the accommodation block under the signal mast painted with the proud Amoco emblem in red, white, and blue—he was ready to do his evening's work. Straight below him was the sea. Off to his left, on the other side of the helicopter, the view from the open side door was of the bridge wing and forty-four white faces, turned upward.

To appreciate Martin's skill as a pilot, and the calculated risks he was taking, it is useful to enumerate the obstacles that stood in his way, the "anomalies," as the military like to say, that differentiated his mission from the parade-ground kind of exercises where ships like the Super-Frelon are usually demonstrated: It was night, with visibility changing from bad to terrible, depending on squalls; winds were force seven, gusting to eight, nine or even ten; temperature was barely above freezing, making for a precipitation that varied unpredictably between snow, sleet, and rain; as low as he was hovering, waves smashing against the *Cadiz* shot up and actually hit him in mid-air—on his return to base, his ground crew found the arklike bottom of his Super-Frelon spattered with crude oil and bits of seaweed hanging from his wheels.

At 11:50 Martin was moving in on his final approach, "playing" his helicopter with a delicately complicated coordination that would put concert pianists to shame. His feet controlled yaw and heading, his hands pitch and roll. At the same time a fiendishly clever series of microcontrols was at the tips of his fingers. Earlier, he had lifted a little green safety flap with a finger of his left hand and flicked the toggle switch that illuminated his fore and aft GE iode projectors, six hundred watts each. He had no radio communication with either the tug or the casualty, but Captain Winter was quick-witted and understood the problems of rescue work at night. As soon as the helicopter threw on its searchlights, he cut his off. The last thing he wanted to do was to blind the pilot and send him crashing into the superstructure. If anything would make the bomb explode, that would.

Next to the toggle switch for Martin's lights was a rounded protuberance that he could move in all directions with a fingertip: "the Chinese hat," the pilots called it, and it controlled the orientation of the searchlights. Steadily downward he inched his eggbeater, until he had one light beaming onto the port bridge wing and the other locked onto the radar mast. Martin was where he wanted to be. Now it was a question of holding her steady. For this he had the help of his flight engineer, who monitored the engine systems, and the co-pilot to his left, who handled the radio and kept an attentive eye on the flight instruments. The one that interested him the most was the radio altimeter. By bringing the Super-Frelon down from thirty meters to thirty feet he was completely fracturing the rulebook, which stated a minimum winching altitude of seventy feet. That was okay for theory, but in this weather seventy feet would mean a wildly looping and gyrating winch cable. Also, *Bravo Alpha* didn't have a high-speed winch. By going down to thirty feet, he could cut winching time by better than half. He told his diver to go.

Just at this moment, copilot Dagorn, who had already called for more helicopters, broke in to say that Brest Marine Radio was asking whether or not the commander of the tanker had given his authorization for the evacuation of his personnel. Ah, bureaucracy.

"Tell them *évacuation en cours*," said Martin, as his diver left their company.

Principal maître Guy Lenabat was a bearded, green-eyed Breton who looked like the world stereotype of the sturdy fisherman when you met him wearing his pea jacket, but at 11:52 that night he bore more of a resemblance to James Bond. His stocky, athletic frame was entirely encased in the black rubber of his wet suit, his face in a diving mask, and his feet in long black fins. Leaving his twin air tanks behind him (he ardently hoped he would have no need for diving overboard), he slipped the nylon harness under his arms, nodded to his winch man, and stepped out the door of the Super-Frelon. The sickly hydrocarbon cloud immediately blanketed him, but the descent went off smoothly, Legall leaning out of the open door and guiding the winch wire by hand to prevent it from swinging. When Lenabat hit the deck he knew that the first thing he would have to do was make order.

"Everyone was out on the left-hand wing of the bridge," he remembered. "Right under me. They were completely panicked. As soon as I got down everyone tried to jump onto the winch at once. Some of them were even down on their knees. They were screaming in Italian, and I couldn't understand a thing."

Lenabat shouted back in French and maybe a little bit of Breton, too. Physically shoving at the mob, using his flashlight like a traffic cop, he herded them back away from the point of the wing to the shelter inside the bridge deck's wheelhouse, and then persuaded them with gestures to sit down on the deck and wait their turns. When they were finally in a semblance of order, he began motioning them forward, one by one. With this chore, and throughout the rest of his long night aboard the ship, he remembers being helped at all times by a bearded man with an air of command about him, very calm. He took him for the first mate. Only later did he learn that it was in fact Mr. Maynard, the admirable Englishman who came for a short visit and stayed somewhat longer. Lenabat's own aura of authority suffered twice in the early stages when his feet went out from under him on the oil-covered deck, made even more slippery by melting snow. After his second spill, he took his fins off and chucked them in a corner. He would probably have to make out an equipment loss report in triplicate for that, but at least he was steady on his feet. He began winching—double time, looping the harness over each new arrival, placing their hands up above them on the cable, then signaling Legall to pull away. After three men had been sent up, someone tapped Lenabat on the shoulder and pushed the next candidate at him. With the noise of the helicopter and the unfamiliar phrases in Italian, the diver didn't know what it was all about until he took a second look—it was a woman! Franca Strano was dressed like all the others in a slicker and life vest. If she hadn't been brought forward out of the crowd, she would have taken her chances with the rotation among the others.

With the big chopper holding rock-steady and the winching going well (to save time, Lenabat "forgot" to hitch up the safety line each time), the stranded sailors calmed and awaited their turns in good order. They seemed to believe Lenabat when he assured them they would all get away, and that more choppers would be there soon. Upstairs, Legall had a moment of horrified surprise, when he briefly turned his glance from below to the interior of *Bravo Alpha.* There, in the back of the machine, everyone he had winched up was huddled on the clamshell of the cargo door, instead of occupying the seats along the two sides. What bothered him about this was that a couple of months previously, without even the weight of refugees upon it, a cargo door of the same sort had chosen to drop away in flight and tumble into the ocean. This time, the door held long enough for him to shoo his visitors away and into the bucket seats.

After half an hour of hovering, Martin felt himself weakening. The nervous strain of holding a thirteen-ton helicopter steady at night against unpredictable winds gusting up to one hundred kilometers an hour, with only a few feet of tolerance in any direction, is difficult to describe, even for a pilot. Most of them search for analogies, but there are none that really fit. It was not only the strain on Martin's eyes that fatigued him, but the pitilessly pervasive tension that gripped him and actually made him wonder if his hands and his feet would go on obeying his brain. Hovering of this sort during training exercises had always been limited to ten minutes, and now, after thirty, his nerves were crying for surcease. He wanted out, but the problem was that Dagorn couldn't take over: On his side, there was no reference point: only the vague white foaming of the sea below. Twice Martin tried to pass him the controls—the helicopter lurching off the stationary in the process—and twice he was obliged to give up and take them back himself.

By 12:35, Lenabat had sent up twenty-eight survivors, one more than the Super-Frelon's theoretical maximum capacity, and Legall was signaling him to stop. Crassin, the flight engineer, had warned Martin that the turbines were at their limit. This time, the cable didn't come down again to Lenabat. Normal textbook procedure required Martin to leave his stationary position by continuing up and forward, into the wind, but now he had the tanker's mast right in front of his eyes: he took her out in reverse, letting the wind fly him backward. That was very, very unorthodox. Theory would not approve. As soon as he had gained a safe altitude, he heaved a sigh of relief, passed the controls to Dagorn, sat back in his seat, and closed his eyes. He ached all over. The French Aeronavale would later claim a world record for his performance: twenty-eight persons winched to safety in forty-three minutes. The record stands today in the Guinness book of records—the French edition, at any rate.

Acting as an airborne buoy, *Bravo Alpha* now hovered above and to one side of the wreck for a quarter of an hour until Martin's friend Michel d'Escayrac roared up in *Bravo Kilo,* an antisub ship that had been hastily cleared of any gear that was liftable. There wasn't much space in *Bravo Kilo*—with the weight of the electronic systems, nine men would bring her right to the edge of her lift capacity—but she was the one that was available, and so she was the one that went.

Below, Lenabat had a chance to take a little rest, if that word may be used here, and get somewhat better acquainted with his environment. He had been concentrating so hard on crowd control and winching that he had scarcely been aware of anything but the noise of the turbines above him, the slick deck, and the pervasive, suffocating atmosphere of oil fumes. Now he could hear the ship dying, and actually feel it—it was moving under his feet, as if it were writhing in pain. The stern was pinned down hard, but the forward half was still in motion, riding up on the rock with a titanic clang and then shuddering back with a sound of scraping and ripping steel, accompanied by sparks and flashes.

"How many are you?" he asked a crew member who spoke French.

"Forty-four," he said.

"Are you all here on the bridge?"

"Yes."

"How did it happen?"

"Our rudder broke. We had a tug, but he let us down."

Thus are legends born. Little did he know that it was because of the tug that the helicopters had been able to come in to save them.

As they were waiting for the second helicopter, a playful wave came along and lifted a lifebuoy free of its bracket, turning on its water-activated beacon light. Perhaps mistaking the flash for fire, a sailor shouted and gestured toward the port bridge wing. Captain Bardari, accompanied by the brave Mr. Maynard, rushed out at full speed. This time it was Bardari's turn to lose his footing. He went down on the run, breaking his fall with his left elbow and forearm and sliding on the oily snow all the way to the end of the wing. For a long moment he lay there gasping in pain, then finally arose and stumbled back to the bridge area, wretched and suffering. As if he needed that, on top of everything else. His wet suit covered with oil and occasionally speckled with an errant snowflake, Lenabat held his flashlight up and made ready to guide the second chopper in.

Lieutenant de vaisseau Michel d'Escayrac and his crew had been smelling crude oil ever since they lifted off from Lanvéoc. He spotted Martin's navigational lights well before he was over water, but then he shared the same worrisome experience of not being able to see Amoco *Cadiz* until he was almost on top of her. In daytime, she was only a risible little sliver of metal amongst the Portsall rocks, but at night, even with all the flashlights on her deck, she was all but invisible. (In fact later, after he had completed his winching, D'Escayrac momentarily lost her by straying off a bit too far in the night.) Now, as he made his approach into the wind, he could plainly see the white foam on the face of the ocean before the wreck came into view. And, of course, he could smell her. The oil vapors were so thick that naval spokesmen later said that the helicopter turbines could well have "suffocated" in the too-rich atmosphere. But it was ignition rather than extinction that was preying on D'Escayrac's mind.

"It was like a fog of oil fumes," he remembered. "We were all a little tense when we came in because we didn't know if the heat from our engines would set it off or not. My approach brought me closer to the superstructure than Martin had been, so when I was at winching altitude the tips of my rotors were perhaps ten meters from the radar mast over on the right. I couldn't see anything at all on the left, except a shower of spray from time to time. It was very *sportif*.

You can wet your shirt in half an hour of flying like that."

D'Escayrac's initiation into lifesaving as a sporting event went off smoothly and quickly, but it was marked by an unusual occurrence—a two-man winching, in which Lenabat accompanied one of the survivors up into the belly of the Super-Frelon and then went back down alone to carry on with his work. The technique is a classical one, usually reserved for injured persons who are unable to hold themselves inside the rescue harness. In this case, though, the "injury" was due only to the bottle—the man was dead drunk. There are many ways to do battle with anxiety, Lenabat thought as he flailed grimly upward with his cumbersomely disjointed burden, but if every sailor reacted to shipwreck by going for the bottle, he was going to ask for a desk job.

While D'Escayrac was hanging over the wreck, Martin darted back to Lanvéoc, disgorged his twenty-eight passengers, and refueled in combat emergency mode, with his rotors still turning. A few minutes after 1:30 A.M. he was back over Portsall and had joined up with D'Escayrac.

"I've lost her!" D'Escayrac cried angrily over the radio. He had been circling above the tanker in a holding pattern to mark the spot, but the wind had shoved him off to the side. Now Amoco *Cadiz* was nowhere to be found, and he had no way of signaling *Pacific* or *Simson* to throw their searchlights on her again, since radio contact had never been established. Down on the tanker's bridge, Lenabat understood what had happened when he saw the aerial ballet over the water. He tried to signal with his flashlight, but in the vastness of the ocean his little beam was worth next to nothing. He waited. It was Martin who found the solution, by circling back and positioning himself in line with the X and Y coordinates on Legall's doppler navigator's table. Setting himself up to stand just short of the point, he made a regulation upwind approach and—bingo!—came in right on top of Amoco *Cadiz*.

Seven men remained to be rescued—Captain Bardari, Mr. Maynard, and five officers. Lenabat was never able to tell who was who (he didn't know them, and didn't speak Italian), but it was clear to him that this last bunch was all officers, as, indeed, it should have been. They were not strangers to emotion, though.

"The strongest one of all seemed to be the guy with the beard," Lenabat remembered, pointing out, as many others have done since, the exemplary behavior of Mr. Maynard. "He was trying to reason with one guy who had lost control and was crying. He kept saying he didn't want to go up and leave the ship. I grabbed him by the shoulders and forced him into the harness."

This last man up into Martin's helicopter may have been Strano, the first mate, but Lenabat never knew. It would have been logical for the first mate to wish to remain with his skipper, but Captain Bardari insisted that he go up, arguing that it would be too cruel for his wife, Franca, to see the last helicopter arrive without him. Up he went. It was at this moment, as the last of his officers were being winched to safety, that Captain Bardari turned to Mr. Maynard and said, "When they go off, I am staying."

"Yes, okay," answered the Englishman without hesitation. "I'll stay with you."

Lenabat spent a few minutes trying to persuade them to change their minds. He didn't like the situation a bit. From the way she was heaving on the rocks, he was sure that the tanker was going to gut herself. The hulk's movements had become more accentuated in the two and a half hours that he had been aboard. Now he had to hold onto the railing to keep standing. It could give way any minute, he was sure—and then what? Even if she didn't explode, the superstructure could be dragged under, and they with it. When he saw that these last two were adamant, he didn't waste any more time. He signaled to his winch man, soared skyward, and disappeared into the cargo hold.

It was a few minutes before two in the morning. Captain Bardari and Mr. Maynard had Amoco *Cadiz* all to themselves. Or what was left of her. They had three excruciatingly long hours ahead of them. Everything was unbearable about their situation. Their ship was gone, finished, broken. They had sent away their last lifeline. Even if there were any hope of saving anything, they couldn't communicate with the tugs anymore, because their walkie-talkies were dead. They switched from channel to channel in the hope of raising *Pacific* or *Simson* but got nothing but silence for the rest of the night. Inside the bridge, the gas was so thick that they feared they would pass out and die asphyxiated. When they staggered out to the windward wing of the bridge they were showered with rain, snow, and oil, so cold that after a few minutes they had to take shelter again and repeat the whole dreadful process. There was no sanctuary.

With the lower doors of the accommodation block blown away, rushing waves hurled themselves inside and forced passage six stories up to the bridge deck, ripping out equipment as they passed and sending odd pieces of furniture, clothing, and all the miscellane-

E. LE DROFF

The wreck of the Amoco *Cadiz* viewed from the town of Portsall

At high tide, the town of Portsall is dead ahead of the sunken tanker.

E. LE DROFF

Left: Captain Pasquale Bardari of the Amoco *Cadiz*

Below: Mr. Maynard (*right*) and Captain Bardari reach dry land after being rescued by helicopter.

E. LE DROFF

The Amoco *Cadiz* lies with a broken back on the shoal the day after ground-ing. The Roches de Portsall are so badly charted and so dangerous that even the locals avoid it in their tiny fishing boats.

E. LE DROFF

Left: Rene Martin, the hero pilot, broke the rules to save lives.

Below: The inhabitants of Portsall view the oil spill in their harbor the day after the disaster.

E. LE DROFF

E. LE DROFF

Right: The day after the Amoco *Cadiz* went aground, two of many ocean-rescue tugs remained on the scene.

Below: A volunteer holds up a sea bird killed by the spill.

E. LE DROFF

The bow of the Amoco *Cadiz* before it went under. Note the anchor chain.

ous seagoing gear of a big ship along in the wall of compressed air they pushed before them. Coming up, the sea roared like a freight train, and receding it echoed like an immense, grossly overproportioned drainpipe. Captain Bardari and Mr. Maynard earned their pay that night, and then some.

In the last hour of their solitary watch, the two men, drenched and frozen to the bone, woozy and woolly from gas fumes—too much hydrocarbon gas causes brain damage, and a lot too much causes death—began to entertain serious doubts as to their terrestrial futures. Even several years afterward, Mr. Maynard retained a vividly clear memory of his hardest hour.

"The noise that was made with the wind roaring in and out was terrifying, and we were feeling pretty grim at this stage. It was right around four o'clock. I crawled out onto the starboard wing in an attempt to get some fresh air because I felt pretty bad, and I can remember seeing what I thought was flashes of lightning in the sky, which could indicate that another squall was coming through. But, looking up, I couldn't see any clouds at all. I just couldn't make out where the light was coming from.

"I recall looking at the sky and thinking, 'Where the hell is it?' because I could see stars all around, and you cannot have stars all around and a squall. In fact, when I looked forward I could see what was causing it: In fact, the ship was breaking in two, with a screech of metal and a shower of sparks that lasted about ten minutes. The metal was ripping and flaring and flaming and popping. So I called to the captain—I cannot remember the exact words—and said something like, 'Here, Guv'nor, this thing's just fell in two.'

"He came out of the door very, very quickly with a lamp—a large, intrinsically safe damage-control lamp. We shone it forward and we could see that the ship was broken and breaking in fact right across. I think the captain said to me, 'What are we going to do if this bit sinks?' I planned to go off and try and get a life raft up on to the bridge, and when I looked around they had all gone. They had been washed away, as had the lifeboats. We had nothing left at all, in fact. And so I fired our remaining three flares."

It wasn't the flares but the concern of first mate Strano that was responsible for the rescue of Captain Bardari and Mr. Maynard. Strano, who held a master's ticket, had studied enough and had experienced enough to know that Amoco *Cadiz* would not hold together in those seas. And if she didn't hold together, there was no guarantee that the superstructure would stay upright. The skipper and Mr. Maynard had remained aboard on the off-chance that if the grounding was not too bad, and if the weather changed, they might be needed to put lines from tugs aboard, or guide lightering vessels in to her. But Strano realized that such hopes were ephemeral.

Back in the warmth of Lanvéoc, he made his case strongly enough so that the base commander consented to send out one more Super-Frelon mission. Or rather, the same machine once again. This time *Bravo Alpha,* which had already brought back thirty-three men, was piloted by principal maître Michel Omnes. At 5:00 A.M., with the sky still not giving the least hint of dawn, he was over the wreck and ready to winch. The two men out on the bridge wing were not in a mood to refuse the ride. There would have been no point in remaining. It was obvious that the tanker could never be refloated. She—it—was a goner. And if it is a certified, ancient gesture of heroism to go down with a stricken liner or a valiant warship, it is quite another matter for a minor domestic of a multinational giant to accept death from gassing, drowning, or incineration while stranded upon a leaky oilpot. For what—the greater glory of Standard Oil of Indiana, Inc.?

It is one of the minor historical curiosities of the Amoco *Cadiz* affair that Pasquale Bardari was not the last man off his ship. As *Bravo Alpha* hovered overhead, Mr. Maynard heatedly insisted that the skipper go up first, and after one of those slightly comical after-you-Alphonse protests he acquiesced. It was without question more logical that way, because his injured left arm was virtually useless. Mr. Maynard could help him into the harness and try to break his fall, should he slip back out. The winching went off without incident, and by 5:05 A.M. they were swooping back toward Lanvéoc, with just enough time for one last glance downward toward the position of their ship. Through the rain and the blackness of the night they could discern nothing but swatches of white spume being blown across the tops of the waves.

Amoco *Cadiz* continued writhing and grinding up her metal innards, sending occasional clashes of sparks out into what remained of that night, but as things turned out she never did explode. It probably would have been better for Brittany if she had.

12.

The Pollution

The northern coast of the Breton peninsula is a workaday kind of place. It has neither the glamour of the Normandy coast nor the sex appeal (however overripe it may be) of the Côte d'Azur. Its beaches are coves rather than the endless tracts of sand that seem to appeal to tourists, its towns small and unprepossessing (St. Brieuc tops the population chart with some 55,000 inhabitants), its nightlife limited mostly to sleeping and its days to work. Its physical layout bears a resemblance to the coast of Maine, and its natives share much of the gruff reserve that has traditionally characterized Maine folk. The work of erosion over millions of centuries has left mostly rock behind it, granite and metamorphic formations that reach out into the sea as if inviting battle. The sea accepts, the battle is perpetual, and the sea usually wins.

The entire coastline is irregularly slashed with inlets of salt water of varying size, from the huge roadsteads of Brest to the more modest abers—miniature fjords of shallow seawater that peter out as inland marshes. Between these two extremes is a whole vocabulary of indentation: bays, bights, estuaries, inlets, coves. What harbors there are, are small and severely affected by the tides; the postcard spectacle of wooden boats lying on their gunwales in the mud at low tide is a familiar one here, with the result that the larger, oceangoing fishing craft are virtually unknown. It is an area of *petite pêche,* coastal fishing generally within sight of land: in and out of harbor with the tide, for daily harvests of sole, turbot, mullet, sea bass, mackerel, skate, sea spiders, and the like. Closer by the rocks are shellfish like crabs and cockles and the small but gastronomically prized Breton lobster. In many of the abers and creeks are oyster beds, and just below the high-water mark, clinging to the rock and shingle, is about ninety percent of the seaweed (used for fertilizers and industrial thickeners) harvested in France. Tourism has heavily developed there since the war, as has a certain amount of industry, but the Coast of Legends, as it is sometimes called, is above all sea oriented: long before Celts, Gauls, or Romans set foot there, its prehistoric populations fed from the sea and venerated it for its inexhaustible resources of life. "The bountiful sea" is a hackneyed image, but if ever a shoreline deserved the description, this one does. Or did.

They had had some warnings before, and even some quite serious ones. The problem here is geographical and geological, and it is simple in the extreme: with the exception of the North Sea deposits, Western Europe has virtually no oil of its own; Occidental civilization today runs on oil. The oil is down south, and after it is bought it has to be carried up north; and the obvious, natural route to the heart of Western Europe is up through the English Channel. So the VLCCs and ULCCs plod past the Breton peninsula every day, brim-full of the coveted black poison, fighting for space with a couple of hundred other boats, navigating perhaps well and perhaps badly, suffering the same kind of mechanical weaknesses that make cars stall or can-openers jam.

The serious warnings had begun eleven years earlier, almost to the day (March 18, 1967), when the *Torrey Canyon* motored gently onto an obdurate reef off the Scillys, across the Channel in English territory. The English, helped along by currents and winds, were good enough to share their misfortune with the French, and some 30,000 tons of Kuwaiti guck left its viscid calling card on Brittany's northern shore. More recently, the *Olympic Bravery,* a brand-new Onassis-owned VLCC on its way north for laying-up in Norway (no customers) drifted onto the rocks off Ouessant and vomited up 1,200 tons of bunker fuel. Her grounding struck many as suspicious—get rid of a useless boat and pick up the insurance money—but nothing was ever proved beyond the engine trouble that caused her to come a cropper. Nine months later, an East German clunker named *Boehlen* went down off Brest and lost 9,000 tons. But there never had been anything like this, nothing to prepare them for Friday morning, March 17, 1978.

If Amoco *Cadiz* didn't exactly make all other oil spills look like puddles, it dominated them with the majesty of a super job done super-well. There have been greater amounts of oil poured into the marine environment through acts of war (the tragedy of the Persian Gulf is owed entirely to the suicidal bellicosity of Iraq and Iran); through collisions at sea (as when the tankers *Atlantic Empress* and *Aegean Captain* ran into each other off Tobago in July of 1979); and through oil-well blowouts (Ixtoc I in the Gulf of Mexico). But no ship ever inflicted such damage upon a shoreline as did Amoco *Cadiz* to Brittany. Nor, for that matter, had a ship of such a size ever managed to bring her cargo so close in to shore—a mere two kilometers. Blind and helpless, with her crew mere spectators, Standard Oil's monstrous oilpot had done a magnificent piece of navigation in finding the channel to Men Goulven, a channel shown on no map and unknown even to the local fishermen.

The result was spectacularly awful. Amoco *Cadiz* delivered her soup to Portsall just as it was when she sucked it up in the Persian Gulf—direct from producer to consumer, as it were. There was so much of it, so liberally offered, that the oil flowed pure into Portsall harbor. One woman likened it to the end of the world when she awoke the next morning. It was an apt comparison, because the spill there, at that early stage, was more than simply dirty, more than dangerous to marine and shore life: It was frightening. Hydrocarbon gas dominated the air that morning, and the simple act of breathing felt unhealthy, almost obscene, like the repulsive act of breathing in the odor of the dead after natural calamities or acts of war. At high tide, Portsall harbor was a placid black pool; when the tide was out, the mud on the bottom, the seawalls and breakwaters, the beaches and the bottoms of boats were all blanketed with a filthy, glistening foreign skin. With time, the stuff penetrated two meters down into the sediment. But even more eerie than this was the silence. The surf, the heartbeat with which Bretons live almost as intimately as their own, had been reduced to a muted slap, a soft, sick noise. People reacted strangely in the pervading atmosphere of angst. Anger came quickly when the natives saw what the ship had done to them, but there was also despair. Many persons who made their livelihood from the shellfish and seaweed were ruined, or at least thought themselves to be. One young man who had gone deeply into debt to buy a new fishing boat tried to commit suicide, but fortunately bungled the attempt. Another one, it was reported on national television, became so frenzied at the sight and smell of the oil that he powered his car right into a lagoon. And why not, after all—it must have looked just like a parking lot.

No one had any idea of what to do. Where do you start when you have that much muck upon you, and so much more coming in with each tide? At first, in Portsall, they just stood on top of the sea-wall and looked. Then they tramped across lots to the shore and trained binoculars and telescopes out at the wreck. She was pointing her bow right at them, and at low tide she lifted out her bulb, the ungainly, chinlike protuberance first placed beneath the bows of VLCCs by Japanese designers as a means of improving ships' hydrodynamic efficiency when empty and riding high in ballast. Although she was broken in half forward of the bridge, her superstructure still was lined up quite straight then, and she looked for all the world like she had just been parked there, at her berth, in close for the sake of convenience.

The dance of the helicopters began on Friday morning. Now that there was no more need for the heroics of lifesaving, though, their missions were a good deal more mundane. For the best part of a month helicopters regularly overflew the wreck, but in the first week they were a perpetual swarm. Journalists energetically competed for air space with government officials, politicians, pollution experts, gendarmes, representatives from Amoco, Shell, and at least two salvage companies, naval officers, insurance people, foreign visitors, and VIP joyriders. Residents of Portsall regarded them at first with the tentative relief born of wild hope—helicopters seem so official and purposeful—which soon turned to disparaging cynicism as the days went by and it became apparent that they were all just looking, out of curiosity as much as anything else, and didn't know any more than they did what the hell to do. Soon the airborne flotillas became dubbed *les parisiens,* or *les touristes,* and the Portsall people took refuge behind a facade of bitterly ironic humor, describing the place as "the dirtiest village in the world." The owner of a local restaurant put up a sign: "No fish but the oil is free," but Mayor Legendre was too tired and too sickened for bravura displays of Gallic wit.

"The authorities are impotent," he said. "We're ruined. The mainstay of the village economy is fishing and the tourists. Nothing is being done. Nothing."

Unfortunately, he was quite right. In the beginning, an indescribable bureaucratic confusion reigned in Brest, local headquarters of most things, as well as in Paris, national super-headquarters for all things in this most centralized of European countries. It was instantly demonstrated that the much vaunted Plan POLMAR (for pollution maritime) was in reality little more than a collection of phone numbers and a few risible stockpiles of largely useless materials. Later investigations showed that POLMAR involved no less than eight ministries, each one having its own priorities and jealously guarded prerogatives, and was capable of dealing with a slick of no more than eighteen and a half kilometers. Just as circumstances had conspired against Pasquale Bardari and his vessel to hopelessly aggravate an already terrible situation, so did they ashore with the French administration: Only one week before the grounding, March 9, a governmental decree had given the *préfet maritime* vast new powers over French coastal waters. In the Second Maritime District, Vice-Admiral Coulondres was made entirely responsible for the Atlantic coastal waters: administrative policing, enforcement of laws, protection of persons and property—everything. He owned the sea, but in spite of the years of anticipating these new responsibilities, for which the navy had been clamoring, his service was woefully unready when the disaster happened.

When some semblance of organization evolved for the cleanup effort, as many as eighteen different administrations became involved. In the absence of effective coordination among them, the wrong decisions were taken or, more often, no decisions were taken at all. Local officials, the ones who suffered the most and to whom the suffering turned for help, were completely shut out and left in the dark. "Leave everything to Paris" had been the centralizing byword of just about every French government since Louis XIV (except that in his case it was "Leave everything to Versailles"), and Amoco *Cadiz* proved that Paris was utterly, almost comically unprepared, in the image of the admiral in his Château above Brest. Moreover, that mid-March was a period of indecision par excellence in France, because it was election time. As if the intersecting of all the other circumstances around the breakdown of the Amoco *Cadiz* were not already horrible enough, it had to occur between the two rounds of some of the most crucial parliamentary elections since World War II, with the country's entire future political orientation at stake. The first round had been voted on Saturday, March 11, and the second, the final determination of who won what, was scheduled for Saturday, March 18. It may not be fair to say that no one in the political brotherhood gave a damn about the sullying of the Côte des Legendes in the two days following the grounding of Amoco *Cadiz*, but their concern was secondary at best.

The hull of the big ship had been ruptured in several places in its grounding, and one by one over the next several days the bulkheads separating the cargo tanks gave way. Contrary to an automatic assumption, the oil did not leak out of the rent bottom, but rather from the top. It was only logical: Oil floats on water. Consequently, the helicopters that flew low enough and close enough witnessed the depressing spectacle of fountains of crude eight and sometimes ten meters high, burbling up through holes and aeration vents on the Rustoleum red deck of Amoco *Cadiz*. As the stuff hit the water it rapidly changed color from black to the reddish brown characteristic of what pollution people prettily call "mousse," a fifty-fifty mixture of oil and water, and which was soon to become grimly familiar to shore dwellers from Pointe du Raz to Paimpol. (The gastronomic inspirations of the scientists didn't end there. American investigators working under the aegis of the National Oceanographic and Atmospheric Administration and the Environmental Protection Agency coined the expressions "mousse frappe" and "mousse shake" to describe the form the gunk took when it encountered a highly energetic surf zone. Later, French and Belgian volunteers cleaning up beaches, struck by the consistency and yellow-brown hue of mousse mixed with sand, spontaneously began referring to it as "mayonnaise.") Weathered old mousse from slicks that had broken up or had been dispersed or partially sunk took on the aspect of the congealed globes, or tarballs, that are all too familiar to beach-goers nowadays. The final metamorphosis of the Amoco *Cadiz* cargo was the rainbow-hued sheen floating on the surface after the heavy stuff had been washed ashore or dropped down to say howdy to the population living on the ocean floor. This iridescent film, exactly the same as you see when a clumsy pump attendant spills gas or oil on the ground of a service station, worried ecologists for its ubiquity and the uncalculable damage its light-blocking (or filtering) powers could do to the process of photosynthesis and hence, by extension, to marine plants and phytoplankton. For as long as two months after the event, the sea was still covered in many places with this sheen.

With the option of towing eliminated from the start—she was too deeply impaled, in waters too shallow, and the weather began breaking her up almost immediately—speculation turned to the possibility of bringing in a fleet of smaller tankers to her side for pumping, even as she remained stuck fast to the rocks. Still another plan envisaged hoses being strung out to her on pontoons, barges, or improvised platforms, and attached to portable pumps secured to the tanker's deck, or even to her own discharge pumps. God knows there was enough maritime might to inspire hope that something could be done: By the day after the wreck, in addition to *Pacific* and *Simson,* the French navy tug *Centaur* had arrived, and the *Guardsman* from England and no fewer than four from the Dutch company Smit: the *Houston,* the *Polzee,* the *Hermes,* and the *Bank.* Shortly afterward the big new French tug *Abeille Normandie* cruised in from Cherbourg to Brest with its 16,500 horsepower. By Friday also, Shell International had made arrangements for three lightering tankers to make a course for the Portsall rocks. Amoco, equally fast on its corporate feet, rustled up four self-contained high-delivery immersible pumps in America and flew them over when they discovered that there were no such units available in France. That same day, Chicago confirmed a primary salvaging contract with Smit, naming Bugsier as subcontractors.

The press was pouring into Brest and besieging the Standard Oil Building in Chicago. As the man in charge, Rinkema had to take most of the onslaught, leaving Captain Phillips free to handle the operational side of things. Meeting succeeded meeting, and in between them came phone calls and interviews. By that afternoon, Rinkema and his fellow executives came to an inescapable conclusion: He would have to get to Brest himself, "to take the heat," as he put it. He sent an exhausted Phillips and Clair home to get a little rest, carried on himself to a late evening's work, and finally returned home, physically and emotionally drained. That was a good preparation for what lay in store for him in France.

On Saturday morning the tanker received its first recorded visitor when Captain Heinrich Detlev, a Bugsier salvage expert, borrowed a rubber dinghy from *Pacific,* zoomed across the bounding main, drove up to *Cadiz*'s bow, climbed up the anchor chain, and hauled himself aboard through the hawse hole. (Detlev had asked the French navy to drop him on the deck in a helicopter, but faced with their refusal he simply took the matter into his own hands. His hands were just the right tool for the job: the size of hams, attached to arms approximately equal in girth to the Amoco *Cadiz* anchor chain. Around Bugsier, no one laughed when Heinrich Detlev said he was going to take matters into his own hands.) He stumped up and down the deck in his rubber boots, sizing up the damage and working out the best places for attaching pumps if they ever reached the stage of lightering her. When he ventured aft, toward the sullied superstructure, he gazed over the gap separating the two sections: By then it had already grown to thirty meters. Oil was spurting up in tall fountains. The ship was still writhing and grinding. Detlev made his way forward again, looked down into the fo'c'sle storage locker to see that *Pacific*'s white tow chain had been stowed down there, grunted, and returned to his hawse hole, his anchor chain, and his rubber dinghy. If the weather improved, he figured, she could be lightered, but if not, well, he tended to agree with Jean Quivoron.

The first problem with lightering, even before the weather, was the shoal itself all around Amoco *Cadiz*, badly charted and so dangerous that even the locals avoided it with their tiny fishing boats. It was clear that no captain of a lightering vessel would risk his ship among Roches de Portsall until a proper hydrographic chart of the area had been drawn. Before anyone could begin taking soundings, though, before even the arrival of Amoco's famous pumps, nature made it all academic by sending the storms back to Brittany. By Tuesday, March 22, five of *Cadiz*'s tanks were leaking heavily, and by Wednesday the remaining eight had been broached. By Friday, one week after Portsall's rude awakening, it was estimated that the tanker had already vomited up eighty-five to ninety percent of her cargo. The day after, French navy divers rode helicopter winches down to her deck and opened as many hatches and valves as they could. By then, there was no course left but to make sure she got it all up.

Dazed and suffering, first Portsall and then the other wounded towns of the Breton coast began to get organized to dig themselves free of the invading muck. The means at their disposal were laughable: shovels, rakes, plastic buckets, and garbage cans. But ironically enough—horribly enough—the following months were to prove that these laughable means were the best methods available for cleaning the shore. In the age of moon rockets, there was no invention more efficient than medieval elbow grease. Most of the modern equipment failed miserably. The prime example of deficient technology was the skimmer, a vacuum device developed in several variations since the *Torrey Canyon* disaster. The idea is simple: From land-based or boat-based suction pumps, booms and gathering devices reach out to the surface of the water and slurp the oil up from the top. The problem is that the skimmers work with true efficiency only when they are employed on perfectly smooth waters, like swimming pools. Unfortunately, the Breton coast is full of waves, and the waves were unusually high that March of 1978. Except for the rare places where the oil gathered in puddles, the skimmers flopped.

The less sophisticated the equipment, the greater was the success. With typical French inventiveness, the local farmers discovered that they had at their disposition a device much more useful than the high-technology skimmers: manure pumps. Designed for the purpose of keeping pig farms approximately clean, these rustic machines proved to be very effective at pumping mousse, mousse shakes, and mayonnaise, which have approximately the same viscid texture as pig excrement. What had begun as a gesture of solidarity by a few peasants in the vicinity of Portsall soon became a popular tool and then a necessity of national priority. Several hundred tractor-pump-tank combinations were pressed into service along the polluted coast, rented (as were all available cistern trucks) out of the POLMAR budget. The picturesque appearance of these rigs up and down the Breton coast moved a jaded Parisian journalist to muse to an official at POLMAR's field headquarters in Ploudalmezeau, "In the eleven years since *Torrey Canyon,* the only notable advance in pollution control has been the pigshit pump." The POLMAR man swallowed hard and nodded.

For more than two weeks after the grounding of Amoco *Cadiz,* the winds blew steadily from the west and northwest, pushing the sluggish oil slick up along the coast at a rate that some mathematical whiz figured at three percent of the wind's speed. In the first twenty-four hours, wind speed hardly mattered, since the oil was so hugely prolific that it just slopped ashore pure, directly polluting a zone of seven or eight kilometers around the wreck. Underwater, the fish population at least had the option of swimming away, but in the sister fjords of Aber Benoit and Aber Wrac'h, the stuff came in as heavy and undiluted as it did in Portsall, killing not only the cultivations of lobsters and oysters, but birds and crabs as well, and even the worms in the mud, and razor clams, cockles, and limpets. Along with the still-water sea marshes, the abers proved to be the most fiercely scarred victims of the Arabian Light crude. Observation in the following years showed that nothing cleans the shore like the sea itself, the constant "scrubbing" effected by the in-flowing surf, mixed with sand churned up from the bottom. But in the calm, surf-free estuaries of the abers, the oil simply sat on the surface of the water, then settled onto the bottom at low tide, percolating downward a meter or more into the sediment, where the oysters and shellfish lived.

By the Sunday after the grounding, the slick had grown to hideous proportions—seventy by twenty kilometers—and by Monday it reached the town of Roscoff, a famous watering place that, ironically, had always made a point of advertising its pure air and pollution-free waters. Roscoff's excellent hotels and restaurants (specializing, naturally, in fish and the locally raised oysters and lobsters) were a traditional tourist magnet, as were its "helio-marine centers," where the now-fashionable "thalassotherapy" techniques of treating aches and pains by seawater and algae had been pioneered. The fact that the University of Paris had maintained a biological station there since 1872 was both ironic and extraordinarily useful from a scientific point of view. The Station Biologique de Roscoff (which is also associated with the Centre National de la Recherche Scientifique) had been sending biologists, oceanographers, and students on work projects up and down the Breton coast for more than a hundred years, meticulously charting the flora and fauna in a kind of ongoing census that made that section of the littoral one of the best-studied in the world. The availability of this "before" information meant that the "after" situation—the state of the marine life six months, a year, ten years beyond the event of the oil spill—would afford a precise and unusually detailed yardstick for measuring the effects of the pollution. Never before had a spill occurred in such a thoroughly studied area. From that standpoint, at any rate, it was a true scientific goldmine.

Nor was the Roscoff center alone in taking advantage of the opportunity for study. Chemists, marine biologists, geomorphologists, and representatives of even more arcane disciplines crowded onto the beaches not only to count the dead birds (the inevitable front-page picture everywhere in the world), but to inspect sand, soil, rock and sediment, plants, fish, worms, microorganisms—all the thousands of varieties of life in the hugely varied environments offered by the cold, rich waters and the propitious geography of the Breton littoral. Particularly fast on his feet was Professor Claude Chassé of the Institute of Marine Studies at the Université de Bretagne Occidentale in Brest. Instantly recognizing the importance of the event and the opportunities it offered, Chassé sent as many students and assistants as he could lay hands on to the beaches of the northern coast, even before the pollution arrived. Their rapid studies of the oil-free situation provided the invaluable background against which the pollution could be compared. Chassé's studies, which carried on for years afterward, are among the most important for establishing the ecological losses that can be directly ascribed to the grounding of Amoco *Cadiz*. Later, they were to form the backbone of the claims made against Standard Oil by the polluted communities of the Finistère and Côtes-du-Nord departments.

There was one other goldmine created by the wrecking of the Amoco *Cadiz,* but it was as ephemeral as a shooting star: a mini-boom in tourism. The month of March is always a bad one in Brittany, combining rain with low temperatures and generally unpleasant weather. The tourists stay away in droves. But suddenly, with the grounding of the tanker, every hotel and restaurant within fifty or sixty kilometers of Portsall was filled with a new, unexpected, and surprising clientele.

In Ploudalmezeau, fifty-five-year-old Raymond Floquet, owner of the tiny, eight-room Hotel Una, which has a grocery store instead of a lobby downstairs, was amused at first to have radio reporters filing their stories by telephone from his sitting room, but within a few days the fun disappeared when his entire hotel was requisitioned for the housing of POLMAR brass. In Portsall, things were considerably more raucous in the Hotel Beg Ar Mor of thirty-seven-year-old Jacques Letard, a large, rotund, and jolly sort who looks like the innkeeper from a Flemish painting. He not only filled every one of his fifteen rooms with officials, but from one day to the next found himself moving without warning from the few workmen eating his off-season twenty-two-franc menu to feeding the heteroclite, fractious mob of puerile loudmouths known as the Parisian press, who were united only in their hunger, their expense accounts, and their unanimous demand to be served immediately, if not sooner—that and the scramble for news.

Floquet vividly recalls the moments when a cry from the doorway, or a simple rumor that the wreck was moving, would empty his dining room in an instant, as the cursing, jostling guardians of the freedom to inform raced out to their rented cars, one arm free to carry their gear and the other engaged in elbowing the competition out of the way. Half-eaten meals, half-drunk bottles, and often film canisters, jackets, hats, and even cameras would be left behind with the unpaid bills, but the mob usually returned, to turn the dining room into an office for their typewriters and video and sound equipment. But, like many others before him, Floquet found the secret for dealing with the press and making them behave: he gave them assignments. When his wife, Yvonne, could no longer cope with the orders in the kitchen, he simply drafted a few journalists from his dining room, ordered them into the kitchen, and set them to work washing mussels and peeling potatoes. When the complicity of camaraderie was established, he was able to command them like a sergeant-major. His smoky, overcrowded dining room, as noisy as a boiler factory, became the Portsall Press Club, and the only thing he regretted afterward was that he had not raised the price of his twenty-two-franc menu with the arrival of the Parisians. He certainly should have, because there is no doubt that most of them became magically transformed into seventy-five-franc menus when they were reported on the expense accounts back in the big city. Floquet ended his Amoco *Cadiz* saga with an aching back, a lot more francs in the till than usual for the month of March, Arabian light crude all over his furniture, and the solid determination to close up tight for the next oil spill.

By the weekend, it was virtually impossible to find a hotel room in Brest. Scrambling for them was an unlikely horde of journalists, scientists attracted to Portsall like a compass to lodestone, pollution consultants, salvage representatives, inventors with miraculous gimmicks to peddle, and ambulance-chasing lawyers who "happened" to be on vacation in Brest for the March rains. And then, of course, there were the company men. From both Shell and Amoco appeared imposing delegations of vice presidents, lawyers, house scientists, public-relations men, and executives of all descriptions, looking slightly uncomfortable and out of place, with their Chicago suits and Midwestern vernacular, in gloomy, gray, Gallic Brest. Rinkema arrived on Sunday, March 19, leading an eighteen-man task force, and proceeded to take the heat with admirable aplomb at endlessly repeated press conferences arranged by the aw, shucks, PR man Meyerdirk, and usually starring a rather harassed Captain Phillips. None of the company men spoke French, so the relations with the indigenous press (which makes a point of pride of not speaking any English) were thoroughly chaotic. Every afternoon, the press conferences went on with the same litany, the only change being that the numbers decreased from day to day: We estimate that the ship still holds 100,000 tons . . . 70,000 tons . . . 30,000 tons. They kept at it until there was nothing more left inside her and nothing more left to say.

Through it all, the company lawyers hovered. Even this early—and a good deal more strikingly in the years that followed—

it became apparent that if the tanker spilled poison over Brittany, it disgorged nothing but greenbacks for the "whereas" brotherhood. The only real winners in this biggest and most complicated of pollution disasters were the lawyers, and tens of millions of dollars were spent in legal fees after Men Goulven reached out and grabbed the tanker. The lawyers were everywhere in Brest that March, watching attentively, copyreading statements, whispering in ears, correcting phraseology, keeping track of the nuances: God only knew how many uncounted millions of dollars would be involved with this horror before the smoke cleared; and if no one knew with any precision just then who would eventually be suing whom, it clearly behove everyone involved to watch his ass with the greatest of care.

The company men were wearing kid gloves in Brest, and the lobby of the Hotel Continental, where they gave their press conferences, was lined from wall to wall with eggshells, on which they treaded with infinite tenderness, balancing an instinctive terror of the press (got to give the beasts something to eat), with the imperatives of what was good for the company (don't give them anything). There was the matter of Captain Bardari and his crew, for example. You can speak to Captain Bardari as much as you wish, the company men repeated innocently—he is a free man, and we don't tell him what to do. But Captain Bardari was as unavailable as if he had been sequestered in a vault at 200 East Randolph Drive. Neither he nor his officers nor his crew felt like commenting. It was a striking coincidence. At times the company atmosphere managed to border on the comical. I remember speaking with a marine biologist in the employ of Amoco who was so upbeat in his manner and predictions that he all but told me that oil was good for beaches. He had the team spirit, there was no doubting that.

The oil slick continued inching westward, slathering beaches and westward-facing points of land as it went, reaching far into creeks to leave coatings of semisolid muck asphyxiating everything in its path, playing havoc with the systems designed to suck it up or keep it at bay. Two weeks after the accident, there appeared to be serious danger to the Gulf of Saint-Malo, the Channel Islands of Jersey and Guernsey, and—who could tell where it would stop?—to the island abbey of Mont-Saint-Michel. Then the wind shifted around and began blowing from the southwest and pushed the oil out to sea. It carried as far as sixty kilometers into the Channel before the winds turned around, blew easterly, and pushed it back in the direction it had come from, back toward Amoco *Cadiz*. Now the eastward-facing beaches and points of land were polluted in their turn: The entire coastline from Portsall to Paimpol was painted with brown-yellow sludge that from the air looked like a giant bathtub ring. Normandy and the Channel Islands were spared, but the shifting winds brought the oil out to the end of the Breton peninsula to the west of Portsall, shoved it down past Pointe de Saint-Mathieu, Le Conquet, across the Brest roadsteads, and finally, in mid-April, as far as Pointe du Raz. In all, some four hundred kilometers of coastline were polluted by the time Amoco *Cadiz* finished her work. To be fair to Standard Oil of Indiana, it should be added that at least a few of those kilometers were kindly donated by the seafaring brotherhood. It is one of the saddest commentaries on twentieth-century ethical deportment—can civilization survive without virtue?—that some new and unexpected oil slicks appeared from the north and the west while *Cadiz*'s cargo was over east. The new slicks were the result of opportunistic action by passing tanker captains, who seized upon Standard Oil's misfortune to illegally flush out their tanks and dump the crude oil residue into the sea. And just to demonstrate that the possibilities of ideological expression are multifarious, a captain of a passing Soviet ship, the *Atko*, did his part for the class struggle by dumping his glop, too, along with the capitalist exploiters. The newly vigilant French navy detoured him into Dieppe harbor and fined him 40,000 francs.

If the directly observed fish kill appeared to be relatively small (endangered, they could swim away, which crustaceans and shellfish couldn't), investigating scientists were carefully reserved about the future, since the spill occurred at spawning time, and no one could predict the effect of the hydrocarbons on the infinitely delicate larvae. But, as usual in these cases, it was the innocent seabirds that offered the most frightful spectacle. It was a hardened soul, indeed, who could bear with equanimity a visit to one of the score of bird clinics improvised by the universities and nature protection societies, and largely staffed by students. They were more like charnel houses, really, because almost all the birds brought in rapidly died. Perhaps only one in a hundred could be saved, and the kindest thing that could be done for most of the poor, flopping, struggling beasts was to deliver them by mercifully wringing their necks. The young executioners had tears in their eyes as they performed their terrible duty. About 3,500 of them were brought in and counted, but of course they were only a portion of the total, which Chassé and his colleagues tried to estimate with precision in the following years.

Eighty-five percent of these were shag cormorants, guillemots, razorbills, and puffins, and they really didn't need the favor: The last three of these species were already considered rare or in danger in French waters, thanks to the "normal" course of our civilization's pollution.

Four dates marked the hopeless disintegration of Captain Bardari's oilpot. March 24: A second break appeared, quite far forward, at about the point where bulkheads separated the first and second row of tanks; now she was in three pieces. March 25: The navy divers opened as many hatches as they could. March 28: The neap tide of the vernal equinox carried the sea (and hence the oil) to the highest possible point inland. March 29: The navy bombed the hulk with depth charges.

It was well and truly the end of Amoco *Cadiz*. After the neap tide had done its work, and the oil could go no higher, the mobilization for the cleanup could be made total. The reason for the bombing was to ensure that every cargo tank had been thoroughly blown open and the crude emptied: No one wanted any oily surprises for the near or distant future. The depth charges, launched from the ever-attentive Super-Frelons, smashed the central portion of the ship into a scrap pile. The only evidence that it was once a VLCC was the Amoco-red tip of the smokestack, the summit of the bridge, its wings skimming over the waves, and—far ahead—the point of the bow where Strano had so suffered to pull the heaving line through the fairlead. Canted upward at a forty-five-degree angle, the bulb jutting from under the rake of the dirty silver bow, the remains of Amoco *Cadiz* looked, appropriately enough, like a dying fish gulping air. With the passage of years, this local landmark finally disappeared altogether. The angle at which the bow bulb hung on the rock grew more and more steep, until finally, in the dark and silence of some anonymous night, it rolled over on its back and subsided downward beneath the waters. By now, the tidy ocean has erased its memory entirely, and covered it over with sand.

The French love clever experimentation almost as much as arguing politics. The national passion for pottering, making do, finding unexpected solutions for complex problems—*"le système D,"* they call it—is rooted in the national consciousness as a part of the country's patrimony, with examples running from the practical (Napoleon's cook inventing chicken Marengo when he was short of supplies) to the glorious (the Paris taxis ingeniously pressed into troop transport service in the Battle of the Marne) to the visionary (the latest revolutionary backscratcher presented by the latest unknown genius of an inventor). In Brittany, the inventors and experimenters flooded in as the schools of fish swam away, seeing riches and fame just around the corner of this God-given opportunity. They were, unfortunately for Portsall and the other suffering towns, mostly of the third category cited above.

The gent who suggested that two aircraft carriers with a big line between them tow the oil puddle out to sea echoed a persistent theme of bright ideas that had to do with the navy. Thousands of earnest observers, some of them illustrious, had wondered why the navy could not have stopped the drift of Amoco *Cadiz* with some big warships, ignoring the facts that 1) the navy had no warships out in the Channel then, and could not have gotten any out there in time even if it tried, and 2) warships are made for war, and not for towing, and would have failed even more miserably than *Pacific*. Mayor Legendre permitted himself a wry laugh when remembering the nationally known mariner and ecologist who had suggested exactly this approach. His laughter was tinged with bitterness when he spoke of some of the others who came to see him that March.

"There was this one fellow who appeared one morning, very well-dressed, very businesslike, and very much in command of himself. It was almost as if he were a minister or an admiral. He came in one morning with his hat and cane, strode up to me, and said, '*Monsieur le maire, ça suffit.* I have the plan. Everything is prepared.' *Ah, bon,* I said, and he said, 'Yes—we shall attack England with thirty ships.' That's interesting, I said, but who are you? 'Why, Napoleon Bonaparte,' he said. I had him conducted out of town.

"Then there was the elegant, upper-class lady from Paris—very sixteenth arrondissement—who drove to Portsall in a magnificent car and appeared at my doorway in a fur coat. She was more interested in health problems. '*Monsieur le maire,*' she asked, 'do the natives have any contagious diseases?' Oh yes, I told her—you can have your choice between the plague, diphtheria, and cirrhosis of the liver. This one left town of her own accord. Then of course I had the inevitable Jesus in his buckram tunic, who told us to kneel down to welcome the end of the world, and the anarchist who screamed his hatred of society with every dead bird he found. We got rid of him with a couple of bottles of red wine. We had a good deal more trouble with a professional ecologist from Paris, who had adopted a Breton name for the occasion and came to help with the cleanup. But this one was against all mechanization, and to prove his point, he sneaked in one night and blew up an earth-moving machine we had out on the dunes. He finished his ecology career in jail."

The cleanup was, as economists like to say, a labor-intensive undertaking. It is impossible to come up with an exact count of the hands that took part in the cleanup, but the generally accepted figure is around 10,000. This includes the navy men in their boats, the soldiers (most of them baffled draftees who could ponder long on the many and varied ways of serving one's country), the hired hands (tank-truck owners, peasants with their pig-pumps), the volunteers, and, of course, the local population itself. They made a motley army, but they worked with admirable dedication all the same, "Chinese style," with their hands, wielding rakes, shovels, plastic buckets, brooms, and garbage cans. It was physically and spiritually exhausting to fill little buckets, tip them into bigger buckets, and then lug them up to gathering points, but hand-removal of the gunk was by far the most salubrious for the flora and fauna. (The most passionately ecological of the volunteers who came to Brittany often cleaned the crevices of rock formations with wooden spoons, and a few of them were seen busily scooping away with cockleshells.) This kind of purist determination was all too often offset by the get-it-over-with crowd who allowed themselves to be satisfied with the sight of apparently clean water and oil-free beaches, which were only masking the ugly truth. On the bird sanctuary of Ile Grande, for example, bulldozers made the edges of marine marshes look clean, but by scraping away topsoil and ground cover they facilitated an erosion that later destroyed much of the marsh that they were trying to save. Likewise, many municipalities took the short-sighted approach of simply covering fouled beaches with fresh sand (guaranteeing a delayed-action surprise for tourists a year or two later), and too many hurry-up mayors sent fleets of bulldozers and earth-moving equipment to do the job that should have been reserved for the hand workers. In so doing, they often churned the beaches' substrata into prairies of "mayonnaise" and largely contributed to the erosion of the shoreline beyond.

If the Stakhanovites of the cleanup were the ecologists with the cockleshells, they were also the six hundred foreign volunteers (Belgians, mostly, but they also came from Britain, Holland, and Germany) who spent their Easter vacations in the rain and fog of Brittany, wallowing in crude oil during the day and shivering in unheated tents at night. Nor should the French families who spontaneously contributed money and clothing be forgotten, any more than the manufacturers who donated boots, slickers, and other cleanup gear, or the truckers who drove them to Brest from forty different French cities. But the real heroes were the Bretons themselves, who after a brief reaction of aimless despair, proceeded to give battle against the intrusion with an energy and determination that do credit to all the best Breton traditions of stubborn courage in times of adversity. They are the ones who refused the bulldozers and chemicals, and cleaned their beaches and coves with shovels and buckets and fire hoses, and who sopped up the oil with straw and rags and even old newspapers. The truest image of the fight against the pollution is neither the helicopters endlessly turning over the wreck of the Amoco *Cadiz* nor the navy's dispersant boats chasing after oil slicks nor even the squads of soldiers marching back to improvised barracks in filthy, oil-splattered slickers. It is the sight of a row of old men in fishermen's boots, silhouetted against a gray horizon, patiently raking an enormous, shimmering tidal flat with wooden scrapers.

As they raked and shoveled, others—lawyers, politicians, scientists—were already at work, each in his own specialized way, to estimate the damages in terms of hard cash. Sometimes with care and accuracy, often in sorrow, and occasionally with the delectation of opportunists who spot a rich vein and follow it as far as they can, the estimators began counting the real and imagined losses with one eye on their calculations and the other on that great Carrara marble tower in Chicago, the symbol of Standard Oil's egregiously notorious wealth. In those days of angry rhetoric, even responsible public officials and statesmen spoke in terms of big, bad money: not just a recovery of what had been lost, but a punishment, one that would serve as a warning to would-be polluters of the future.

"We're going to make them pay in blood," one Breton leader promised his constituents, figuratively licking his chops.

Somewhat more modest, or realistic, or perhaps just diplomatic, the French government tabulated the direct cost to the state incurred in the wake of the accident—indemnities to fishermen, shellfish farmers, seaweed gatherers, and the like, plus the personnel and equipment involved in the cleanup of the shoreline—at 340 million francs. Like everything else, though, this figure quickly rose. In mid-September, the judiciary department of the French Treasury, legal representative of the government, filed a suit against Amoco in the New York Federal Court for the pretty sum of $300 million.

It was only the beginning of an unbelievably vast legal imbroglio. Shortly after registration by the suit of the Agence Judiciare du Trésor, some local Breton hotels and businesses weighed in with their own, but they were completely overshadowed by the spectacular hydra lawsuit—attacking in all directions, but most energetically against Amoco—filed by an association of seventy-six communities generally identified as the Côtes-du-Nord parties, in which the total of claims came to no less than $1.9 billion. Compared to this, the later suit of Shell International for $22.9 million—they just wanted to recover the value of the lost cargo—seemed positively modest.

Late in April, Amoco, backed by its liability insurers, had deposited with the Brest Tribunal of Commerce a check in French francs equal to about $16,750,000. This sum was, Amoco insisted, the limit of its liability under the International Convention on Civil Liability for Oil Pollution Damage (CLC), which had been negotiated expressly after *Torrey Canyon,* through the International Maritime Organization. The treaty came into effect in 1975, and France signed it that year. In addition to this CLC fund, the maximum that the treaty required ship owners to establish, Amoco, through a supplementary insurance scheme abbreviated as CRISTAL, offered a further $13,250,000 for the cleanup and damage claims. The total of $30 million, said Amoco, was as far as it would go. Ho, ho, ho, said the Bretons, the Agence Judiciare du Trésor, and Shell—that's what you think. Thus was born the maritime trial of the century.

13.

Whose Fault?
The First Conclusions

Less than twenty-four hours after the grounding, Captain Bardari and Mr. Maynard, exhausted and shocked from their ordeal, got a daylight ride over the remains of their ship in a helicopter of the Gendarmerie Nationale. At that point, the obvious plan was to try to pull her free with the flotilla of tugs churning about in her vicinity or, barring that, at least lighter off her cargo; so any ideas or advice they could give (any advice anyone could give) was eagerly sought. Up in the helicopter, after so many hours of struggling to save their leviathan, of being utterly absorbed in its complex mechanical microcosm, the overflight afforded them a renewed sense of proportion, a second lesson in humility, somewhat more spiritual than the one that had been dealt them the day before. Altitude brings back the relativity of things: Seen from a few thousand feet, Amoco *Cadiz* was barely discernible among the Roches de Portsall, where the sea foamed and leaped. When they finally located her, following the pilot's index finger as it pointed downward, she appeared as a mere metallic sliver pointing landward, colored dirty cream and Rustoleum red, a little toy negligently dropped near the shoreline. Only the cloud staining the water off her port side, the color of congealed blood, stretching beyond the range of eyesight, suggested consequences more sinister than the customary folly of pitting human presumption against the elemental forces of nature.

Whatever the long-range ecological effects brought to the Côte des Légendes by this hideous oil spill, the saga of the Amoco *Cadiz* offers us such a rare and clearly delineated object lesson in arrogance, expedience, presumption, and complacency that it can easily stand on its own merits as a symbol-riddled moral tale, a kind of concise catechism as reference for future generations. With *Torrey Canyon,* the previous record-holder and everyman's byword for oil pollution, it was merely a case of bad navigation by an inexperienced helmsman and a skipper who was probably overworked, but with Amoco *Cadiz* the causality is infinitely more complex, the responsibilities much more widely shared. Hardly anyone comes off well in the story of the shipwreck of Standard Oil's barge. Although there was no deliberate malefaction, or even malfeasance, by any single individual or corporate group, there were so many errors of miscalculation, self-deception, and corner-cutting involved that the guilt (if that is the right word) must be seen as virtually generalized: Amoco *Cadiz* was a bad ship, badly managed, badly sailed, badly served in its hour of crisis, encountering a convergence of circumstances so awful as to be almost unbelievable. As fate would have it, even those who were "right" on paper were wrong in the event. The accusations in the shipwreck of the Amoco *Cadiz* and the subsequent pollution horror must point toward Astilleros Espanoles, S.A., the builders; Amoco, the owners; the American Bureau of Shipping, the classification society that certified the ship; the French administration and navy; and finally poor Pasquale Bardari, the captain, a man who deserves much sympathy but is not likely to get any.

As in the most ordinary of murder mysteries, the dastardly deed and the victim were there for all to contemplate as of the morning of March 17. Even the modus operandi, often obscure in many crime stories, was perfectly clear: death was delivered by grounding, and grounding was caused by the steering failure, which set into motion the entire chain of events. There was a nice Agatha Christie touch, too, which revealed someone's taste for the classical: The butler, Pasquale, was the one who was discovered holding the gory dagger when the lights went on.

But was he the guilty party?

Ah, *mon cher—voilà une bonne question.* Beginning with this question and digging a bit further, beyond the appearances, we find our steps leading into thickets and quagmires of complexity worthy of the masters of mystery. It is here, in these swamps and woods, that the Case of the Amoco *Cadiz* moves from the banal to the sublime and shows itself for what it truly is: the best damn maritime whodunnit since Henry VIII of England watched the *Mary Rose* sink like a stone, turned his soft gaze upon the nearest admiral, and asked how come.

As history would have it, the sleuths who eventually turned up to look things over were a good deal less colorful than the Holmses, Poirots, Maigrets, and Spades who accompany foul play between the covers of books. There were two of them, in this case: Sir Gordon Wilmer, retired Lord Justice of Appeal of the Supreme Court of England, working out of London; and U.S. District Judge Frank J. McGarr, who hangs his hat in Chicago. Neither one worked alone, though. Both had plenty of help—and McGarr, in any case, probably a lot more than he wanted.

Wilmer and McGarr were the magistrates who presided over the two major public investigations that followed the grounding, and which provided the bulk of the information publicly available about what happened, how, and why. The first one, quickly convened and expeditiously dispatched—only twenty-eight days of hearings in all, over a period of six weeks—was the Marine Board of Investigation of the Republic of Liberia, carried out in an elegant, white-columned row house, headquarters of the Royal Institute of Naval Architects, in the Belgravia section of London, just around the corner from Buckingham Palace. Sir Gordon, whose air of slightly bored distinction and mellifluously hoity-toity accent made him every foreign reporter's dream stereotype of the upper-class Brit, was assisted in his labors by two Liberians who hardly opened their mouths during the entire proceedings, by R. O. Patterson, a retired American rear admiral, and by Gordon Victory, an understated but terrifyingly knowledgeable English technical expert who previously had been a ship's engineer himself before becoming engineer surveyor-in-chief for the British Board of Trade and president of the Institute of Marine Engineers.

The second proceeding, fabulously, incalculably more complex and expensive than the first one, was the result of the various lawsuits filed after the grounding, all of which were amalgamated into a single monumental trial in the U.S. District Court for the Northern District of Illinois, on the twenty-fifth floor of the Everett McKinley Dirksen Building in downtown Chicago, just a fifteen-minute walk away from the marble-clad Standard Oil Building. Over this, for the best part of five interminable years, presided the solid, imperturbable person of Frank J. McGarr, a former Illinois state prosecutor who had been named to his judgeship by President Nixon and who had been a naval officer himself, during World War II. Judge McGarr, who turned sixty and whitened a few more of his already short supply of hair during the trial, was a man of great patience. He needed it—that and an uncommon capacity for the assimilation of information, and for the winnowing of boring fact out of plausibly argued humbug.

Sir Gordon Wilmer's inquiry into the events of March 16, 1978, was less encompassing than McGarr's, but it was nonetheless incisive and, in its own way, more objective than the Chicago proceedings, because no money awards were involved. It gave the lie to some of the common assumptions made about the Republic of Liberia and its maritime regulations. His investigation was carried out dispassionately and professionally, and it provided several key insights into how and why the Amoco *Cadiz* went aground that day. The Liberian Ministry of Finance is clever enough to know that a good deal of the country's credibility as a maritime flag state—a crucial source of revenues for an otherwise impoverished nation—is at play with major accidents involving ships registered in Monrovia. Hence the ministry regularly employs competent men of the sea, mostly American and British, in the Bureau of Maritime Affairs. Similarly, when a major accident occurs, the investigation is led by qualified men of law, supported by excellent technical advisors. Both Liberia, where the ship was registered, and France, where the accident occurred, were signatories of the Safety of Life at Sea (SOLAS) Convention, through which participating states agreed not only to hold such investigations, but to assist one another as well.

So it was on May 16, 1978, only two months after the accident, that Sir Gordon and his associates set to work in London. Representing the interests of Monrovia was Dr. Frank Wiswall, a huge American lawyer who resembled the Michelin man and who worked for Liberia full-time, as one of the directors of the Virginia-based Liberian Services, Inc. Dr. Wiswall, confident, energetic, and learned (his business card lets you know that he earned his doctorate at Harvard), effortlessly assumed the hybrid double-role of advocate for Liberia, out to demonstrate that the Bureau of Maritime Affairs was a serious outfit, and to interrogate witnesses in the manner of a prosecutor to discover what went wrong and why.

He was not the only one with pertinent questions to ask. Through the six weeks of hearing trooped a large and varied cast of characters, including many, many lawyers: for Standard Oil, for Shell, for Captain Bardari and his crew, for Astilleros Espanoles,

Bugsier, and Marine Safety Services, plus observers from America, Germany, France, Italy, and England, all of which countries were directly involved in one way or another in this most international of shipwrecks. One crucial difference with Judge McGarr's later investigation was that, in spite of the SOLAS Convention, neither the French government nor the injured parties of Brittany were represented at the Liberian hearing. There were several reasons for this. For one thing, the rapidity of the convening of Sir Gordon's investigation made it difficult for them to assemble the full force of their accusations against Amoco—because, even then, it was clear that Amoco was going to be the number-one target for the damage claims.

But—and here was a second important reason for the absence of the French parties—the Liberian hearing was not seeking to assign guilt for the purpose of monetary damages. In fact, it had no power whatsoever for awarding damage payments. As a court of inquiry in line with IMO recommendations, it fulfilled Liberia's international obligations but held no interest for the French parties, since they already knew that it was not France that had polluted its own shores, and since Sir Gordon could not award them any damages. They preferred to hold their fire until later, for the big trial, for the "real" one, in the United States—where the money was. There were also some other reasons for the French absence at the London hearing, reasons never expressed in so many words, but nonetheless real and obvious to everyone who was present at the Liberian hearing. From the start, it had been evident that the French did not approve of this court of inquiry, wished it no good, and would have nothing to do with it. This attitude was one manner of expressing a righteous disapproval of the principle of flags of convenience. This approach had received heavy play in the French press, as often as not egged on by government officials eager to point their fingers at scapegoats. Cooperate with the Liberians? *Ah, non!* As a result of this attitude, not only petty but also contrary to the spirit of France's international agreements, inspectors employed by Liberia were systematically shut out from participating in or even observing the preliminary inquiries in Brest, when Bardari and Weinert were arrested by local authorities on charges of voluntary pollution. In spite of repeated requests, French authorities refused to make available to Sir Gordon and his associates any of the original documents removed from the tanker, and even went so far as to refuse the radio logs from Le Conquet. One could not help wondering how much of this intransigence had its roots in the ancient, atavistic mistrust of perfidious Albion, since it was an English judge who was running the board, and everything about the investigation smacked of England. Cooperate with the Liberians? With the Liberians and the English? *Ah, non, non, et non!*

Unable to oblige French witnesses to come to London and not having at his disposal the discovery process through which American litigants compel their adversaries to cough up potentially compromising material, Sir Gordon and his board had to carry out their investigation with far less documentation than Judge McGarr. Even so, the Liberian proceeding proved to be of capital importance for an understanding of the shipwreck, because it contained two crucial elements absent in Chicago: the officers of the Amoco *Cadiz* and a representative of Astilleros Espanoles. At that time, in the spring of 1978, most persons who attended the hearing in the Weir Lecture Hall of the Royal Institute of Naval Architects assumed that these witnesses would appear again in the American lawsuit that obviously was in the offing. But no: For different reasons, they declined. This, then, proved to be the only chance for hearing from two of the most directly implicated parties: the truck driver and the guy who built the truck. It was an edifying confrontation.

The truck hadn't been built so well, it turned out. Over several days of maddeningly complex technical questioning, the Liberian board demonstrated that the Manises gear was not up to all the standards it purported to satisfy, and that if it was strong enough to cope with the normal loads of steering a ship in ordinary weather, it failed drastically in the kind of bad weather that a ship can be reasonably expected to encounter two or three times in its life. It was, in short, underbuilt for the purposes for which it had been intended. Further, there were some indications that it had been poorly assembled as well. But did this mean that the cause of the accident had been elucidated? That it was the Spaniard who did the deed? Not at all. That would be underestimating the infinitely complex nature of this case, of the design of electro-hydraulic servomotors, and of the endlessly inventive hypotheses that lawyers and their rented technical experts can propound. In the Chicago trial, events took an entirely different tack as new evidence was adduced. It was not the fault of the Manises steering gear, argued the French parties and Shell, but rather of Amoco, who had maintained the gear badly. We shall be getting to that.

For the moment, though, let us consider the Liberian inquiry,

Astilleros Espanoles, and the American Bureau of Shipping, which certified the Manises design, perhaps a bit too hastily. That the Manises design was too weak to take the loads imposed on it seemed evident to Sir Gordon and his associates, because it broke when it met the three-hour wave off the Breton coast. Worse, when it did break there was no way to fix it, because it had no effective backup system.

Paradoxical, frightening, but true. The ABS ruling under which *Cadiz*'s gear was built stipulated that auxiliary steering is not required "where the main gear is of the dual power hydraulic type, having two independent pumps and separate leads to the pump prime movers from the source of power."

The Manises system had two independent pumps, all right, with separate leads to the prime movers (rams), but only a single distribution block. When the massive hemorrhage of oil occurred, it proved impossible to make the system work with the second pump (the theoretical backup) because too much air had entered the piping by the time engineers could get there to begin operating the isolation valves, and because one of the crucial isolating points—C valve—was apparently blocked with some foreign matter and could not be closed down entirely. Then other elements of underbuilding came fatally into play: The piping for delivering fresh oil into the system from the gravity tank proved to be too small and constricted to permit enough of a flow to make up for the loss from the leak, thereby defeating the acrobatic purging operation of the four engineers astraddle the rams. When something—perhaps an internal failure within the warren of passageways drilled inside the distribution block—caused the relief pipe to blow away, the situation became hopeless.

Amoco's normal practice was to employ only one pump at a time to activate the four rams, and in fact the ship was in this mode at the time of the breakdown. The rudder moved more slowly this way, going from hard over to hard over in fifty seconds rather than twenty-eight, and while the ship was moving at seven knots instead of top speed—but this was thought to be good enough for the VLCC's normal maneuvering. The rationale for running the ship in the one-pump mode was, as an Amoco engineer explained, one of wear and tear: While one pump was doing the steering job, the other was being rested for twenty-four hours and maintained by engineers like Melito and Assante. In this manner, theory had it, both pumps were kept in tip-top condition, and the nonrunning one was always ready as a backup, a standby in case the other should fail. Explained this way, the one-pump mode sounds reasonable—but what it meant was that the ship was, in effect, permanently running in a subnormal mode.

The Manises brochure put a more upbeat accent on things when describing the multiple possibilities of its design: "The servo mechanism is arranged in such a way that, even with the steering gear working, and the ship sailing, any of the two hydraulic pumps can be dismantled without interfering with the pump which is running."

What the Manises brochure did not point out is that with the gear in the one-pump, four-ram mode, as was the normal practice, the valves in the distribution block connecting the two sides of the theoretically independent units were opened. Thus, the dual system was transformed into a single system. For the four years of her petroleum route drudgery, then, Amoco *Cadiz* had been ploughing the high seas with no backup system, *because she was already in the emergency mode.* Thus, when one massive failure occurred with the distribution block valves open, there was no redundancy, and hence no security: As a result, the Manises spilled out its life blood and killed itself.

But that doesn't end the story of the Manises design. The precise point where the failure happened was at the flange where the high-pressure hydraulic pipe from the port pump joined the distribution block. The flange came away from the wall of the block when an overloaded stud gave way, rapidly followed by four more. The sixth, and last, stud holding the flange to the distribution block bent right over, allowing the pipe to free itself and begin spewing oil.

Why did the studs break? The stresses visited upon them by hydraulic pressures could be immense—probably more than twenty tons per square inch—but they certainly should have been designed to handle any forces that could conceivably be put on them in normal operation. They weren't.

Even for the loads that the designers assumed they would be undergoing—let alone the loads they did get on March 26, when the sea decided to match its muscle with the oilpot's rudder—the studs were too few and too weak. For such high-pressure junction points, both British and American standards required a greater number of studs, and studs that were bigger and stronger. The Manises gear held the pipe to the block by a flange fastened with six studs, each one half an inch (12.7 millimeters) in diameter. For the pressure expected at this point, British and American standards prevailing at the time required eight studs of one-inch (25.4 millimeters.) diameter. So, quite clearly, the studs were too few and too weak.

But that was not all. The flanges themselves, through which the studs passed, were only twenty millimeters thick, whereas the same corresponding British standards cited above required flanges of thirty-eight millimeters, and the American standards required them to be a minimum of thirty millimeters. The flanges were too thin, then, but the story of errors goes on. These same kinds of flanges in traditional steering gear design had been perfectly round, but on the distribution block of the Amoco *Cadiz* they were "flatted" on the sides, that is, lopped off in straight lines left and right. The reason for this was simple: Flanges flatted in this manner can be spaced closer together than perfectly circular ones. The piping takes up less room, the distribution block can be made smaller, more modern and compact in appearance, using less material and is thus cheaper to build. Unfortunately, this flatting creates uneven stresses on the studs. The twenty-millimeter flange, already marginal for the loads imposed on it, became even more so by the fact that it was flatted: Because of its hybrid shape, a flatted flange bends unevenly when it encounters hydraulic pressures, "dishes," and does not distribute the load evenly to all the studs, as a circular one would—the four "corner" studs, located just above and below the flange's flat sides, are obliged to take a greater portion of the stress load than the two center ones. All of these factors when combined meant that the Manises design for the assumed pressures gave a safety factor of something like two to one, where ABS requires at least four to one.

We are almost through with the story of the flanges and studs. Just one more point. (This won't hurt.) With all the highly technical information flying around the Liberian hearing (I have spared you more than you realize), perhaps the most astounding discovery to emerge about the Manises design was one that even the most non-mechanical soul in the world can quickly understand: the steering gear, and specifically the flanges and studs, were designed for a theoretical maximum working pressure of 140 kilos per square centimeter—but the relief valves, the only means by which the pressure in the system could be effectively limited, were set to come into operation at 220 kilos per square centimeter. Put that in your pipe and smoke it.

After the grounding of the *Cadiz,* Amoco finally grew suspicious that something was drastically awry with the steering design itself. Company technicians removed the studs and flanges from the distribution blocks of *Milford Haven, Europa,* and *Singapore.* Metallurgical testing showed that the quality of the steel of the studs varied greatly from point to point (apparently a proof of bad quality control) and that the tensioning of the studs—a crucially important factor in high-pressure hydraulic systems—also varied greatly, from finger-tight to over-tensioned (apparently, proof of bad assembly). This evidence looked damning beyond appeal. The ships were immediately refitted with studs of higher tensile strengths. Still, as far as the Liberian investigators could tell, it did not necessarily prove anything about Amoco *Cadiz,* since her studs went down on the Portsall rocks, and none was available for testing. Studs from sister ships of the *Cadiz* series, plus some nearby studs from the distribution block of *Cadiz* herself, fished up from the hulk by divers, did make their appearances in Chicago. But the broken studs that made it all happen disappeared for good when the ship went down.

Most large, modern ships, as we have already seen—even the old *Queens*—use four-ram, two-pump hydraulic steering systems, but the difference in design detail meant that the others were generally overbuilt, with safety factors well above any possible eventuality. Reliability can be guaranteed either through high safety factors or redundancy of the equipment. The Manises design, as it was employed on Amoco *Cadiz,* had neither.

"The safety factor is being nibbled into all the time," explained a specialist who followed the Liberian hearing. "It is partly because of the aeronautical and automobile industries, I assume. Marine people have gone along to say, 'If they can do it, we can, too,' and you get down to these finely controlled items which work to a much higher percentage of the maximum than in the older designs. But they don't realize that they don't have the exactness of specifications—testing, quality control, tightening-up, and all that. If it's not done absolutely right, you're in trouble. Meanwhile, the pressures are going up, and the safety factors are going down."

The Liberian board's final report said the same thing, essentially, but couched in terms slightly more diplomatic: "The specification of the materials used is important, as better or more suitable materials combined with rigorous inspection and quality control to ensure that all materials used have the correct and uniform characteristics can be one means of improving a marginal design, and these factors are sometimes used to justify a lower factor of safety. In this case, however, there is no evidence of any special materials being used, or of any specially effective inspection and quality controls having been provided. In fact tests on studs taken from the flanges of sister ships, which should have been to the same specification as those on the Amoco *Cadiz,* were found to have material characteristics which varied to an unsatisfactory degree and in some cases were outside the range of specification."

Citing "unexplained discrepancies," the Liberian board's final report affirmed that on a proper ship, with properly designed and maintained equipment, the accident would not have happened, and that the Manises design obviously had not taken into account the pressures to which the rudder could be submitted in its normal course of existence. "As a result," the report concluded, "although similar installations have performed with satisfaction over a fairly large number of ship years, the factor of safety provided was not adequate for the service intended and did not provide an adequate margin of safety."

If Astilleros Espanoles was to be taken to task for the design, workmanship, and materials that made the Manises servomotor a bad steering system, it inescapably followed that a large portion of the blame for this should be shared by the American Bureau of Shipping and by Amoco. Such was the impression left by the London hearings. The ship was built to comply with ABS regulations and approved in minutest detail by ABS inspectors, who awarded it the highest classification that can be given a tanker: Maltese Cross A1E. (Lloyd's, the British classification society, also approved the design.) Likewise, as an old Amoco press release underscored, "Amoco has a New Construction Department which is staffed by naval architects and marine engineers who are responsible for reviewing and monitoring the shipyard's design and construction. Amoco also maintains an inspection team at the builder's shipyard where construction is monitored. Company personnel witness the construction of the vessel."

Why were neither the ABS inspectors nor the highly qualified Amoco inspection team able to spot on the construction site the errors and weaknesses that a few weeks after the accident were so glaringly apparent that Amoco first changed the distribution block studs on its remaining *Cadiz*-class tankers and then finally pulled them out of service altogether to drastically (cost: $960,000) revise the steering systems? One should like to know: why, indeed?

Was it because of ignorance, or was it because a steering system so designed and so operated was simply cheaper? In other words, did Amoco *Cadiz* founder because of stupidity or cupidity? It's a hard judgment to make, but either alternative is just as depressing as the other.

Paradoxes abound in the Amoco *Cadiz* case, and perhaps the greatest one of all is that the ship was badly managed by its corporate owner. Saying this about a huge, up-to-date company like Standard Oil, a veritable pillar of modern capitalism, is almost heretical, like saying Marilyn Monroe had a lousy figure—and yet it is so. The legal eagles and business-school geniuses who honed every department of every subsidiary of the empire to a fine edge of performance seemed to have taken every contingency into account except one: the human beings involved, with their human natures. Human beings can be dynamic executives and devoted drudges, but they can also be presumptuous, complacent, unthinking—in short, fallible. By all evidence, the human beings who should have considered the possibility that the fairlead might be needed for salvage towing and should have seen the design mistakes in the steering gear possessed at least some of these qualities, and certainly the last one. Human error and poor judgment were pointed up much more sharply in the Chicago trial, where the maintenance of the system was put to close scrutiny, but what came through in London already gave a pretty good preview of what could be coming in Chicago. The Liberian hearing was particularly edifying as regards the ties that bound Pasquale Bardari to the demigods in the Standard Oil Building in Chicago. Those few seemingly innocent but menace-charged words in the tanker operations manual about notifying the fellows back at headquarters, and using company vessels for help, certainly colored the captain's actions that day. It would be difficult to find a symbol more eloquent than Bardari's leapfrogging walkie-talkie call to Chicago in the black of night after grounding, from his swaying, tempest-tossed bridge. Hello, boss? *Ave atque vale.*

The enormous tanker was nothing more than a (relatively minor) piece of capital investment in the empire, and its crew pawns in the larger scheme of things, moved about from ship to ship like mutually replaceable bricks in a company wall. The oilpot had no identity of its own, no character, commanded no particular loyalty, or even respect, from Pasquale Bardari or his fellow employees. There was absolutely none of the "good old girl" affection that sailors traditionally felt for the few sticks of wood under their feet that separated them from Davy Jones's fabled locker. This was boring work they had to do, and they did it in the firm knowledge that they were there because they were cheaper than Americans, just as the Koreans later manning Amoco ships doubtless realize that they are cheaper than Italians. Once again, the corporate mentality: It contributed to create the atmosphere of hesitation and pusillanimity that was eminently unpropitious to effective action and serene collaboration with *Pacific,* the tanker's first, last, and only straw.

That Amoco *Cadiz* was badly sailed may be open to argument, at least insofar as most of her last voyage was concerned, down south around the tip of Africa and then up again, until she was off the coast of France. About that part of the voyage we know nothing, because no records have survived. The log books covering that early period went down with the ship, having been stored in the first mate's cabin. As fate would have it, a new log was begun that very day, March 16, and so what transpired earlier will forever remain mysterious. The only documents brought off the ship after the grounding, apart from Mr. Maynard's handwritten scribbles, were a single day's log in abbreviated form and a marked-up chart of the area around Ouessant.

Or was it fate? The stunning coincidence that the new log should just happen to begin on the day of the accident inevitably aroused suspicions of hanky-panky in the minds of skeptics, and in France it was often suggested—often in high places—that in fact there was a complete log, but it was spirited away and "lost" by unnamed parties. In Chicago, where the natives are every bit as skeptical as in France, speculation about a purloined log ran just as high—the suggestion being that the full log would have revealed earlier problems with the steering gear—but nothing was ever proven.

Even without any other incriminating evidence, though, the papers and charts and officers' memories studied at the Liberian hearing showed that the tanker ran a very curious zigzag course on that fatal last day, once turning dramatically westward (the first lube oil drum incident) and twice toward the east (the second lube drum-fire hose incident, and the rogue tanker reported by Captain Bardari). Certainly the captain and deck officers offered plausible explanations for this ponderous darting about, but three troubling facts permit us to suspect that there may have been other explanations as well. First, the positions entered in the *Cadiz*'s deck log indicate that at around 0800—half an hour before the second lube drum incident is alleged to have occurred—the tanker was just about to enter the separation zone between the "up" and "down" lanes of the Channel mouth off Ouessant. In other words, to use the automotive analogy again, she was swerving left out of her lane and into the "mall." Second, no one else—not any of his deck officers, not even his friend Mr. Maynard—except Captain Bardari had any recollection of the rogue tanker that forced him to turn to starboard a second time. Apparently, the captain was the only one to see it, which led to some speculation that it was a phantom ship, invented to explain his tanker's unadvisable proximity to Ouessant when the steering gear broke. Third is the matter of third mate Costagliola's plotting errors, for which, Bardari testified, he gave an oral reprimand: The positions in question show Amoco *Cadiz* to be in the middle of the separation zone. What if Costagliola's positions were in fact correct, and the reprimand for his "mistakes" was only a coverup invented later, in order to prove that the ship had never strayed from within the "up" lane? It is as good an explanation as a phantom tanker seen only by the captain.

Under questioning by the Liberian panel, Captain Bardari changed his story from time to time, and the investigators were never able to fully satisfy themselves about where the big ship was when. It was apparent that the record keeping was casual and sloppy to say the least, and that logs and charts were written up later to look clean, rather than entered minute by minute, as they were by the more meticulous crew of *Pacific*. With regard to this, Sir Gordon and his associates were less diplomatic.

Beginning with a swipe at the "lamentable failure" of the officers to keep any proper record of the courses actually sailed, the Liberian report clearly suggested that someone was lying when it evoked the conflicting evidence given by various officers, which engendered a "lack of confidence in the accuracy and truthfulness of their evidence."

This was pretty rough stuff, but it got even rougher: "Having regard to the confusion caused by the conflicting evidence of the various officers the Board finds it quite impossible to arrive at any finding as to what the Amoco *Cadiz* really was doing, and what courses were being steered, between 0726 and the time of the breakdown at 0946. The impression left on the minds of the Board is that none of the officers concerned during this period was paying proper attention to what was going on, and none of them preserved any reliable recollection as to how their vessel was navigated. This, coupled with their failure to make any relevant entries in the ship's log (other than the 0726 position), renders it difficult to regard them as reliable witnesses, or to treat the evidence which they gave as to the subsequent events otherwise than with a good deal of reserve."

In other words: Either they were lying, or they were incompetent. Either way, the choice is hardly flattering.

Aboard *Pacific,* the crew performed magnificently, but that is what is expected from the special breed of sailors who hire out on the oceangoing salvage tugs. They are tough and fearless men who are paid good wages to live out stretches of boredom in port, followed by breathless periods of nonstop work, discomfort, and danger at sea. And, as we have said before, it is an old and honorable trade. There is nothing of the jackal or the pirate about Hartmut Weinert, his officers, or his men. In this light, they were unconscionably maligned after the grounding, and it is time the record was set straight: *Pacific* was the only succor—the only hope of succor—available that day to Amoco *Cadiz,* and the tanker was lucky to have her at that. Had the *Cadiz* been a few more hours behind schedule, the tug would have been up in the Straits of Dover, out of reach.

Captain Weinert, the arch-knave in most popular accounts of the shipwreck, emerges almost completely clean from an unbiased examination of the events of March 16, 1978, and, indeed, this is precisely what happened with both the Liberian hearing and the later trial in Chicago. Certainly his character was impetuous, intolerant, and even scornful (his systematic denigration of "the Italians" makes for uncomfortable listening), but those very qualities probably made him a good salvage tug captain. One is struck by his resemblance to Shakespeare's formidable Hotspur, the hero-villain warrior of *King Henry IV,* especially in the context of the battle against the sea, as viewed from a tug or a VLCC:

> *. . . I remember, when the fight was done,*
> *When I was dry with rage and extreme toil,*
> *Breathless and faint, leaning upon my sword,*
> *Came there a certain lord, neat, and trimly dress'd,*
> *Fresh as a bridegroom; and his chin new reap'd.*
> *Show'd like a stubble-land at harvest-home;*
> *He was perfumed like a milliner;*
> *And 'twixt his finger and his thumb he held*
> *A pouncet-box, which ever and anon*
> *He gave his nose and took't away again*

It is interesting to speculate on what would have happened if *Pacific* had not been in the vicinity and the French navy had been officially notified, even as early as 0945, when the breakdown first occurred. The simple truth is that the entire French administration would have been impotent to do anything about it, short of sinking the tanker with one of the navy's nuclear subs (if it could get there on time). The navy's sole available tug, the little *Malabar,* would have been hours too late and, had it hooked up and tried to pull the VLCC, would have been like a pygmy in the ring against Muhammad Ali. Seeking solutions after the fact, many naive souls suggested that a big warship might have been able to stop the tanker's drift, but the idea only makes experienced sailors laugh. Even if such a providential craft had been available, which it was not, it, too, would have been helpless to deal with the bulk of *Cadiz.* Beyond the question of simple size, warships are not suitable, either, in maneuverability or in structural reinforcing, for towing. Nor do they carry the immensely complicated towing gear. Even if they did, and a hypothetical destroyer or cruiser had managed to make fast to the tanker, she probably would have uprooted her bollards from her deck at the first heavy strain. No: There was no way out beyond *Pacific.*

After examining the relative merits of the French administration, Standard Oil, Bugsier, and the American Bureau of Shipping, the Liberian investigators finally turned their light on the drama's most central figure: the butler, Pasquale, he with the dagger in his hand. Was it he, after all, who was the guilty one?

Well, yes and no, they concluded, just to make things clear. In the light of what happened that day, and what was later established during Sir Gordon's hearing, it was difficult not to feel a great deal of empathy for this obviously good man and conscientious professional who was overwhelmed by events not of his own causing. Many of his actions on the last day of his run from the Persian Gulf deserve comment, and some censure, which the Liberian board did not fail to heap upon him. He contributed his bit to Portsall's gloomy awakening, no doubt about it, but even so the feeling is inescapable that from the moment those five half-inch studs, which should have been three-quarter-inch studs, snapped down in the bowels of his ship, he was doomed. It was all over at 0945. If it had been another man who happened to be assigned to the oilpot by Chicago for that trip, then, probably, he would have been the one to become famous. It was only the roll of the dice that determined that the man to suffer shipwreck and ignominy would be Pasquale Bardari.

There are elements of a Thomas Hardy novel in his undoing—a blameless man being destroyed by brutish, implacable forces of nature—but even more apt seems to be the comparison to Greek tragedy. It requires little stretching of the imagination to assign the roles: The Gods are the unseen executives in Chicago, the omnipotent corporate string-pullers who signed letters and telexes, and for whom Pasquale Bardari counted as little more than immigrant labor, a heavyweight truck driver; the chorus could be Radio le Conquet and the semaphores, watching events and calmly commenting on them throughout the day over VHF; the hero, of course, is Captain Bardari, fate-stalked and eventually crushed. Like Oedipus, he was left freedom of choice, but the freedom was limited by circumstances and beyond his full understanding. He made some decisions and didn't make others, thereby sealing his fate. And most surely, in those wretched, cold, and terrifying few last hours alone with Mr. Maynard aboard the heaving hulk of what he probably saw as his last command, he must have felt as did the messenger who appears after Oedipus' blinding:

All the ills that there are names for, all are here.

Captain Bardari's fatal flaw was wishful thinking. Or, if you wish to be kinder, call it optimism. Either way, he was led to commit several capital errors, which were shown with glaring clarity in the London hearing. Chronologically, his errors began at about 1015, when he returned to the bridge after his first inspection trip to the steering flat with Mr. Maynard. It was probably normal for a captain to assume that his engineers could fix the machine, but nothing prevented him at the point from changing his earlier security message to the more urgent "pan" (obviously, with oil gushing all over the steering flat, this was a serious breakdown), and asking available tugs to stand by. Any salvage tug in the world would treat a "pan" message under those circumstances as a general assistance call, and come steaming up to the casualty on pure speculation, on the off-chance of a big job. A standby call would have cost Bardari nothing, and it would have been prudent: After all, he could actually see land from his position. A call for tugs at that moment would have brought *Pacific* to his side an hour sooner, and *Simson* three or four hours sooner. This point, the matter of his early judgment, was the first demonstration of his wishful thinking. Perhaps—perhaps—a more pessimistic master might have asked tugs to stand by.

At 1115, when engineer Assante delivered him the news that the steering gear was irreparably smashed, he finally asked for tugs. Normal. Could he also have put his engine astern then, in an attempt to back into the wind and keep farther from shore? He could have, and it might have helped some, but he was nagged by the fear that the reverse motion might make the swing of the rudder worse, to the point where the whole monstrous slab of iron would fall away, doing God knows what damage to his screw and the bottom of his ship. It doesn't seem reasonable to deny him this anxiety, but the upshot of it was that he lost an hour of reverse steaming while *Pacific* was blasting over the waves to his succor.

The famous "haggling," which was so amply reported in most of the world's press, wasn't haggling at all. It was simpler than that: a refusal on the part of Pasquale Bardari to accept the traditional terms of salvage at sea, the Lloyd's Open Form, which Captain Weinert had every right to expect and demand. And even if for some inexplicable reason Captain Weinert had not insisted on the LOF, the case would have gone to arbitration in London anyway, by Admiralty court. Bugsier would have put in a salvage claim, and it would have been arbitrated by the Admiralty court instead of Lloyd's. So Captain Bardari was doubly wrong in this aspect of the case. It is far from certain that an immediate acceptance of LOF would have made any difference, but a serene cooperation between him and Captain Weinert might just have tilted the balance favorably, and maritime history would have been spared the sad and slightly ludicrous spectacle of two estimable skippers floating toward doom while screeching and backbiting like two marketplace fishwives.

Captain Bardari's failure to prepare his anchors for dropping may be put into the same category as his failure to put out an earlier "pan" message: In all likelihood, this action would have done nothing to prevent his shipwreck, but it would have been postmortem evidence that he had tried everything possible. Apparently the anchors came to his mind only as a last desperation measure after dark, while *Pacific* was trying to get a line across astern, after he had already passed the buoy of la Grande Basse de Portsall. By then, only the port anchor was available to him, because the starboard one was under a meter or so of water, and cruelly assailed by the prevailing weather. No deckhand could have been expected to hurl himself into that dark, frigid, and hellish corner of the bow to try clearing away the cables and block holding the anchor in place. But if Captain Bardari had sent Vaudo forward that afternoon, when there was plenty of daylight and more favorable weather, he could have cleared away the blocks from both anchors, to make them ready for almost instantaneous dropping. They probably would not have held the ship—VLCCs usually are anchored only when dead in the water—but it was another recourse that he had failed to try.

This did not end the speculation—the what-ifs—about the anchors aboard Amoco *Cadiz*. Afterward, many were those who wondered whether he could not have tried an emergency stop during those long, frustrating hours when *Pacific* was retrieving and putting into order her towing rig. The scenario most usually evoked had him preparing and dropping both anchors, which ought to have had the effect of bringing his bow around to the wind—that is, facing out to sea. And then could he not have held his position by running his main engine forward, into the gale, "steered" by his anchors and held stationary by his screw? Perhaps yes, perhaps no. Maybe both anchors would have had no more effect on altering his heading than the single port one did when he was a few minutes from grounding. But this possibility just added to the already overburdened basket of options never attempted. In any case, the result certainly could not have been worse than the one that finally happened.

If the Liberian board censured the obviously slack discipline among the *Cadiz*'s bridge officers that had resulted in the odd, unpredictable, and inaccurate keeping of records, they were harsher with one last major error, calling it "a gross dereliction which cannot be excused." This is the matter of the missing SOS call. All through the day, as matters grew progressively worse, Bardari never publicly committed himself to anything more urgent than the security call, apparently thinking of the evidence—the admission that he was in critical danger—that might later be used in fixing the Lloyd's arbitration settlement. Not even when he was dropping his anchor as a last gesture of desperation, not even when he was ordering Vaudo and his men back in from the deck, not even when his ship first grounded, did he cry mayday. But even more surrealistic than this is the fact that, apparently, he never even asked *Pacific* to send an SOS for him after he had gone hard aground. He fired red flares, and tried to raise help through the useless hand-cranked lifeboat radio, but never asked Captain Weinert by walkie-talkie to radio an official SOS. And yet he did make that boat-hopping proxy call to Chicago, by walkie-talkie. This is so incongruous as to beggar understanding. Could it be that he was asking Chicago for permission to send an SOS? No. It is not conceivable. That would be too grotesque.

If Oedipus learned wisdom by magnanimously accepting his new, shattered life, Pasquale Bardari may grow personally as a result of his terrible experience. Without question it should make him a better and wiser sailor. The Liberian board reasoned in these terms, restoring his skipper's ticket after three years, reasoning that he had suffered enough. Apparently the gods at Standard Oil felt the same way. Bardari remained a skipper of Amoco vessels for several more years until he finally retired to his native Pizzo.

One man whose future will see no shortage of employment is the extraordinary Mr. Maynard. This English supernumerary, completely foreign to the crew and operation of Amoco *Cadiz,* having no more reason to be aboard than to run through the lectures and safety demonstrations which he knew so well, bore himself in a manner so far beyond the call of duty that in time of war, had he been in the military, he would have earned a high medal. Beginning as only a helper with English language transmissions, he gradually imposed his calm, powerful personality throughout that long day until he had become, in effect, Captain Bardari's equal and surrogate. He did honor to the greatest traditions of the greatest seafaring nation of them all. If there were no medals forthcoming from Her Gracious Majesty's merchant marine authorities, it is pleasant to see that Mr. Maynard's bosses recognized the merits of their most estimable employee: Sixteen months after his day of bravery, P&O Lines, the parent company of Marine Safety Services, promoted him to safety manager for their entire cargo division.

In the summer of 1983, recognition came—at long last—to René Martin, the daring young man on the flying eggbeater named *Bravo Alpha.* Revered by his crew members, admired and envied by his fellow helicopter pilots around the world, few of whom have ever carried out an airborne exploit as deftly courageous as his rescue of thirty-three members of the Amoco *Cadiz* crew, Martin apparently had been viewed as just another functionary by the sedentary geniuses in charge of things at the Aeronavale. He never received any personal citation, medal, or sign of official approval beyond the slap on the back of his base commander. There was no admiral who saw fit to reward him, no government minister who thought twice about all the Super-Frelons to the selling of which his flying skill eminently contributed. On the contrary, Martin remained in his rank of lieutenant de vaisseau for almost eight years in all, five of them after his midnight heroics, when he deserved to have been promoted on the spot. It was only in the summer of 1983 that the naval authorities, in all their wisdom, saw fit to make him a capitaine de corvette. About time.

14.

The Riposte

"Nous allons devenir célèbres."

If ever there was a completely fulfilled and accurate prediction made in those days, this was it: We're going to become famous. Mayor Legendre of Portsall, only at the beginning of his calvary, was struck by the words of his hierarchical superior, Alphonse Arzel, a national senator who was also mayor of Ploudalmezeau, as the two of them viewed the helicopters buzzing over the cadaver of the oilpot a couple of kilometers from where they stood.

Famous they were, indeed, as of the morning of March 17, and the notoriety proved to be enduring. During the first few weeks, as Legendre struggled to deal with the overwhelming mess and the indescribable bureaucratic chaos that constituted the response to it, when he was pumping crude oil directly from the surface of his picturebook harbor, he had to wait three and a half hours for the trucks transporting the muck to make the sixty-kilometer roundtrip to Brest. Why? Because the roads were choked with tourists fighting their way north, in the best traditions of a Jacques Tati comedy, to have a look at the stricken coastline and the boat that had done the job. Likewise, Legendre found himself obliged to post gendarmes all around the perimeter of his town in order to stanch the flow of gawkers, who threatened to disturb the already precarious efficiency of the ad hoc cleanup operations that he had managed to assemble. It took ten days before the northern coast had any semblance of organization, and by the end of the month the combination of soldiers, sailors, volunteers, and paid workers was fully engaged in the long, hard job of helping the sea to cleanse itself.

While the central government took it upon itself to foot the bill for the cleanup and to offer a certain amount of indemnity to fishermen, oyster farmers, and seaweed gatherers, the Bretons realized that if they were to collect damages for their wounded ecosystem and the business and tourism revenues lost in the aftermath of the "black tides," they would have to do it all by themselves. The government just wanted to get back what it had spent, and apparently had no interest in anything beyond that. The result was that two different French entities, parallel but separate, took up the legal battle against the polluters in the years that followed. Often these entities cooperated, but the electricity of contention that crackled between them was a persistent reminder of the gulf that separated the Bretons from the central government.

It was time for an entirely new cast of characters to enter the picture: the lawyers. Now that the action itself had been played out, and the press and television had returned to Caroline of Monaco, Idi Amin Dada, Sophia Loren, and other matters of abiding interest, it was the moment for the saga of the Amoco *Cadiz* to enter its most complex phase: the legal aftermath. Now it was no longer a question of the adventure of the ship and her crew, but what was shaping up as the most important ecological lawsuit ever undertaken, with the greatest amount of cash award imaginable, winking dimly but irresistibly like a holy grail, there at the end of the tunnel, plus the added possibility of setting several historical precedents. Gleefully warming their tenor voices with whoops of "whereas," "res ipsa loquitur," and "objection, Your Honor," the lawyers came charging out of the walnut paneling of a thousand offices, briefcases at the ready, primed for the hunt.

In the mad tourbillon of the early days at Brest, the ambulance-chasers had their brief moments in history and then slunk away, generally empty-handed. There were a few brief fires of legal action for individual suits on behalf of persons and businesses who had suffered prejudice from the oil, but it was clear that this was mere epiphenomenon. The real action, the big-league stuff, was going to come from the central authorities in Paris on the one hand, and the Breton communities on the other. The Paris action was handled by the Agence Judiciare du Trésor, the juridical service of the Ministry of Economy and Finance, and it undertook its task in the shadows, keeping its own counsel, moving with the secretive and ponderous dignity of administrations everywhere.

The proceedings of the Breton parties were a different story altogether, much more baroque and freewheeling, carried out by men and women imbued with the inventive excitement of pioneers, rushing into an adventure in which they knew they were breaking new ground—ground that, if treated correctly, might yield a rich harvest of greenbacks, the best crop of all. The first person of note to enter this picture was a thirty-seven-year-old Parisian lawyer named Christian Huglo, a man who had achieved a certain fame as a very successful champion of industrial pollution victims. Called to Brest by the mayor's office, he was already in the thick of things by the Monday following the accident, and the dossier that he took in hand that day was like the first grain of sand of what was destined to become a vast legal beach, stretching endlessly to the horizon.

Maître Christian Huglo was not a man to waste time. Rocketing back and forth around Brittany observing damages, meeting with mayors, city councilors, and politicians for the Finistère and Côtes-du-Nord departments, he soon became a familiar figure around the peninsula, with his disheveled, shirt-sleeves appearance, his nervous pacing—the sign of many cases pleaded in many courtrooms—and his chain-smoking of tiny Davidoff cigarillos, which over the years had altered his speech pattern from a normal vocal flow to a staccato series of hissing gasps between puffs of sweet-acrid smoke. Maître Huglo seemed to approach life and career through clenched teeth, and his mannerisms brought to mind Rod Steiger imitating Peter Lorre playing a Frenchman, perhaps Napoleon.

Today, Huglo remembers 1978 as one of the hardest and worst—but at the same time most exalting—years he had ever spent, marked by endless shuttles between Brittany and Paris, consultations with eminent professors of constitutional matters, meeting after meeting with angry and confused Bretons, memo after memo, for a constant effort of explanation and persuasion, all the while fighting against the slings and arrows of Parisian bureaucrats, opposing politicians, and his jealous *confrères* in the legal game. It was the year of the big decisions: Whom should he sue, where and in what manner? Between frantic journeys and sleepless nights, he and his associate, Corinne Lepage, decided to take an approach radically different from that of the Agence Judiciare du Trésor, which finally limited its lawsuit to Standard Oil and Amoco International: Sue everyone and see what happens. Thus, he decided to take on not only these two corporate bodies, but Amoco Transport Company as well, and Astilleros Espanoles, and the American Bureau of Shipping, and Bugsier, too. No one was to be spared. Let the chips fall where they may.

The important chips lived in America, that was obvious. Both Huglo and the porcupines at the AJT realized that the venue for their suits would have to be across the Atlantic, where Standard Oil sat on its mattress full of money. A trial in France, they knew, would stand good chances of ending with a severe judgment against the polluters (in law, as in basketball, the home court advantage is not negligible), but even a big victory in France would be hollow: Standard Oil possessed virtually no property of consequence there, so there was nothing to lay hands on. No: If money was to be taken, it would have to be right inside the lion's den. They would sue in the United States. And for this, they would need the help of American lawyers. Huglo scratched his head, called around for information, and came up with a name that would later become anathema inside the Carrara palace at East Randolph Drive: Curtis, Mallet-Prevost, Colt & Mosle, Counselors at Law, 101 Park Avenue, New York, New York 10178. September 1978 was just around the corner, and a suit would have to be filed before the six-month statute of limitations took effect. Soon, it would be time for Batman and Robin to enter the scene.

Meanwhile, French Prime Minister Raymond Barre, the navy, and the plethora of ministries involved with the sea and pollution had been busily securing the barn door even tighter. Only a week after the disaster, Barre ordered the navy to maintain a twenty-four-hour watch, both by air and sea, over the shipping lanes, and tankers were warned to keep to the outer edge of the traffic separation rail from which the Amoco *Cadiz* had strayed, to never approach closer than seven nautical miles of the French coastline, and to report in by radio when they arrived off Ouessant. In mid-May the *préfet maritime* tightened up the navigation instructions with new rules for entering and leaving harbors and giving advance warning of possible troubles aboard ship. In July, divers from the Marseille-based salvage and engineering firm of Comex, carefully watched by a platoon of gendarmes maritimes, went down into the hulk of the tanker and, in a feat of unusual skill and daring, located and cut away the broken distribution block and its associated piping. This gear, brought to the surface and immediately impounded by French authorities, underwent exhaustive analysis by both Amoco and the French Laboratoire National d'Essais in the continuing quest to determine exactly what had caused it to blow. The divers were unsuccessful, though, in locating the most important pieces of all: the six studs that had failed. Lacking them, all later judgments of the soundness of the Astilleros design and materials would have to be done by extrapolation, from analysis of the other studs and flanges on the same block, and those from sister ships. From the very start, even before the Comex men went down, persistent and sarcastic innuendo suggested that "someone" (no names, please, but follow my regard) had made sure that the broken studs had vaporized from the face of the earth, and would never be seen again.

The maritime trial of the century took its first baby steps in mid-September, when the Agence Judiciare du Trésor, through its American lawyers, filed suit for alleged damages of $300 million against Standard Oil in the U.S. District Court for the Southern District of New York. Two days later, the Conseil Général des Côtes du Nord, as Huglo's grouping and its miscellaneous hangers-on had decided to call themselves, weighed in with its own suit in the same court. In all, the damages claimed by all the different parties totaled more than $2 billion.

From this point on, our cast of characters developed a whole new series of stars, in the persons of the American lawyers wrestling inside the unbelievably labyrinthine can of worms into which the case developed when it was actually brought to court. This dizzying juridical swirl defies simple presentation, but the broad lines of the skirmishes fought by the American "whereas" brotherhood are roughly resumed as follows.

After the two big suits were filed in September, Standard Oil of Indiana, Amoco International, Amoco Transport, and Captain Phillips (whom the Côtes-du-Nord parties had also decided to sue) filed an action in the U.S. District Court in Chicago to limit their liability according to the long-standing rule of admiralty law that a shipowner could not be held responsible for amounts greater than the value of his vessel and his interest in its cargo. Since the scrap heap on the rocks of Portsall was by then worth zero or less, and the cargo had already been paid for by Shell's captive insurance company, this idea looked like a particularly attractive proposition, as viewed from the fiftieth floor of the Standard Oil Building. In December, Bugsier made the mistake of bringing one of its salvage tugs, the *Atlantic,* into port in Norfolk, Virginia. When the news of this providential arrival came to the big ears of Curtis-Mallet in New York, they promptly obtained an order of attachment, to hold the ship until Bugsier produced a letter promising to appear in court to argue its case in the Amoco *Cadiz*'s grounding. Hardly had *Atlantic* been freed, though, than Amoco seized her in turn, alleging that their oilpot went aground because of the Germans and their badly managed and unseaworthy tugs. After a second letter of undertaking, the tug was finally free to leave Norfolk and get back to work. Around this time, the Côtes-du-Nord people were also filing suits in New York against Astilleros Espanoles and American Bureau of Shipping.

At the limitation proceedings initiated by Amoco in Chicago, the French parties roared in and filed suits of their own, not only contesting the limitation, but claiming damages of more than $2 billion. At this, Amoco filed counterclaims and third-party claims against France, alleging that the republic had assumed responsibility for the cleanup, and by handling it negligently had either caused or aggravated the damages. Things were getting complicated. In a praiseworthy effort at simplification, a multidistrict hearing stayed the suits elsewhere and assigned one judge—the now-famous Frank J. McGarr—to hear it all in one place. Logically enough, that place was the U.S. District Court for the Northern District of Illinois, in Chicago. The New York suits were dropped.

Astilleros Espanoles vigorously insisted that American courts did not have jurisdiction over them in this case, but McGarr ruled against them by issuing a default judgment saying, in essence, you are guilty if you do not show up for the trial. In itself, this was a first big victory for Amoco, meaning that the Spanish shipyard could be held liable for part or all of any damages assigned against Amoco. (The victory was hollow, though: How could Amoco possibly collect?) Astilleros appealed McGarr's ruling all the way to the U.S. Supreme Court, but they lost every time. The result of all of this was that, although the shipyard was deeply and intimately involved in the case, it refused to come to Chicago, and never argued its position in the big lawsuit. Whether this was due to cool decision by rational-minded executives or the legendary prickles of Spanish pride is not known, but most observers had the distinct feeling that they had decided to play a single erroneous card—and lost badly in the showdown.

"I would guess that Astilleros feels confident that it doesn't have any assets within reach that Amoco can grab," observed Benjamin E. Haller, the principal U.S. lawyer for the Republic of France. "If Amoco can't find any assets within the U.S. to execute on, its only recourse would be to bring an original action in Spain or any jurisdiction where Astilleros has assets, asking it to enforce the judgment."

Good luck.

As for American Bureau of Shipping, it dropped out of the legal scene on the eve of the trial, when it decided to settle with the Côtes-du-Nord parties, for a sum that remained secret. ABS hotly denied that this settlement could be construed as an admission of guilt, however: An early settlement was simply a way of avoiding years and years of astronomic legal fees. In the Côtes-du-Nord camp the settlement was the cause for considerable jubilation and not a small amount of self-congratulation, but ABS spokesmen did their best to deflate the balloon: "One would be hard pressed to categorize the payment as anything more than a 'nuisance value' settlement," explained Kenneth E. Sheehan, an ABS vice-president.

With ABS out of the picture, Judge McGarr simplified further by throwing out the suit against Captain Phillips, reasoning that any responsibility for the grounding imputable to him would have to be assigned to his employer. Now Amoco filed a claim against Bugsier, counterclaims against France and the Côtes-du-Nord parties, plus a third-party claim against Astilleros Espanoles, alleging faulty construction. The final simplification came when Judge McGarr decided to break the trial into two distinct segments, the first dealing with liability—who was guilty—and the second to determine the value of the damages suffered by France and the Breton towns.

Well, that is roughly the way it went. What it finally came down to, in terms that can be understood by the normally constituted human being, was this:

—France was suing Standard Oil and Amoco International, to get its cleanup and compensation money back. (France was not suing Amoco Transport, though. By this legal pirouette French attorneys adroitly stepped around the bind of the CLC, which France had signed, and which let the registered owner off the hook with the 77-million-franc limitation clause.)

—Shell was suing Amoco to get payment for the cargo.

—Amoco, while defending itself with fierce efficiency, was accusing Bugsier and Astilleros Espanoles of causing the wreck and France of doing a bad job of cleaning up the mess.

—Côtes-du-Nord was suing everyone in sight, ostensibly for payment of real damages incurred but in reality to inflict exemplary punishment on the polluters, in order to strike the fear of God into all the world's owners of oilpots.

—Bugsier was just defending itself.

One very salient fact that emerged from these various legal maneuverings was that no one (apart from Amoco, for obvious reasons) was interested in attacking Astilleros Espanoles for the breakdown, and no one (except Bugsier, which had to defend its conduct of the tow) cared about finding fault with Captain Bardari. This marked the major difference between the Liberian inquiry—which had assigned most of the blame in precisely these two directions—and Judge McGarr's trial. For all intents and purposes, Côtes-du-Nord and the Agence Judiciare du Trésor pretended that Astilleros Espanoles, uncontested manufacturer of a faulty steering gear, and Pasquale Bardari, who incontrovertibly had made several key mistakes, simply did not exist. Why? Money, *mon cher:* Astilleros was in Spain, and possessed no capital or properties of interest outside on which the damaged parties could lay their hands. As for Bardari, his skipper's pay wouldn't be enough to cover the pollution even if he lived for a thousand years. What the French wanted (and Shell, too) was to take the Standard Oil Building like the Bastille, and ride the elevator to the thirtieth floor, where Mr. Swearingen was sitting on his mattress full of money. Nothing else counted.

From September of 1978 the pretrial skirmishing carried on through the winter, and it was not until July of 1979 that the entire monumental machine was ready to get started. As tortuous as the preliminaries had been, though, they were nothing as compared to what was about to come. The beginning of the beginning of the serious stuff came with the opening of the discovery phase.

The process of discovery is a peculiarly American institution, dating from a reform of federal rules in the thirties, and aiming at achieving the most equitable trials possible. Although it is absolutely fundamental to the legal process, it is little understood by laymen in America, and virtually unknown in foreign lands. By enabling opposing attorneys to order the production of documents, even the most incriminating ones, specific or general, from their opponents, discovery insures that all sides of the case being tried can be displayed in the light of day. Thus, for instance, the French parties were able to demand from Amoco all documents, letters, reports, and the like relevant to the company's maintenance of the Astilleros steering gear, and Amoco was able to make France, sovereign republic though it was, cough up literally tons of papers concerning the country's preparation for and battle against hydrocarbon pollution. Failure to produce the requested documents or efforts to dissimulate them are punished harshly and swiftly. New York lawyers still speak with awe of their prominent Wall Street colleague who was purely and simply disbarred—that is to say, deprived of his livelihood—for having "forgotten" a damaging paper in his desk drawer. In addition to forcing production of documents, discovery allows for written interrogatories to which the opponents must reply and for pretrial testimony by chosen witnesses, in the form of sworn depositions. All of this is specifically designed to permit the "fishing expeditions" of the opposed parties, which will produce all the evidence, all the facts, and hence the truth, so that justice may be done. It has the added advantage of doing away with the last-minute surprises and gamesmanship so dear to writers of legal fiction.

Discovery, then, was a revolutionary innovation in the American judicial system—but it incalculably added to the complications of an already complex and time-consuming apparatus. (This reform alone probably doubled the employment opportunities for lawyers in America, which may go toward explaining the country's presently overpopulated legal trade.) All parties involved in the Amoco *Cadiz* case needed no encouragement to leap into the swimming pool of discovery feet first. More than one hundred depositions were taken, in France, Italy, Germany, England, and America, and literally tons of papers, representing hundreds of thousands of documents, were flown to New York, Paris, and Chicago on demand of the warring law firms. In all, the discovery period lasted nearly three years, during which hundreds of lawyers, clerks, secretaries, and assistants pored over the excruciating detail of everything from maps and manifests to memos, contracts, bills, and technical brochures. It was painful, time-consuming, and expensive, but nonetheless fruitful, especially for the Agence Judiciare du Trésor and the Côtes-du-Nord parties, because during the process they discovered exactly what they had been looking for: evidence that the breakdown of the

Servomotore Electrohidraulico de Cilindros Rectos Manises was caused not just by any inherent fault of design, as it had seemed to the Liberians, but by Amoco's grossly negligent maintenance of the system and refusal to make the necessary repairs. With this evidence, unavailable to Sir Gordon Wilmer and his associates, the Chicago trial broke new ground and put Amoco in a very embarrassing posture. By this evidence alone, discovery fully proved its value.

The liability trial itself did not begin until May of 1982. It lasted slightly more than six months, after which the law firms involved drew up the posttrial papers, summing up their arguments as succinctly and persuasively as possible, for consideration by the judge in making his verdict. The first of these papers—posttrial briefs, proposed findings of fact, appendices, and replies to their opponents' briefs—were filed on a poignant date: March 16, 1983, exactly five years after the grounding. By the middle of May all the filings were finished, and Judge McGarr was left alone with five neat stacks of documents, behind which lay rooms and rooms of material and infinities of argumentation. Now it was up to him to come to a conclusion. That, as everyone knew, would take a while.

Of all the multitudinous Americans who flowed into Brittany in those days as the big lawsuit was being prepared and brought to its six months of flowering in 1982, Barry Kingham and Peter Wolrich were doubtless the most important for the cause of the seventy-six communities that by common agreement had gone to court with the collective name of Conseil Général des Côtes du Nord. Crack legal guns for the firm of Curtis, Mallet-Prevost, Colt & Mosle—Kingham was already a partner, although the younger Wolrich had not yet achieved that distinction—they were to become familiar figures as the guardian angels of the Breton cause, the knights who were to lead the battle against Standard Oil in Judge McGarr's courtroom. Still only in their thirties and suffused with the energy and dedication common to youthful champions of a cause that was not only just, but paying their salaries as well, Kingham and Wolrich were impressively thorough and tireless workers, building their case methodically throughout the years of discovery until everything was in place and they were certain that they had a hammerlock on the head of the monster. Kingham was reserved, stern, chill, and austere of appearance, with a huge shock of Kennedyesque hair screening the upper half of his noble brow, flinty and bespectacled in spite of his youth, handsome of mien and fanatically fastidious of attire. Wolrich, his deputy, sixteen months younger, was both shorter and slighter, but considerably more accessible of manner: helpful, outgoing, and even prepared to smile on occasion (provided no one was looking). Both of them were clearly men of unusual skill and dedication, and it was an added plus, a nicely symbolical accident of history, that they physically resembled, like two drops of water, as the French say, Batman and Robin. Their Batmobile was from Hertz or Avis as they drove over the ancient historical roads of Brittany in quest of justice, but it was easy to picture them swinging vengefully down on villainous polluters on the fine, long threads of their intelligence. All that was missing from the picture were the bat masks and the blue long underwear. Kingham compensated by a sternly wooden gaze and Brooks Brothers pinstripes.

On Tuesday morning, May 4, 1982, Kingham and Wolrich were finally called upon to begin the performance they had been preparing for nearly four years. In a vast, walnut-paneled courtroom on the twenty-fifth floor of the Everett McKinley Dirksen Building in downtown Chicago, they and the lawyers for the other parties involved in the maritime trial of the century took their places before Judge Frank J. McGarr. In the seating area reserved for the public was a fifty-five-person delegation of mayors from the sullied villages along the Breton coast. They had winged in to make a symbolic demonstration of determination and solidarity that cut across political lines. As they watched the first witness being sworn in, most of them were expecting the trial to be over and the verdict pronounced by the end of 1982. But at the end of 1983 they were still waiting. American justice may grind well, but it grinds fine, and exceeding slow.

15.

The Maritime Trial
of the Century

Wrapped in their thoughts, girt in their tricolor sashes, the Breton mayors beamed proudly as one of their very own, Jean-François Leborgne, mayor of Le Conquet, took the stand as the very first live witness in the maritime trial of the century. Leborgne was not on the witness stand for his political function, though. Judge McGarr was interested in him because of the job by which he earned his living: the present chief of Radio le Conquet and duty operator at the time of the Amoco *Cadiz* grounding. In the course of that first day's proceedings, however, the mayors' pride turned to apprehension, then nervousness and finally downright consternation when their fellow public servant came under the fearsome fire of Frank Cicero, otherwise known around Brittany as Old Nick.

Frank Cicero! The name is graven in the memories of a thousand Frenchmen, today still, as indelibly remembered as if it had been branded into their flesh. Most of those who had anything to do with the French side of the trial automatically turned crimson at the mention of his name, and around the hallways of the Agence Judiciare du Trésor the secretaries and errand boys whispered that his feet were cloven and that he carried his tail wrapped up neatly inside a custom-tailored pocket of his pinstripe suit. Worse than Satan was he, because he was both the devil and the devil's advocate: Frank Cicero—star performer of the huge law firm of Kirkland & Ellis, prominent citizen of the Second City, luminary of the Illinois Bar Association—was the lawyer in charge of the stable of lawyers who handled the case for Standard Oil and all its corporate off-spring that were involved with Captain Bardari's oilpot.

Elegant of dress, sharp of feature, and incisive of manner, Cicero was as keen and quick and canny as a cross between a fox and an IBM PC, and he drove his opponents to distraction with the thoroughness of his preparation and the skill with which he argued his case. Few doubted that this could be a reincarnation of his (slightly better known) Roman antecedent, Marcus Tullius, or that his *Pro Amoco* was in every way equal to the other guy's *Pro Milone* or *Pro Murena.*

From that first day, it was clear what Cicero was aiming at. The denigration of the competence of the French authorities at all levels was central to Amoco's argumentation, every bit as much as the contentions that the breakdown of the steering gear occurred because of negligent design and construction by Astilleros Espanoles and that the grounding was caused by *Pacific*'s improper handling of the tow. In sum, Amoco's position, as set forth with virtuosity by Satan himself, was that the company was an innocent virgin, being set upon and victimized by a band of villainous rascals, and as such should be found entirely free of guilt in the polluting. It was the others who had caused the damage to the Breton shore, not Amoco. Even though the French side exploded with righteous wrath at the "presumption" and "indecency" of this approach, Cicero's arguments were not altogether lacking in plausibility, especially as concerned the preparation of the government for coastal calamity and the inefficacy of Plan POLMAR—excoriated in embarrassing detail in reports issued by the Senate and National Assembly after the disaster.

For the attack against Captain Weinert and *Pacific,* Cicero had an unlikely ally in the Côtes-du-Nord camp, who were also charging negligent towing, in accordance with Maître Huglo's strategy of suing *tous azimuts,* in the manner of General de Gaulle's *force de frappe.* Regarding the liability of Astilleros Espanoles, Cicero made use of much of the same evidence that had been adduced in the Liberian hearing. The fact that Astilleros chose to boycott the American action made his work easier in this respect: There was no one to contradict him when he demonstrated what he found to be wrong with the Manises design and construction.

A situation that was impossibly complicated from the start (a Spanish-Liberian-American-Italian boat spilling Dutch cargo on France, with Germans and English also involved) had been made even worse by the fact that one nation (France) had signed and ratified the 1969 Brussels Convention known as CLC, while the other (the United States) had signed but not ratified it. CLC, therefore, was law of the land in France but not in America. There was a nice, ironic parallel to this, too: Just as the Lloyd's Open Form had been conceived as a means of avoiding unseemly squabbling over money between captains, CLC, rushed through in the shock of the *Torrey Canyon* wreck, had been intended as an instrument for quickly compensating victims of oil pollution and, thereby, avoiding lawsuits and unseemly squabbling over money.

The problem with CLC was threefold: Its compensation limits were too low, it wasn't clear to whom it applied, and since one nation recognized it and the other didn't, maybe it didn't apply at all. This made perfect terrain for squabbling, and the lawyers on all sides went at it with relish. The compensation, the limit of 77 million Poincaré francs for which CLC held shipowners liable in case of pollution, was a figure that the treaty makers in 1968 and 1969 thought would amply cover any claims. In the ten years since their work, though, oilpots had grown monstrously bigger than *Torrey Canyon,* inflation had eroded what had seemed like a magnificent sum—and pollution victims had become a good deal more feisty. By March, 1978, 77 million Poincaré francs looked paltry, and so no one was of a mind to accept it. The Plaintiffs were determined to go beyond CLC.

As Judge McGarr's monumental trial finally got under way, everyone who was anyone was there, with the two glaring exceptions of Astilleros Espanoles, who had decided to stalk away in a high hidalgo huff, and Pasquale Bardari, who had declined to appear.

The confrontation between justice and the *Cadiz*'s skipper had not been an altogether happy one. After his early arrest by the juge d'instruction in Brest, the French proceedings against Bardari for voluntary pollution had vegetated, left in abeyance as the bigger trial in Chicago ran its course. But the initial charges had not been dropped, and the fact that they remained hanging over him was to prove pertinent for the Chicago action. As we have seen, his testimony in the Liberian hearing sometimes appeared confused and contradictory, and when it was over he received a severe reprimand. (And, although it didn't prove anything legally, observers in Sir Gordon's court were struck by the fact that Bardari and his crewmen preferred only to "affirm" their testimony, while Popeye-Weinert did not hesitate to take the oath.) Now, as the maritime trial of the century was being prepared, Captain Bardari, acting on the advice of his New York and Paris lawyers, declined to appear or testify. His crew members had agreed to submit to sworn depositions—that is, to testify under oath and give evidence that could be officially introduced into the trial—but Bardari used the still-pending Brest proceedings as a justification for refusing to do the same. The single attempt at a deposition at which he appeared, on July 9, 1980, in Naples, was illuminating. At the first question pertinent to the case he responded by reading a prepared statement handed to him by his American lawyer:

> After consulting my attorney for everything which is foreseen and can be applied by French laws, including Articles 104 and 105 of the Penal Procedure Code and article 206 of the Civil Procedure Co⌐ for what is force to and applicable by Italian laws including Arti⸗ 246 of the Civil Procedure Code, I take advantage of my rightr ⸗ cording to the European Convention for the Protection of Human Rights and using my rights according to the Fifth Amendment of the United States Constitution, I respectfully refuse to answer to this question.

Michael Snyder, the lawyer representing Bugsier, was hopping mad. Not only had he lost his time in flying to Naples for the deposition, but he was now about to lose his potentially most useful witness for confounding the Amoco charges against Captain Weinert. He had been supremely confident that a confrontation in the courtroom between Bardari and Weinert would as much as end the case against Bugsier—and now the opportunity was being denied him. After fruitlessly trying to get some information—any information—out of Bardari, and always receiving the identical response ("Same answer," a reference to his earlier statement), Snyder found himself in the following edifying colloquy:

MR. SNYDER:

Q. Do you have any knowledge of anything said to the master of the tug PACIFIC on March 16, 1978?

A. Same answer.

Q. Are you making this answer written on exhibit Number 3 to my questions because you have been subjected to any physical or emotional duress . . .

MR. RAY SMITH (Bardari's lawyer): I object to the form of the question.

MR. CICERO: Same objection.

MR. SNYDER:

Q. . . . by any person?

A. Privilege of consultation between client and attorney.

MR. SNYDER:

At this point, it becomes clear to me that I am on a fool's errand . . .

MR. CICERO: Speak for yourself, Mr. Snyder.

Frustrated but still game, Snyder ended the one-way interview with a voluntarily cryptic salutation:

Thank you, Captain. See you in two to five years.

"Rambaud, his French lawyer, flew over to explain why Bardari couldn't testify," said Snyder later, fairly dripping with contemptuous disdain, "because that testimony could implicate him in the Brest proceedings. But when we questioned him on the seriousness of the penalties Bardari faced in Brest, he admitted that, under the worst possible circumstances, Bardari would be facing no jail sentence at all, and only a small fine. The only way he could be jailed was if he had polluted France voluntarily, and no one was accusing him of that. Weinert was furious when he heard Bardari wasn't showing up. He and the other people from Bugsier were jumping through hoops for the court. Weinert was facing the same accusations in Brest—but he didn't take the Fifth Amendment. He wasn't afraid of this trial."

For outsiders, Bardari's refusal to participate in the trial looked terribly damning: He was, after all, the most important single witness of the entire unhappy saga. On the face of it, this appeared perfectly absurd. Amoco's unbending argument was that Bardari was perfectly within his rights, that they had no power to oblige him to come (even though at the time he was commanding an Amoco ship, the *Texas City*), and that the court should not draw any adverse inference from his absence. He was protected from self-incrimination by both French law and the U.S. Constitution, and his failure to appear ought to be no more damaging than the fact that he had preferred to only "affirm" at the Liberian hearing.

That was not the way Michael A. Snyder saw it at all. He was not prepared to allow Bardari or Amoco off the hook, and insisted that "every inference" be drawn adversely to Amoco, who "clearly" controlled their employee. Citing several previous cases to buttress his argument, Snyder pointed to a long-standing principle of maritime law that held that the failure of a party to call an important witness to testify, or even to make a deposition, raises the presumption that his testimony would have been unfavorable to that party. This, of course, was the commonsense conclusion to which nonlegal outsiders immediately jumped—Amoco, having experienced his performance in London, didn't want Bardari in Chicago—although they were perhaps not prepared to follow Snyder in the complete detail of the inferences that he proposed, which included the proposal that the *Cadiz's* skipper was "incapacitated, or possibly intoxicated, on March 16, 1978." (Snyder's reference was to the beer that Mr. Maynard and Captain Bardari had drunk with their lunches.) Occasionally, the game being played out before Judge McGarr grew rough; and if Snyder's elbow appeared to be flying here, it looked very much like retribution for an earlier slur that Cicero had directed at Captain Weinert. We will be getting to that soon.

Judge McGarr played Sphinx on the matter of the inferences to be drawn from Bardari's glaring absence, suggesting that it could be a matter of some importance, but one on which he had not made up his mind.

"Well, first," he told the assembled lawyers, "we have Mr. Bardari, a key witness by anyone's view of this case, the captain of the ship. Weinert's testimony made him and his crew out to be incompetent. He testified at the Liberian hearing. And I have some speculation in my own mind as to why he isn't here. I really don't know. Because he was at the Liberian hearing and I don't know the bona fides of his refusal to be here."

With the exception of Snyder, though, no one else seemed overly concerned by the absence of the drama's principal actor. It was definitely not in the interest of France, Côtes-du-Nord, or Petroleum Insurance Limited to show that the shipwreck had been caused by personal errors of the captain. The captain had no money.

Of all the members of Frank Cicero's Amoco team, it was no doubt the terrible Ms. McDole who horripilated most thoroughly everybody on the other side of the fence. Tall, blonde, angular, and inevitable, Sidney Bosworth McDole, aged thirty-five when the trial got under way, pursued her duties as Satan's second with all the fiercely determined singlemindedness of a Standard Oil zealot, shining with especial brilliance during the long days of depositions when she guarded Amoco's interests like a duenna, clashing with opposing lawyers with metronomic regularity, assailing them with objection after objection, relishing a combat in which the petty was often called upon to vanquish the picayune, wreaking havoc upon her adversaries' strategies by sheer unyielding waspishness, and often succeeding in destroying their composure as well. If Frank Cicero was the Devil, Ms. McDole was Medusa, basilisk, and succubus, all wrapped up into one lovable bundle, and her semantic brawls with the men on the other side of the case were memorable masterpieces of juridical melodrama, worthy of a footnote in an anthology of legal curiosities. Clad in elegantly fashionable duds, her three degrees (Vassar, Middlebury, and Northwestern) an implacable righteousness, and an eighteen-karat gold ladies' Rolex, Ms. McDole possessed the extraordinary ability to make her opponents climb walls and chew up documents in rage and to wither wills with her wivern gaze. Lawyers for France and Côtes-du-Nord consistently charged this most dreaded and least gentlemanly adversary with "leading" during the depositions, especially those having to do with crew members of the ill-fated tanker. By leading or "instructing," as it also was called, they meant her repeated objections to the questions of opposing lawyers, interjections that she placed at such times and in such a manner as to indicate to the witness how he should answer (or not answer). All too often, they complained, Ms. McDole disrupted the orderly proceeding of the interrogation and caused what should have been a productive line of questioning to turn sterile. So acrimonious did these exchanges become that lawyers for the French side were reduced to anguished threats to bring her tactics to the attention of Judge McGarr. At times, the transcripts of the depositions read more like schoolyard harangues—I'll tell teacher!—than interchanges among mature specimens of *Homo sapiens*.

When Joseph C. Smith, one of America's top admiralty lawyers, who had been hired to represent Shell's interests, attempted to wrest some technical information out of Nicolo Giampaolo, one of the engineering staff who had wrestled with the mortally wounded steering motor, the confrontation became a masterpiece in frustration and obfuscation. Was it planned that way? Who knows? But it is certain that both Ms. McDole and the poor, thwarted Joseph Smith earned their salaries that day, if not necessarily enormous amounts of mutual esteem. The vignette begins as Smith, occasionally joined by another lawyer, Terence Gargan, is angrily charging connivance between Ms. McDole and Giampaolo, the man she has been assigned to guard.

BY MR. GARGAN:

Q. What did you say?

A. I have already said it before.

Q. I didn't hear it.

A. I'm sorry. I have already said it before.

MR. SMITH: He's taking instructions from Ms. McDole not to answer the question, and that's obviously why she made the objection.

Now, the question was not asked before. Mr. Gargan has laid a foundation for it, and I wish you would not interrupt his examination.

You're wasting a lot of time here, Ms. McDole.

MS. MC DOLE: The witness may answer the question. I'm not instructing him not to answer the question, Mr. Smith.

MR. SMITH: Well, it's quite obvious to me, when you make an objection, he's not going to answer the question.

MS. MC DOLE: He may answer the question.

MR. SMITH: Will you interpret that to the witness, what Ms. McDole just said, that he may answer the question.

(translation)

THE WITNESS: I said it. I have already replied to this question before, and I don't intend to reply again to this question.

MR. GARGAN: Read it to him again.

(Whereupon the reporter read the following:

Q. "Could you tell us how you placed the wrench on the first stud that you were attempting to remove?")

BY MR. GARGAN:

Q. Mr. Giampaolo, you have to answer these questions as best you can as they're put to you. You don't have a choice of deciding whether or not you're going to answer the questions.

If you don't know the answer, then you say, I don't know the answer or I don't remember, but you have no choice of deciding whether you're going to answer a particular question or not.

Do you understand what I just said?

(Whereupon the reporter read the following for the interpreter:

"Mr. Giampaolo, you have to answer these questions as best you can as they're put to you. You don't have a choice of deciding whether or not you're going to answer the questions.

"If you don't know the answer, then you say, I don't know the answer or I don't remember, but you have no choice of deciding whether you're going to answer a particular question or not.

"Do you understand what I just said?")

THE WITNESS: No.

BY MR. GARGAN:

Q. You don't understand that?

A. No. I didn't quite well understand.

MR. SMITH: Repeat it. Would you read it back again? Mr. reporter, read it back sentence by sentence so that it can be translated by the interpreter.

(Whereupon the reporter read the following: "Mr. Giampaolo, you have to answer these questions as best you can as they're put to you. You don't have a choice of deciding whether or not you're going to answer the questions.

"If you don't know the answer, then you say, I don't know the answer or I don't remember, but you have no choice of deciding whether you're going to answer a particular question or not.

"Do you understand what I just said?")

THE WITNESS: I said, I have not well understood the question.

BY MR. GARGAN:

Q. Okay. But do you understand the sentence that I just said?

A. No.

Q. What is it about the statement that I have just made that you do not understand?

A. I don't know. But what I mean to say is I have not understood perfectly the question that you have placed before.

Q. But we are not talking about that. I asked you if you understood the sentence which was just read and translated to you.

A. No.

MR. SMITH: Read it to him again.

MR. GARGAN: Yeah. Let's read it to him again.

(Whereupon the reporter read the following:

"Mr. Giampaolo, you have to answer these questions as best you can as they're put to you. You don't have a choice of deciding whether or not you're going to answer the questions.

"If you don't know the answer then you say I don't know the answer or I don't remember, but you have no choice of deciding whether you're going to answer a particular question or not.

"Do you understand what I said?")

THE WITNESS: Yes.

MR. GARGAN: Now, I want the record to reflect that this was repeated three times till finally the witness acknowledged an understanding of the sentence, okay?

(Reporter Crites nodded head affirmatively)

BY MR. GARGAN:

Q. I would like you, Mr. Giampaolo, to describe for us the way in which you placed the wrench on the stud the first time, as best you recall.

A. Well, exactly, I don't remember which was the first stud I placed the wrench on, but I know for sure that I have placed the wrench the proper way to remove the broken stud.

In case any benighted soul in the French camp had the naïveté to imagine that confronting a powerful adversary under the rules of American justice would be easy, the illusions were dispelled even before the trial itself, and much of the credit went to Ms. McDole. Poor Terence Gargan. As history would have it, he was the one upon whom the brunt of the lesson fell most often and most heavily. Would you like another example of a schoolyard harangue? Of course you would. This one, fittingly, begins with the magic word: *objection.*

MS. MC DOLE: Objection.

MR. GARGAN: Wait. Wait. If you're going to make an objection, I would ask the witness be excused from the room. This is clearly going to be an instructive type of objection, and I am not going to stand for it.

MS. MC DOLE: Well, I'll make my objection as I see fit, Mr. Gargan.

MR. GARGAN: Right.

MS.MC DOLE: I object to the form of the question.

MR. GARGAN: That's it.

MS. MC DOLE: I object to the form of the question on the ground that it's not clear what studs you're talking about. Are you talking about the broken studs?

MR. GARGAN: The witness is not having any problems answering these questions.

MS. MC DOLE: I will make my objection.

MR. GARGAN: Okay, you have it.

MS. MC DOLE: Fine. Let it be translated.

MR. GARGAN: I want to indicate on the record, this is clearly an instructive type of objection, and it's clear the intent and so forth, and we have gone through this any number of times now.

MS. MC DOLE: You can form that question, Mr. Gargan, without having any objection; you know that.

MR. SMITH: Ms. McDole, let him conduct his examination, please.

MS. MC DOLE: Fine. Let him allow me to make the objection.

MR. SMITH: You have made it.

MS. MC DOLE: Can it be translated, please?

(Whereupon, the reporter read the following:

MS. MC DOLE: I object to the form of the question.

MR. GARGAN: That's it.

MS. MC DOLE: I object to the form of the question on the ground that it's not clear what studs you're talking about. Are you talking about the broken studs?

MR. GARGAN: The witness is not having any problems answering these questions.

MS. MC DOLE: I will make my objection.

MR. GARGAN: Okay, you have it.")

Upon occasion, it seemed miraculous that the opposing lawyers did not come to blows. It can only be surmised that American law schools offer courses in self-control. Either that, or they were all afraid to take a poke at Sidney Bosworth McDole. No doubt she held a doctorate in karate as well. Barred from physical action, they were reduced to venting their rage with shouted words. After one quarrel, the court reporter inserted a poignant little paragraph into his transcript that was at once an admission of defeat and an anguished cry for help:

(Whereupon Mr. White, Mr. Strickland and Ms. McDole, all speaking in English at the same time, and Interpreter K'Danet speaking in French at the same time, and after listening to the tape recording made by Mr. Seyrat, Reporter Crites was unable to decipher what anyone was saying for a period of about 30 seconds.)

Of course, all this skirmishing finally ended with the judge, who was obliged to read the transcripts and weigh, as judiciously as possible, who was right and who was wrong and who was harassing whom. Years later, when the trial itself had ended and everyone was waiting for Frank J. McGarr to render his verdict, many outsiders, especially the poor, victimized Bretons, burning with impatience as the months and months went by, wondered what was taking the judge so long. Had they known what he had to put up with, they would have been more understanding. Among other things, he was reading transcripts of depositions, such as the 167 pages for Giampaolo, in which Ms. McDole objected 66 times, or the 260 pages dedicated to another of the engineering staff, Vincenzo Conversano, in which she objected 124 times. This was the kind of weighty judicial material that McGarr was studying:

Q. Okay. Now, on the morning of the 16th of March, how did you first learn of the problem with the steering gear?

MS. MC DOLE: Objection to the form of the question. Lack of foundation and lack of specificity as far as what you mean by "problem."

MR. SMITH: May I interrupt you at one point, please. In order to preserve your objection, all you have to do is object.

If the person asking the question has to know the basis of your objection, they will ask. But, I regard your objections, other than objections as to form, quote, unquote, instructing the witness.

Now, will you please stop doing it?

MS. MC DOLE: I will make my objections the way I deem proper.

MR. SMITH: Well, Judge McGarr is going to hear about this.

MS. MC DOLE: Fine.

MR. GARGAN: Translate everything to the witness.

When it was all over, when the discovery had finally run its seemingly interminable course, when all the depositions had been taken, all the documents digested and the strategies finely honed, the parties involved could get down to presenting their cases. This was where we came in, as Frank Cicero was circling around Jean-Francois Leborgne, waiting to strike and sink in his fangs.

Cicero, developing Amoco's arguments over the months, had to be both agile and bicephalous, always fighting on two fronts and in two directions: on the attack, with his countersuits against Astilleros, France and Bugsier, and on defense in attempting to disprove the grave charges leveled against Standard Oil and its subsidiaries by France, Côtes-du-Nord, and PIL, Shell's captive insurance company. Appropriately, he broke down into two categories the thrust of his case: technical and jurisprudential.

On the technical side he sought to prove approximately the same thing that had already been demonstrated at the Liberian hearing: that the Manises design was inherently flawed, not up to the standards it was advertised as respecting and too weak to support the kind of seas that a VLCC might reasonably be expected to encounter in its working life. Further, his reasoning ran, ABS certified the ship, while Amoco's own marine architecture department and on-site inspectors at the Cadiz shipyards had nothing more than a generalized overview of construction, with no responsibility for the sort of detail that caused the failure on the distribution block.

Amoco's opponents heartily scoffed at the ravished virgin defense, and did not hesitate to throw Cicero's sarcasm back into his face. Just as he had made merry with the French navy's alleged inability to see Amoco *Cadiz* right in the middle of its most sensitive strategic area (his manner of affirming that they did see it, but failed in their duty to do something about it) so did his opponents with the ravished virgin hypothesis: Standard Oil, the multinational giant, with more experts than you could shake a stick at, being taken in like a hick by a bunch of little old Spanish scallywags? Come, come . . . But even more curious, they found, was Amoco's attitude toward the American Bureau of Shipping: Surely, if the ship grounded because of a faulty steering gear, was not the guilt for its faulty design equally applicable to the certification society that had been hired to check on the builder and approve its work? So why, then, did Amoco not sue Astilleros Espanoles and ABS, as the Côtes-du-Nord parties did? In his posttrial papers, Cicero mentioned the ABS certification only in passing, with a mere gentle swipe of the paw, and then went on with his exposition. Why such solicitude? What was going on here?

"They need ABS too much," gasped Huglo, by way of explanation. What Huglo and other adversaries pointed out was that Amoco's entire fleet was certified by ABS, which created a delicate symbiotic relationship: Among other things, ABS inspectors determined whether or not a damaged vessel could remain in class; whether drydockings could be deferred; when inspection intervals could be extended; and when expensive machinery teardowns (for internal inspection) could be waived. For a shipowner, an unfavorable finding from an ABS man is approximately like a Michelin inspector with heartburn for a French restaurant. Vessels must remain in class to keep their hull and liability insurances in force. Without insurance, no vessel sails. So perhaps Cicero, his opponents reasoned, preferred to take it easy on ABS, all the more so since, as a nonprofit organization, they had little money to offer for the grabbing. Further, attacking ABS could be a punch into a hornet's nest: What other damaging evidence against Amoco might not the organization bring before the court in its defense, since it knew the Amoco fleet so intimately? And there was one final, saucy point in all this supposition: It has long been common knowledge that throughout the Western world the shipowners and the classification societies are "one big, happy family," as a French insider explained it to me. You scratch my back, and I'll scratch yours. As evidence of this symbiosis, it came out in the trial that Captain Phillips—the very same Claude Phillips who sat in the southeast corner office of the fiftieth floor of the Standard Oil Building—was a member of the board of managers of the American Bureau of Shipping.

Armed with an enormous battery of graphs, curves, figures, and miscellaneous data from his assistants, Cicero went even further than the Liberian board in pinpointing a precise technical explanation of just why the high-pressure pipe had burst. Put briefly, the Amoco contention was that incompetently engineered relief valves caused repetitious oscillating pressure, which ultimately blew open an underdesigned system, through metal fatigue in the studs that failed. Instead of cleanly relieving pressure surges caused by the sea's violent contact with the rudder, the valves actually increased pressures, "chattering" in a mechanical rhythm that eventually broke the studs in the same manner that a beer can or a piece of plastic breaks when subjected to repeated bendings.

Naturally, Cicero had models to demonstrate how this hypothesis worked, and eminently learned gentlemen to come to the bar and testify that, yes, indeed, this could be the only correct interpretation of the events of that fate-charged morning of March 16—just as the lawyers for France, Shell, and Côtes-du-Nord had their own mirror images of such erudition at their command, saying, nonsense, old chap, it was only *this* way that it all happened. Since the failed studs had never been produced, it was all ex post facto conjecture, anyway, and Judge McGarr had to regard the rented experts with the same illusionless eye he would reserve for the hired psychiatrists who come to the bar in cases of mass murder and mayhem, place their hands over their hearts, and offer perfectly contradictory testimony as to the mental health of the particular Son of Sam who happens to be in the dock.

It was on the matter of maintenance, though, that Cicero had to expend his most prodigious sums of intelligence, craft, and energy, because maintenance was the Achilles' heel at which all his opponents took aim. The question of faulty maintenance had arisen in the years of discovery, during which hordes of lawyers, legal clerks, and researchers pored over the more than 500,000 documents that had been pried loose from Standard Oil's corporate fist: revelatory, compromising, and sometimes astonishing material on which they based their attacks on Amoco, and which had not been available to the Liberian investigators. Cicero insisted that the vessel had undergone all the routine repairs and inspections that are normal for such a ship, and that as far as the Amoco and ABS inspectors who visited her regularly could tell, there was no need for anything more. He scornfully dismissed the argumentation of his adversaries as a semantic house of cards, based on hindsight and speculation. This, of course, was his job, and he handled it well, but it did not prevent that speculation from looking dangerously well-founded.

Cicero's technical exposition contained two final accusatory assaults, one against Bugsier and the other against the French republic. Amoco *Cadiz* would not have grounded but for the improper conduct of *Pacific,* her master, and his employers in Hamburg, he held, since Captain Weinert did not exercise reasonable care in conducting the salvage operation. Sidestepping the matter of Chicago's long-distance control over Captain Bardari, he maintained that the tug had been called promptly at 1120, as soon as the engineers had told him that the gear could not be fixed, and that from then on, Weinert, his crew, and the Bugsier front office consistently screwed everything up: by trying the first tow at a ninety-degree angle from the bow (he should have done it astern); by taking an unreasonably long time in retrieving the broken gear and setting up the second tow (*Pacific*'s winch, he said, was not working properly); by "recklessly" bungling the job of getting the Kongsberg line across for the second tow (the time was lost because he drove the tug badly, not because of the tanker's inexperienced crew); by choosing to tow from astern this time (Bardari wanted it from the bow); and, finally, by deliberately letting Amoco *Cadiz* go to her doom ("Weinert undertook to cut the Amoco *Cadiz* adrift").

This, too, was something new that had not been posited at the Liberian hearing. If the breaking of the first tow might legitimately be called accidental, Cicero maintained, the second one was deliberate: Weinert gunned *Pacific*'s engines so long and so hard that the shackle holding the towline to the tanker eventually gave way. And he knew it would happen that way. He did it on purpose. But why? For what conceivable reason would the captain of a salvage tug who stood to earn, personally, $10,000 or $15,000 for a single day's work endeavor to end it all that way after having labored at it for eight hours or so? The answer, according to Cicero, was fear.

"He wanted to get the hell out of there," he told me with a shrug.

During the trial, Cicero leaned heavily on this explanation for the parting of the second tow, charging that Weinert had posted a seaman on *Pacific*'s workdeck with the flex (the electric grindwheel) for the most contemptible of motives. This precaution, which salvage tug masters take as a matter of course when their vessels are in danger of being pulled onto the rocks, was thus interpreted as an act of cowardice, the implementation of which was avoided only because Weinert managed to break the tow with his engine's horsepower. It was a dubious charge at best, but Cicero's strategy from the start had been to limit Amoco's responsibility as much as possible, and to spread it around where it couldn't be avoided. Weinert must have appreciated the slur, and ardently wished for a gentlemanly confrontation with his accuser, preferably in some dark back alley in Hamburg.

Mr. Maynard, the admirable Englishman, a man who was clearly in good faith, as honest as he was courageous from the beginning to the end of this affair, may have thought no one could doubt his word about the events of March 16, but, if so, he obviously hadn't reckoned with the relentlessly inquisitive energies of Michael Snyder, the lawyer who argued the case for Bugsier. A graduate of the U.S. Merchant Marine Academy, Snyder had been a man of the sea before turning to law, and his oceangoing experience collaborated with a nimble wit to make an afternoon on the witness stand an experience that for a sailor was roughly akin to steaming through a minefield. Frustrated in his ambition of dining on a main course of Bardari ("the elusive Captain Bardari," he called him, openly suggesting that it was Amoco, and not his lawyers, who had prevented him from coming to testify), Snyder turned his appetite instead toward the devouring of the unsuspecting Mr. Maynard. It turned out to be a banquet that the Englishman is not likely to forget.

Constantly referring back to earlier depositions and his testimony in the Liberian hearing, Snyder wove such a filigree of contradictions and inconsistencies around poor Mr. Maynard's recollection of what had happened and who had said what to whom that by the time it was over he might well have preferred to be back on the bridge of the oilpot off Portsall, where people were nice to him. Reviewing the witness's naval experience, Snyder demonstrated that his knowledge of salvage tugs and towing was minimal in general, and nonexistent for VLCCs, seriously undermined his credibility in judging whether or not *Pacific* had been pulling, and showed the court that from the tanker's bridge in that weather it would have been in any case virtually impossible to make an accurate estimation of just what was going on a thousand feet or so up ahead by the bow. (It was because of Snyder's destruction of Mr. Maynard that the Amoco side was finally driven to concede that *Pa-*

cific had been pulling all along, after all.) Snyder ploughed on until, just a few minutes before it was all over, he brought Maynard to this satisfying exchange:

Q. Now, your overall assessment of the tug is that it did a damned fine job, isn't that right, sir?
A. Yes, sir.

Captain Weinert proved himself to be such a strong and impressive witness that he rarely needed help from his counsel, Snyder. Even Cicero, in spite of his reserves of intelligence and craft, occasionally stumbled when attempting to match maritime knowhow with the German. In Hamburg and Chicago, supporters of the Bugsier cause cheered long and hard after the confrontation when Cicero had Weinert on the witness stand and was laboring to make him admit that he chose to make the first tow connection from the bow without considering all the relevant factors: in other words, that he had been reprehensibly negligent, or incompetent at his work. Illustrating his thesis with a large, hand-drawn chart of the area, Cicero had been suggesting that a tow from the stern would have been the right course of action, and that Weinert was too impetuous or stubborn to have seen that.

"Now, isn't it a fact," Cicero demanded, "that as you approached the Amoco *Cadiz* and undertook that tow, you gave no consideration to various other alternatives, but rather as you approached the Amoco *Cadiz* that day you had already decided that you were going to attempt to turn her head to port?"

"To port?" wondered Weinert, quickly catching what was either an error or a trap. Cicero responded: "Excuse me, to starboard."

At this point Snyder broke in with an objection, but he had hardly spoken his words when the burly Weinert burst out of the witness box, seized the marker with which Cicero had been illustrating the positions of the two vessels, and slashed lines left, right, and center to show what he had known from the start: The only way to tow was from the bow, and to starboard, away from the coast, into the wind.

"Here is Ushant," he said, in an emphatic, rapid-fire delivery of Hamburger English. "Here is the Le Four Channel, and here is Channel de la-Helle. And from here, and the same here, is the shore. From here was only the way to bring the ship this way. I cannot tow him here. Here is low water. Same here. And later here the current here is very hard, going to the Le Four Channel."

Weinert put down the marker and returned to the witness box. There was a long silence. Now it all seemed perfectly clear. Obviously, Weinert had to pull from the bow, and try to turn the tanker to starboard, to the right, into the weather and away from land. Straight was impossible (land dead ahead), to port hardly any better (the geography of the coast brought the land looming up that way, too), and backward from the stern was definitely inadvisable, since boats "shear" when towed from behind, striking off in mad and unpredictable directions—all the more so when they are deprived of their rudders—and put enormous strains on the towing line. When, for the second tow try, Weinert finally did hook up aft, it was only because he had run out of room up front, and the shoals were only minutes away.

Cicero brought up several more points to suggest that Bugsier and Weinert had been rash and unprofessional in handling the rescue, and further, that *Pacific* was an unseaworthy ship equipped with defective material but, faced with the Germanic thoroughness and perfectionism of the entire Bugsier operation, he was clearly breathing heavily in thin atmosphere to make points with Judge McGarr. The fruit of his labors was not always so convincing. It must have been with a sinking feeling that he saw McGarr shake Weinert's hand as he left the room at the end of his testimony. It was evident to everyone present, even the opposing lawyers, that the captain of *Pacific* had deeply impressed the judge.

Cicero's attack against France picked up most of the criticisms that had been leveled against the government in the Senate and National Assembly reports, as well as those of the hundreds of individuals who, in one capacity or another, had felt the need to point out the numerous failings and insufficiencies that could be imputed to the central authority in Paris and all its provincial lackeys. Among the documents he introduced as evidence was the scathing commentary that Maître Christian Huglo had written for the Paris daily *Le Monde* before becoming counsel for the Côtes-du-Nord parties. Cicero's dart was well-chosen in this case, and it plunged deeply beneath the thin skin of the boys in the Agence Judiciare du Trésor, effectively sowing dissension in the ranks of the odd coalition army that was besieging Standard Oil. The Huglo article, directly impugning the government's handling of coastal protection, was perfectly entitled for Standard Oil's purposes: *La Responsabilité de l'Etat*. Its opening sentence could scarcely suit Cicero better: *"Dans l'affaire de l'Amoco Cadiz la responsabilité du proprietaire du navire n'exclut pas celle de l'Etat ..."* ("In the Amoco *Cadiz* affair, the liability of the vessel's owner does not exclude that of the State ...").

Cicero took that ball and ran with it, making good yardage. Around the Agence Judiciare du Trésor the functionaries seethed and stuck pins in little Christian Huglo dolls. France's conduct was negligent, Cicero argued, in failing to prevent the shipwreck in the first place, and then in bungling the cleanup job so badly that the oil spill took on disastrous proportions. One after another, he pressed his points forward, as pitilessly and inevitably as the tides, always following the strategy of spreading the liability around: The French government knew of the risks posed by the endless parade of tankers in the Channel, publicly undertook to parry them, but failed in its duty and did nothing to stop the grounding; by refusing to use modern dispersants on the slick, France caused an extension far wider than would have happened otherwise; by failing to identify and prepare plans and matériel for safeguarding especially sensitive areas, the oyster beds of the Abers and the bay of Morlaix became polluted; and the cleanup effort on land was botched through use of destructive and ill-advised techniques, such as the bulldozers that scraped away the flora of the salt marshes of Ile Grande.

"They come and rape us and then try to tell us afterward that it was our fault because we were too good looking," grumbled an indignant Breton who followed the trial's progress. "It's indecent."

France, the Côtes-du-Nord, Bugsier, and Petroleum Insurance Limited answered Cicero most devastatingly with the fruit of their years of culling through the documents of discovery. What they found was very, very strong—infinitely more so than any evidence that had emerged against Amoco from the Liberian hearing. Now, as the trial ran its course and the main players began laying down their cards, it seemed less and less certain that the explanation of the grounding lay in Astilleros Espanoles' original sin of providing Amoco with a flawed steering system. As the plot thickened, the gaze of the observer was now led away from the Spanish builders and the butler, Pasquale, and brought upstairs, to the private quarters of the lord of the manor, inside the great, white, eighty-story chateau on East Randolph Drive. And there, it was not only dirty underwear that appeared, but certain embarrassingly quirky habits of Lord Amoco, as well. His Lordship, it turned out, was vain, proud, authoritarian, acquisitive, venal, and parsimonious. He was immensely rich, but he had certain, ah, *péchés mignons.* He liked young ships, but he could be downright avaricious when it came to spending money to keep them in style. Whodunnit? Maybe it was His Lordship, after all.

The charges against Amoco followed the same path: Amoco had inspectors on-site during the construction of the four ships of the *Cadiz* series, and they allowed several gross errors to pass; all four ships of the series showed serious steering-gear problems from the start, defects that required drydocking and remachining, but these defects were not properly corrected, because doing so would have cost money; this shortsighted policy of delaying necessary repairs was most especially conspicuous with the Amoco *Singapore* and Amoco *Cadiz,* the two vessels on time charter to Shell International Petroleum Company for $28,000 per day; the various crews of Amoco *Cadiz* maintained the steering gear in a manner so shoddy that they caused the system to break. In short, then: Amoco *Cadiz* was unseaworthy, Amoco knew it was unseaworthy, but even so the company tolerated and even encouraged maintenance practices that directly caused the shipwreck—in the sole interest of saving money.

Of the three attacking claimants, it was Joseph Smith, of the New York law firm Burlingham, Underwood & Lord, arguing for PIL, who made the most concisely convincing case against Standard and its various offspring. His posttrial brief, the document in which he summed up his main arguments for the judge, although only sixty-three pages long, was a textbook model of a well-researched indictment.

Smith began at the beginning: The four tankers, identified as hulls 93, 94, 95, and 96, were named, in order of their building, Amoco *Milford Haven,* Amoco *Singapore,* Amoco *Cadiz,* and Amoco *Europa,* and were put together in Cadiz under the supervision of both ABS and Amoco's own inspectors, who maintained an office at the shipyards. On January 27, 1971, Shell entered into a time-charter arrangement with Amoco for *Milford Haven* and *Singapore* for a five-year period beginning with delivery from the shipyard in 1973. Even before delivery to Amoco, Smith pointed out, steering-gear trouble announced itself aboard both ships: The hydraulic cylinders leaked, and the rams were scored, that is, scratched along their smooth silvery surfaces. During *Milford Haven's* sea trials, oil leaks were apparent to both ABS and Amoco inspectors, and an Amoco naval architect concluded that the master lube oil tank, feeding the gravity tank above the system, was too small. Likewise, the gravity tank—a commodious reserve for hydraulic oil—had no low-level alarm. Below, among the machinery of the steering motor itself, the oil-draining pumps worked badly because the belts driving them slipped and the main rams, pumps had a tendency to overheat. As a result of these observations, Amoco authorized the builder to install 1,500-liter lube-oil storage tanks on hulls 94, 95, and 96, as reserve supplies to compensate for the high rate of leakage from the hydraulic systems.

Scarcely had the second tanker, Amoco *Singapore,* returned from its sea trials, before delivery to the buyer, than its steering gear was removed because, as with *Milford Haven,* its rams were heavily scored. To fill this hole, the steering system that had been earmarked for *Cadiz* was rushed into *Singapore,* and *Cadiz* inherited the gear that had been meant for the last boat, *Europa.* (The logic of this game of musical chairs continued throughout the series, and *Europa* eventually inherited the rebuilt gear that had been removed from *Singapore.*) As early as the spring of 1974, Amoco engineers expressed concern about the bothersome tendency of the rudders of the VLCCs to swing around in port, when the pumps were shut down. An inspector recommended a careful check of the safety valves and to purge the steering system of air. Already then, before the ships had begun carrying oil, there was talk of air entering the steering systems.

Milford Haven, the first hull delivered, performed so badly that Amoco laid it up for lengthy repairs and substituted *Cadiz* in its place. *Cadiz* went on sea trials in May of 1974, and experienced the same ram-scoring problems as her predecessors, *Milford Haven* and *Singapore.* (The cause of these repeated scorings seems laughably simple, even to a layman: The steel rams were grasped, at their point of exit from the cylinders, by bushings made of cast iron. Cast iron being harder than the steel of the rams, small protuberances or iron slivers on the bushings scratched the rams as they slid in and out of the cylinders. With time, tiny scratches became deep scorings, longitudinal channels running the length of the rams. Naturally, oil can escape from such orifices, and air can be drawn in. At length, the scoring problem was solved on *Milford Haven* and *Europa,* the two ships that remained with Amoco while the other two were chartered out, by the straightforward expedient of substituting bronze bushings for the cast-iron ones. Bronze is softer than steel, so the new bushings could not cut the rams. Even so, when Amoco *Cadiz* sailed on her last run from the Persian Gulf, she still had the old cast-iron bushings and the leaky rams.) On her first time out for the company, an Amoco engineering coordinator sent a memo to Captain Phillips with some gloomy news: *Cadiz* had "experienced more major failures on her trial and maiden voyage than the *Singapore* did," and the first on the list of failures was steering-gear rams.

That was just the beginning of the black comedy whose plot Smith played out for the judge. Already, *Cadiz* was looking like the proverbial lemon that irate car owners try to send back to the factory for repair or replacement. Shortly before *Cadiz*'s maiden voyage, while undergoing tests off Lisbon, her rudder stuck fast in the hard astarboard position, and a month later, in mid-June of 1974, the same thing happened again. In July of 1974, Amoco officially notified the builders that they would not accept *Europa,* the last of the series, until her steering gear—the very one that had been lifted out of *Singapore*—had been made sound. It was fixed by the switch from cast-iron to bronze bushings. In October of 1974, *Milford Haven* underwent the same operation. Thus, both of the tankers that Amoco had in service for its own use were made safer than the pair that was rented out to Shell.

In December 1974 and January 1975, *Singapore* had problems with her steering-gear pumps but continued on to her load port with only one pump operating—a clear violation of ABS safety rules. Why? Presumably for the same reason that kept both of the chartered tankers on the go almost permanently: Stopping for repairs meant "down time," immobilization that lost the company $28,000 a day. Amoco teams scrambled to find the underlying causes for the unsatisfactory performance of the steering systems, and theorized that dirt might have clogged oil filters, and that drainage pumps might be driven inefficiently by slipping belts. The problem of dirt and impurities working their way into steering systems—dirt and grit are mortal enemies of all hydraulic systems—was first evoked for Amoco *Cadiz* in mid-January of 1975, when an inspector reported that conditions in the steering flat were always bad, and made worse by leaking overhead steam pipes: Hydraulic machinery doesn't like rust, either.

In March, the same inspector reported that the scoring of *Cadiz*'s rams had worsened over the preceding three months, and that the portside forward ram was in really bad condition. On the last day of that same month, an electric motor that drove one of

Cadiz's steering-gear pumps failed. Not having a backup motor to cut in instantly, the crew sent the motor ashore to Cape Town, South Africa, for repair, with the understanding that it would be airfreighted for pickup in Dubai. By continuing on to the Persian Gulf with only one pump-motor set operable (which meant no emergency backup), the tanker was in violation of ABS rules. In June, Amoco advised Astilleros Espanoles in a memo dealing with guarantee items that "present rams are scored and cause rapid packing wear and leak oil excessively, resulting in excessive cleaning and expenditure for replacement oil. Repair satisfactorily or replace."

In September, another Amoco inspector reported that *Cadiz*'s steering system was leaking oil, and that the rams were not in good shape. By the beginning of 1976, Captain Phillips had been advised that Shell was pressing for a drydocking and overhaul of the two ships it was renting, in order to ensure that they continue to give safe and efficient service. Drydocking and repair costs are paid by ships' owners, not the charterers. A schedule was set up: *Cadiz* would be brought in for drydocking after her eighth voyage, in March or April.

Late in January of 1976, an Amoco ship superintendent named Robert J. Zimmerman flew to Dubai to join the ship for an onboard inspection while she was on her way up the Persian Gulf for loading. His report, dredged up through discovery, was revelatory in many ways: the constant, pervading presence of the long strings of company authority; the pressure for economies of all sorts (Zimmerman pointedly explained that the limousine he took from Philadelphia to New York was cheaper than a plane); the human tensions and clashes among the crew; and, most tellingly, the prevailing attitude toward down time and repairs, as obvious with him as it was with Bardari's gun-shy approach to the dreaded, expensive LOF. Flying from New York to London, Zimmerman arrived in the middle of the night in Dubai on January 27, and met the next evening with Captain Bardari, who was to be relief master on this trip. Bardari was obviously distraught, having personal problems, and the poignancy of his situation showed through the bureaucratic language:

1800–2000 with Captain Bardari, 1/AE, 2/AE, 2/0, discussing CADIZ in general. Bardari just lost mother in sudden death and has very ill wife; mentally not in good shape to take over as master as well as youth. Will watch his conduct on board to determine possible recommendation for Cape Town relief.

Zimmerman boarded the ship the next morning while it was underway at eleven knots and immediately met with the master, Captain Fedele, like Bardari an Italian. In spite of his liking and respect for Captain Fedele, Zimmerman found much that was wanting aboard his command, and could not help noticing, that day and afterward, that there was a certain amount of conflict within the crew.

1200–On bridge with Captain Fedele. No immediate problems. No remaining unhappy people. Appears R/O [relief officer] getting off very unhappy but general crew morale excellent. C/E [chief engineer] Frazzita getting along excellently with Captain Fedele and C/O [chief officer] indicates has happy home.

1320–1800–General inspection of vessel with C/E Frazzita, Captain Fedele/Captain Bardari and C/O. Main deck pipelines and forward 50% main deck fresh paint. Steam lines no corrosion master treatment. Captain Bardari promised this trip. No leaks noted and Engine Department made up fabricated expansion joints on deck line, one more to do. 956201 on Item 6 on AS 1/2/76 listing of guarantees satisfied, take money credit, no work outstanding. Deck storerooms not good. Many open cans of paint. Foam Room, safety equipment and pumprooms fair.

Engine storerooms fair, steering gear fair. Definite decline in cleanliness in last three months all over but Engine Room and top of fidley near inert gas installation especially.

Zimmerman continued in this technical vein throughout most of his report, in a tone that left the impression of a vessel that was barely acceptable. Indeed, a few pages later he came out and said it: "General condition fair but certainly declining by *Cadiz* previous standard." The food aboard was less good than on the other "Italian" ships of the Amoco fleet, and he was struck by an assistant engineer who would not eat when the master or the chief engineer was in the mess room.

Another tour with Bardari, Fedele, and the chief engineer the following day, confirming his earlier impressions, gives us a few graphic glimpses of life aboard a VLCC:

General condition disappointing. Deck painting progressing well but lubrication not good as before. Galley and pantries and steward storerooms very dirty. Blood dried on deck and bulkhead of butcher shop and many open tins and containers of used food in every area. Noted this ship feeds the same vegetable greens (peas, string beans, brussel sprouts, etc.) for both lunch and dinner indicating Steward is cooking only once a day and leftovers are a large part of each meal. I wonder what comparable costs are here against the SINGAPORE or MILFORD HAVEN where food is good.

By that evening, moored to the huge man-made island, they had completed taking on cargo, but high winds and a thunderstorm prevented the ship from proceeding onward with the journey. At five o'clock the next morning, with the storm still blowing twenty-five-knot winds and eight-foot rollers against the ship, Amoco *Cadiz* could not move away from the sea island, even though she had her own engine and five tugs pulling. If ever a captain needed an object lesson in the fantastic, unmaneuverable mass of a VLCC, the storm gave it that day. It was scarcely any wonder, then, that *Pacific* labored in vain to turn the tanker two years later. What is surprising was that Captain Bardari and Mr. Maynard, caught in a storm far worse than this blow on the gulf, should have assumed *Pacific* was able to do the job and was only going through a cruel charade of pulling and letting go, in order to force LOF. Unhappily for all concerned, that was no charade.

With moderating weather, the tugs finally freed *Cadiz,* and as she moved down the channel to the open gulf, Zimmerman continued his inspection, spending a couple of hours discussing technicalities with the ship's electrician. Then he came to have a look at the steering gear. His report on this aspect of the ship's equipment furnished Amoco's opponents with one of their finest and most telling points, one that hurt cruelly as it was placed into evidence. After describing the performance of the electric motors that drove the pumps, he came to matters more pertinent—the old, familiar problem of the unsatisfactory hydraulic system:

Rams leakage is quite high and believe should repack glands in yard. Will write item to do so. Rams are deeply scarred and will continue to cut pitting, but oil loss cost against extended time required to carry out the replacement of bushes [bushings] and the required polishing is not mentioned in Guarantee List of January 2,

1976, Item 3. I recommend that we take cash credit and defer repair until some extended availability period after charter expires.

There it was, the perfect reflection of what France, Shell, and Côtes-du-Nord had seized upon as the cornerstone of their attacks: Amoco, in its obsessive insistence on keeping the chartered ships in service, gambled with their safety in the hope that they would keep going until the repairs could be effected after the charter period, when they were no longer earning $28,000 a day. It was a terrible charge, and an effective one. There would be more examples of this same attitude, as the three attacking litigants did not fail to point out. The upshot of it all was that *Cadiz* never did get the bronze bushings, the repacking, or the rams polishing that she needed.

On March 10, 1976, Amoco received a bid from the Lisnave Shipyards in Lisbon for the April drydocking. The total of $220,290 included a long list of repairs and rectifications, but several "extra items" had been taken off the final list. Among them was the one for steering-gear packing renewal. The reason for this cancellation was that such major steering-gear repairs would have required two crews to work for fourteen days, while Amoco insisted that the drydock-ing—off-hire time—be completed in just eight working days. As a result, the tanker sailed from Lisnave in April with the same old cast-iron bushings and the same ram packing without having the rams machined or polished and without the steering-gear pumps being opened for internal inspection. As Zimmerman had so rightly written, the cost of replacing the oil that leaked from the hydraulic system was minimal compared to an extended drydocking. Effi-ciently managed and cost-effective, the big oilpot went back on the Gulf run.

Over the next year or so, Amoco experts reported several ab-normal symptoms of steering-gear behavior: overflows of oil from the gravity tank, distribution-block valves that were possibly leak-ing, improperly functioning pumps, low oil pressure in the rams, and uncontrolled rudder movement while the ship was moored in port. The symptoms were worrisome enough for the company to engage an independent hydraulics expert to come aboard and in-spect the system. He recommended that the distribution blocks be taken from the VLCCs and their valves carefully checked. This, of course, would immobilize the ships. His suggestion was rejected.

In May 1977, Chester J. Bysarovich, Director of Marine Engineering, reviewed for Captain Phillips the problems that had plagued all four VLCCs, recognized that their efficiency record had been poor, but pointed out that a policy of making many repairs during voyages had prevented major stoppages. He further suggested that *Milford Haven* and *Europa,* working on Amoco's account in a low market, could be taken out of service for full-scale repairs and upgrading of equipment, including modifications of the steering systems. Subsequent to his recommendations, in August, *Europa* went to a shipyard in Singapore for extensive work. In December, *Milford Haven* did the same. Not *Cadiz* and *Singapore,* however; they remained on the Gulf run.

As *Europa* was receiving her proper going-over in drydock, Bysarovich sent a memo to Captain Phillips that was even more forthright than Zimmerman had been about the pervading concern for economy and cost efficiency. This memo, dated August 23, 1977, was probably the most compromising document unearthed through discovery:

C. D. Phillips
Mail Code 5006
1978 Goal
The primary goal for 1978 is to keep the AMOCO CADIZ and the AMOCO SINGAPORE operating without any down time that would put these two chartered-out vessels offhire. These two vessels will not be scheduled for their drydockings and biennial repair period until the expiration of the charters. This will mean doing various surveys during cargo operations.

The charter hire of $28,000 per day per vessel multiplied by the estimated time in the shipyard of 30 days per vessel is equal to $1,680,000 of incoming money that otherwise would not be realized.

In September, Captain Phillips showed that he had taken cognizance of Bysarovich's recommendations with a handwritten addendum: "Very good! Hope we can reach this goal."

Bysarovich himself had an addendum to his note about the 1978 goal:

AMOCO CADIZ
This vessel normally should be scheduled for drydocking in April 1978. The charter expires in June 1978. An extension of certificates

will be requested until August 1978 depending upon the vessel's schedule. Drydocking will be scheduled accordingly.

On the same day that he received this information from Bysarovich, Phillips passed the good word on to his boss, Rinkema, in a similarly upbeat memo:

1978 Goals
The cost reduction goals for Marine Operations during 1978 follow. The total goal of $1,980,000 should be attainable in 1978.

3. Extend the period between shipyarding the M/T AMOCO CADIZ and M/T AMOCO SINGAPORE until after the Shell charter has expired. This will eliminate loss of revenue of $1,680,000.

Aboard ship, out in the real world, where weather and sea rarely consent to follow the graphs and curves of business offices, the difficulties continued. In September and October of 1977, two Amoco inspectors visited *Cadiz* and found the same problems that Bysarovich had written about. *Milford Haven,* one of the two "company" ships, looked to be in even worse shape: in November her starboard steering-gear pump failed while at sea, and then, during sea trials directly after her major overhaul in December, it happened again. While the replacement parts were on order, for pickup in Dubai, the tanker plodded on down to the Persian Gulf with only the port pump set working. Again, this was a violation of ABS rules, but it was becoming a habit by then.

Milford Haven's pump casing was found to contain metallic particles. Since this was obviously related to the two failures, Chicago sent messages to the three other VLCCs of the series, instructing the masters to have the steering-pump oil sumps opened up and cleaned, and to report back to Chicago on the results. *Cadiz* acknowledged the message, but said the instructions were not understood. Consequently, they were never carried out. In January of 1978, Bysarovich brought aboard *Singapore* a technician from the German manufacturer of the steering-gear pumps. He found one to be normal and the other damaged, for unknown reasons. Bysarovich then sent an Amoco engineer to Dubai to board *Milford Haven* and install new parts for the broken starboard pump. It stubbornly refused to work right, and the pump was eventually set right by a manufacturer's representative in Genoa. The Amoco engineer was in the Persian Gulf area as *Cadiz* loaded up for what was to be her last earthly voyage, but he was otherwise occupied, and never got the chance to board her and inspect her pumps, as he had been scheduled to do.

Sea Voyage Abstracts of Amoco *Cadiz* showed that during the month of February 1978, her steering gear had been leaking an average of more than twelve liters of oil per day. (Normal leakage for such a system is around a liter a week.) Clearly, something was wrong. Even if there had not been such a long history of previous troubles, this rate of leakage—ironically, heavy enough to cause concern for the cost of replacement oil—would have been a warning to the most obtuse of observers. Captain Phillips was far from obtuse. He instructed Bruno Pillepich, an Amoco engineering inspector, to board the tanker around March 10, as she passed off Las Palmas, to investigate the reasons for the excessive leakage, and to see about an overhaul of the starboard pump. Bad luck: Pillepich missed the rendezvous at Las Palmas, and only Assante, Franca Strano, and Mr. Maynard made it. Pillepich flew to London and took a train to Brixham, England, in order to board the ship when she arrived at Lyme Bay. She never arrived, and he never had the chance to see what it was that was wrong with her steering gear.

Men Goulven and the other rock formations off Portsall finally made it all academic, but for the sake of history we can add here that Amoco *Cadiz* originally had been scheduled for drydocking in April of 1978—but that date was pushed back until August. Why? Because the Shell charter expired in June, and no one wanted to lay up a money earner while it was on charter. As it turned out, June was the month in which Rinkema, sobered by the *Cadiz* disaster, ordered the three remaining Amoco VLCCs laid up to have their steering gears modified and strengthened. Cost of the operation: $960,000. Pity no one thought of it sooner.

In summing up its doleful litany of Amoco's multiple malfeasances, Smith's PIL posttrial brief leaves the enumeration of detail behind to offer a generalized indictment that is the stuff of which headlines are made:

> Amoco was aware of the combined design/materials defect in the steering gear ram cylinder bushings. Amoco insisted that the bushings for EUROPA be changed prior to delivery. Amoco insisted that the builder pay for and install bronze bushings on MILFORD HAVEN during the guarantee drydocking. Amoco did not change the bushings on SINGAPORE and AMOCO CADIZ, the two ves-

sels chartered to Shell. The obvious explanation for this delay is the fact that both vessels were under charter to Shell and were providing considerable revenues to Amoco.

A few pages later, the final paragraph of the indictment comes as close to eloquence as a legal document can come:

> Amoco stopped VLCCs during voyages or at loading or discharge ports to make repairs. No reason can be offered by Amoco for not making the repairs and modifications when repairs could have, and should have, been made, except to avoid losing the charter hire. Amoco pushed its luck, gambling that AMOCO CADIZ's steering gear would hold together until after the charter had expired. Amoco lost.

If, in the Liberian inquiry, the various design and construction defects of the Manises steering gear—the differences between working pressures and relief valve settings, the absence of redundancy when running in the one-pump mode, the undersized studs, the too-weak, flatted flanges—were authoritatively demonstrated, the mechanics of the breakdown itself remained a question mark. Having none of the discovery material on hand, the Liberian investigators were reduced to broad supposition when it came to explaining precisely how it all happened. Not so in Chicago. There, everyone had a finely detailed and convincingly argued exegesis of the scripture of hydraulics to offer Judge McGarr. These presentations fell into two categories: the voids theory and the low-cycle fatigue theory. The first one, espoused by France, PIL, and Côtes-du-Nord, showed that the blame lay with Amoco. Hardly more than a passing thought went to Astilleros Espanoles, except to dispute Amoco's claim for exoneration through fault of the builder. (By refusing to show up at the trial, Astilleros thoughtfully obviated the need for anyone to attack them, once McGarr had rendered his default judgment.) The second theory, argued by Cicero, absolved Amoco and awarded the cause of the blowout entirely to the builders: "No fault by the Amoco parties had any causal relationship to the steering gear failure."

Now, then: Without wandering too far into the sloughs of technicality, it is possible to sum up both explanations in terms that are within the grasp of laymen. The voids theory relies on the fact that hydraulic systems are akin to racehorses or beach-strutting muscle men: They can deliver enormous power, but they are notoriously susceptible if they are not treated just right. High-pressure hydraulic systems may not suffer from colic or hurt feelings, but they need very careful attention, and in particular, they have to be kept very clean. Dirt and grit entering pumps, piping, and cylinders can cause undue wear, stoppages, and backups of the oil supply, and a hydraulic system trying to work without the right amount of oil in the right places overheats and overloads and becomes dangerously inefficient. There is worse: Dirt and grit can allow air to enter the closed circuits. And air, as the four engineers astraddle the rams discovered that Thursday morning off Ouessant, is the mortal enemy of hydraulics. If enough air gets into a four-ram steering system, voids—air bubbles, if you like—can develop inside the piping. Normally, what should happen when a big wave comes along to bully the rudder is that the clever Spanish machine, completely filled with fluid and therefore protected by the incompressibility of oil, immediately reacts by pumping a countervailing thrust of oil pressure back against the force, neutralizing it. But if there is an air bubble in the lines, the protection by oil's incompressibility is briefly lost, and the titanic shove of the wave sends a blast of pressure against the rudder and rudder shaft, which in turn imparts it to the rudder stock, against the rams, and then into the piping, making a fist of accumulated energy traveling in one great, single surge. Blam! When the surge reaches the weak spot of the undersized, flatted flange, held to the distribution block by undersized bolts, the whole damn thing goes blooey, and the Manises begins bleeding to death.

All right, then: How would the voids have occurred within the piping network? In the answer to that question lay the whole force of the arguments of negligence imputed to Amoco. This was the reason why PIL, France, and Côtes-du-Nord pounced on the same documents unearthed through discovery and presented similar arguments based on them. The voids came about, they all maintained, because of precisely what we have seen in the past few pages: Amoco's money-saving obsession of keeping faulty boats running because they were chartered out, delaying drydockings, and canceling necessary repairs on these money-spinners while carrying them out on the other two ships.

Further—and this was of equal importance to the anti-Amoco arguments—the claimants were able to show that the on-board engineering personnel failed to carry out the instructions of the steering-gear manufacturer in regard to the cleanliness of the system: In all the years since delivery, the oil in the Manises had never been changed and never tested for cleanliness (the dreaded intrusion of particulate matter), and the various oil filters in the system had never been cleaned, changed, or inspected. To return to our equine analogy, this was like feeding a thoroughbred on garbage, stabling it in its own filth, and then expecting it to win races. What happened—probably happened, at any rate, and the claimants made it sound frighteningly plausible—was a cumulative bungle by Amoco, in which numerous corner-cuttings, postponements, and expediencies for the sake of saving money, allied with the normal human quotient of complacency and procrastination, added up to a steering gear that lay on the knife edge of disaster, and was just awaiting the right wave to come along and push it over. Look at the way this argument builds toward the disaster.

From the start, Amoco knew that the Manises gear was a problem, and a heavy leaker of oil. The cast-iron bushings began scoring the rams as soon as the ship began steering, and through the apertures of scoring, air could enter the system. Minute iron particles from the scored rams washed back and forth throughout the system, precipitating down to the filters, which became clogged. Clogged filters in turn impeded the flow of oil at critical moments, especially in the famous number 9 valve, through which replacement oil was supposed to flow from the gravity tank, most importantly when the engineers were trying to purge air and get fresh oil back into the rams. The small pumps whose duty was to recirculate oil up to the gravity tanks were driven by an old-fashioned system of leather belts, instead of chains or gears. The belts slipped, making the pumps work badly, the consequence of which was that on one side they weren't delivering enough oil and on the other side unpumped oil was backing up, causing problems with the main rams' pumps. Engineering crews filled the gravity tank with fresh oil by the medieval expedient of a step ladder and a bucket, thus allowing many opportunities for air and impurities to enter the system. In sum, the claimants' argument ran, the system was contaminated by a steadily rising rate of impurities, which was reflected by the steadily rising rate of oil leakage. Oil leakage out meant that air could get in, through the same places. And air inside caused the voids, which caused the flange to go blooey.

Not at all, responded Cicero, not at all. The claimants pored over hundreds of thousands of documents to find just a few hints of minor peccadillos. In reality, Amoco *Cadiz* was properly manned and well maintained. What happened was low-cycle fatigue, and that was all the fault of Astilleros Espanoles.

Cicero's explanation postulated a failure of the studs not through a single blast of pressure, as with the voids theory, but through many thousands of repeated oscillations of pressure, caused by the chattering of improperly designed relief valves, within a system that was fully filled with oil and contained no air bubbles. His adversaries calculated that the wave that slapped the Manises down would have had to be sixty feet high (which, they insisted, they were not that day) in order for Cicero's chain of events to be plausible, but just as his opponents had presented for their theories, he trotted out his rented experts to testify for his.

The voids-versus-fatigue controversy caused the greatest and angriest showers of sparks of contention, because it was the crux of the trial. A finding by McGarr for voids, everyone knew, was virtually certain to cost Amoco millions upon millions of dollars, because it would mean that the breakdown was, in all likelihood, the result of bad maintenance and delayed repairs. If he found low-cycle fatigue more plausible, most of the hopes of the sullied Bretons would have been dashed. So bitter did the clash of theories become that Kingham, in the papers he filed with McGarr, did not hesitate to call one of Cicero's principal scientific witnesses a liar. It was an unusual move, considering the decorum that ordinarily reigns in American courtrooms, but the stakes were high in Chicago, and the personal involvement intense. Many professional reputations were put on the line in the Amoco *Cadiz* lawsuit.

On the question of jurisprudence and corporate responsibility, the attacking parties were hardly any gentler with Standard Oil's sensibilities than they had been on the technical side. Inevitably, they got around to the baffling thicket of company names and addresses and places of business through which the profits of the oilpot navigated, as skillfully as legal departments could devise, all the while avoiding taxes and responsibility to the maximum. Contemptuously dismissing the legalistic fabrication of "dummy corporations" and mere "paper entities," the claimants aimed straight at Standard Oil of Indiana, which was, as Kingham put it, "intimately involved with the Amoco *Cadiz* from cradle to grave." The Côtes-du-Nord brief echoed a common charge in maintaining that "Standard is liable as the entity which controlled all others in its corporate family, manipulating them solely for its own benefit," and that it "exercised control over the purchase, design, construction and operation of the Amoco *Cadiz* itself." The tanker's grounding, then, Kingham reasoned, must be every bit as imputable to Standard Oil as its birth and day-to-day life. "Standard cannot avoid this liability by seeking refuge behind the hollow shells of its subsidiaries."

Poring over discovery's documentation and then questioning various Standard Oil officers, the claimants brought to light a corporate fantasy world in which supposed meetings of purported corporations had been invented of a piece by Amoco lawyers, most notably by Randall T. Clair, the legal department advisor who, notebook in hand, had shared the long hours of the breakdown and the grounding with Captain Phillips. One particularly curious detail brought to light was that at the time of the supposed sale of the ship by one of the corporate entities (Amoco Tankers) to another (Amoco Transport), the first company did not even exist, and the Amoco employees who were listed as being its officers could not recollect having participated in any of the meetings of its board of directors. (Nor does it exist today, for that matter. Amoco Tankers' short but happy corporate life has been terminated.) It was, decidedly, an odd kind of wonderland that had evolved over the years as Standard Oil pursued its activities of buying oil in one place and selling it in another.

Amoco Transport, on the other hand, at least had the merit of existing at the time of the sale, the claimants admitted, but it was a fragile life, indeed, purely on paper and entirely as a vassal to International. Of course, this was exactly the opposite of what Cicero contended. According to him, International was only an agent of Transport, a kind of servant, because there was a "consulting agreement" between them, by which International agreed to render services to Transport. Stuff and nonsense, retorted France, PIL, and Côtes-du-Nord in three-part harmony—how can a company be the servant of its subsidiary? This is nothing more than a game of shuffled papers. "The apparent sole purpose of Transport," wrote Kingham with cruel lucidity, "was to hold title to Standard's international fleet." The same conclusions, but even stronger, were presented by the lawyers for France, who demonstrated that every aspect of the management of Amoco *Cadiz* was handled directly by International, and that Cicero's claims of independence for Transport were mere "window dressing" by the agile and omnipresent legal advisor Clair.

True to the conventional stereotypes of national images, the

Americans who leveled accusations against Amoco were audacious where the English authors of the Liberian report had been reserved, summing up their arguments with a gusto that would have pleased the original Cicero, but that fell somewhat less sweetly upon the ears of his contemporary Midwestern homonym. Perhaps the most convincing with this manner of verbal artillery barrage was Benjamin E. Haller, writing on behalf of the French Republic in his posttrial brief:

> The evidence is overwhelming that the culpable conduct of Standard and AOIC was centered almost exclusively in Chicago. Standard's decision to build the vessel took place in Chicago. Contract negotiations with Astilleros Espanoles, S.A., took place in New York and Chicago. The financing of the vessel was arranged in the United States. During construction, the main blueprints of the vessel, including the steering system and the bow chock, were sent back to Chicago to be reviewed and approved by AOIC. These plans were approved in Chicago. Maintenance of the AMOCO CADIZ was controlled by Claude Phillips, a citizen of Illinois, and by the AOIC marine engineering group which was situated in Chicago. The decision not to change known defective components of the steering gear system was made in Chicago. Decisions to defer drydocking of the vessel were made and approved in Chicago. The policy which sacrificed sound maintenance for higher profit with regard to the vessels chartered to Shell, including the AMOCO CADIZ, was made in Chicago and carried out by the Chicago-based ship superintendents when visiting the vessels. AOIC's inadequate contingency plans and operations manual were formulated in Chicago. The improper selection and training of the Master and crew originated in Chicago and was in the hands of the Chicago personnel whose neglect left the crew inadequately trained.
>
> Perhaps most importantly, Chicago was the center of activity on the morning of March 16, 1978, when Phillips, Clair, counsel for Standard, and others, who were in contact with the AMOCO CADIZ and with the principals of the tug PACIFIC usurped the Master's authority and negotiated the terms of salvage.

When in the spring of 1983 the arguments were finished and all the parties involved in the case had submitted their posttrial papers to Judge McGarr for his long study before deciding upon a verdict, it was obvious that Amoco had come away from the trial suffering.

In spite of Cicero's ferocious wizardry, the succession of attacks from France, Côtes-du-Nord, PIL, and Bugsier had landed many telling blows. Certainly the maritime trial of the century had cost a fortune—several fortunes, in fact, more than the combined values of the Amoco *Cadiz* and its cargo and its crew's payroll for several years—but it was not without result: Standard Oil of Indiana finished this first part of the trial with a diminished stature and a reputation as sullied as the Breton coast had been in 1978. Business is business, to be sure, but when corporate convenience eclipses fundamental notions of responsibility, when expediency overwhelms simple common sense, something has to be wrong.

But would the judge see it that way? And to whom would he assign the guilt? Such was the anguished speculation searing the bosoms of the dozens of principal lawyers directly involved with the case, despite their poker-face facades. Between May 9, 1983, and April 18, 1984, Judge McGarr went into the long, lonely hibernation that everyone knew would ensue once the last arguments had been argued and the posttrial briefs filed in defense of each side's interests. Or perhaps it would be more correct to liken the judge's withdrawal from the world to a period of digestion, like a boa constrictor who has swallowed a pig or a calf or some other improbably oversized beast. In his case, though, the animal was paper: the tons of evidence, exhibits, and documentation of all sorts behind this longest, most complex, expensive, and potentially significant of maritime proceedings.

For nearly a year, then, the interested parties busied themselves with other things—in France the matter of beginning to assess and document the full amount of the pollution damage became a fulltime occupation—and waited for McGarr to give birth. It's got to come by the end of the year, the optimists assured themselves, but 1983 turned into 1984 without the least hint of a solution. Well, then, the same voices speculated hopefully, he is a man of anniversaries and symbolic gestures, so he's probably waiting for the sixth anniversary of the grounding to announce his verdict. Bad luck: March 16, 1984, came and went, and McGarr remained just as Sphinx-like as ever. After that, everyone involved with the case was reduced to waiting. At last it happened: On April 18, 1984, Judge McGarr convoked the principal lawyers to his chambers in the Dirksen Building. At nine o'clock that morning, Cicero, Kingham, Haller, Smith, and Snyder filed solemnly past McGarr's secretaries into the inner sanctum where he had labored for so long. Each man was handed a thick document, 111 pages long. The 112th page was stapled to the front, like a preface. In fifteen brief lines, it told the whole story. A summary of the summary, the gist of the judge's findings, was contained in two stark sentences:

> The French claimants and PIL are entitled to the full extent of their incurred damages against Standard, AIOC and Transport, which latter defendants are jointly and severally liable therefor.

> All claims against Bugsier are denied.

So there it was. Six years after he had reluctantly presided over his own shipwreck, Pasquale Bardari had perhaps been able to tuck away into some remote corner of memory the horror and fear of his struggle with the sea, but now the full weight of the responsibility that he had borne on his shoulders was being recalled with cruel clarity. More important, though, was McGarr's reminder about the central fact concerning this responsibility: that he had never been given the authority to back it up. It was this, the distant hand of control from Chicago in all matters concerning the Amoco *Cadiz,* that made the French victory virtually total, and Cicero's defeat very like a legal Waterloo.

By absolving Bugsier one hundred percent of any share in the guilt for the shipwreck, McGarr was, in effect, making a pronouncement: that he had decided who had been lying and who had been telling the truth in the two different versions of the events six years earlier. Captain Weinert's honor and Bugsier's treasury, then, were comforted at the same time. Michael Snyder, the lawyer who had championed them both, could not have dreamed of a success more complete. Soon after returning to his office, he made a long, crackly radiotelephone call via satellite to Captain Weinert, who was in the middle of the Pacific Ocean, at work as usual, pulling a barge over the briny deep. At long last, the myth of the rapacious bounty hunter, so favored by the French press, had been laid to rest.

Christian Huglo learned the good news by telephone also, when an exultant Kingham rang directly from the Dirksen Building. With the difference in time zones, 9:15 A.M. in Chicago translated into 5:15 P.M. in Paris. Sweet numbers for Huglo. He experienced one of those rare moments of professional elation when everything is going just right, and then it was back to business: The news was embargoed for an additional forty-five minutes in order for McGarr to be able to make his announcement first, to the press in Chicago. It was at 1835 Paris time, then, that Huglo emerged from his office to confront the reporters, cameramen, and photographers milling about in his entryway. An hour and a half later he was appearing on the prime-time eight o'clock news, outlining McGarr's decision and diplomatically giving the politicians credit for the work that he, Kingham, and Wolrich had accomplished.

McGarr divided his decision into two sections. The first, ninety-nine pages long, entitled Findings of Fact, was devoted to a minute accounting of everything that occurred on the day of the shipwreck, as well as peripheral events of significance before and after. If ever anyone had doubted the judge's understanding of the redoubtable mass of technical detail involved with the case, the doubt was dispelled with this presentation. Beginning with a description of the complex legal proceedings that had occupied him throughout the preceding years, he went on to describe the history of the design, construction, and certification of the ship, its delivery to Amoco, and its early operational history. The storm, the breakdown, and the two towing attempts were covered in twenty-eight concise pages, concluding:

> At all times on March 16, 1978, Captain Weinert and his crew used their best endeavors to salvage the Amoco *Cadiz* and neither they nor anyone for whom Bugsier was responsible was in any way grossly negligent or guilty of wilful misconduct leading to the grounding of the tanker or the oil pollution damage which followed.

Twenty-eight further pages were devoted to the anatomy of the steering gear, its maintenance by Amoco, and the probable cause of its breakdown. And this section could hardly have been more disagreeable for Standard Oil or for Astilleros Espanoles. Like the Liberian inquiry before him, Judge McGarr pointed to the several glaring defects of design and construction that made the Manises steering gear a questionable product in the first place: a system of relief valves that did not relieve; a lack of a proper brake or other device to prevent the disabled rudder from swinging wildly as it was muscled around by the sea; bushings made of cast iron instead of bronze; studs and flanges that were undersized and deficient. But— and it was here that the American legal process of discovery afforded him precious information that had been hidden from the London hearing—McGarr went on to compound the horror story: To the Astilleros errors of design and building, he added the history of Amoco's astonishingly inadequate maintenance of the steering gear.

This was where Frank Cicero and all his assistants and technical experts were the most bitterly confounded: McGarr accepted the voids theory. Amoco's case was demolished.

Following McGarr's presentation, it is impossible to conclude anything else. The judge's recital of Amoco's sloppy maintenance read like a précis of Smith's indictment for PIL. Amoco, he wrote, never changed the steering-motor's oil as required by the manufacturer, never cleaned the filters, never took samples of the oil for the analysis that could have spotted contaminants, never purged the system of air, never cleaned the gravity tank or sump pump. The steering-gear room was damp and dirty, steam pipes leaked, and condensation was heavy. Further, Amoco never gave its tanker crews proper training in the maintenance of high-pressure hydraulic equipment, and never ran them through drills for dealing with emergency situations. As a result of all this, the system was leaking up to twelve liters a day by early 1978. The maximum permissible loss, McGarr said, should have been no more than one liter a month. (In this, he showed himself to be even more severe than some of the lawyers opposing Amoco, who had argued that one liter a week was an acceptable loss.) Amoco, he continued, deferred the drydockings that would have corrected the defective steering gear only for reasons of economy, with the result that void spaces formed in the hydraulic lines, and the gear blew out when it met with that March storm. One terrible sentence showed how thoroughly McGarr had been convinced by the arguments of Shell and the French parties, and how little truck he would have with Cicero's theories:

> The fact is that a wave generated a pressure peak of whatever magnitude sufficient to rupture *an underdesigned, below underspecification, badly maintained hydraulic steering system.* (emphasis added)

If Cicero's first and greatest defeat was on the technical side, his second, third, and fourth were legal. Entirely following the reasoning of the French parties, especially the excellent arguments put forward by Kingham, McGarr refused to limit liability for the pollution to Amoco Transport, the nominal owner of Amoco *Cadiz.* In spite of the elaborate charade of three separate companies, the simple fact was that "Standard is the controlling parent corporation of a large and intricate corporate structure, the companies of which, including International and Transport, exist and complement one another for the financial benefit of and to carry out the corporate will of Standard." The corporate veil, the smoke screen devised by Amoco's legal department, was well and truly pierced by the judge's commonsense logic: Amoco was responsible for the tortious acts of its subsidiaries, and therefore to the French claimants.

Cicero's third defeat concerned the limitation of damage payments that he had hoped to gain for his clients by invoking CLC, the Treaty of Brussels. Here, Judge McGarr was as straightforward as he had been in the matter of who controlled whom within the Amoco corporate structure. It had been decided that U.S. law applied to the issue of suing Amoco, he ruled, and since CLC was not U.S. law it did not apply. As simple as that—but, he added, even if CLC had applied, its provisions did not protect Amoco International or Standard Oil from lawsuits. Thus, the liability of Transport, International, and Standard Oil was joint and several: The French parties could claim damages from any one of them or all of them.

As if this were not depressing enough for Cicero and his colleagues, the judge reserved one last spoonful of gall by turning away Amoco's counterclaims against France, the departments of Finistère and Côtes-du-Nord, and the communes for negligence in preventing and cleaning up the oil spill. Whatever laws and decrees were in effect at the time of the grounding, he explained, concerned only the French versus the French. French citizens could attack their state under French law, but an American oil company could not.

With all the blows falling successively on his head, Cicero did manage, however, to salvage two points in Amoco's favor. The first was McGarr's concession that when it came time to assess the damages, Amoco's liability could be diminished to the extent that any inept cleanup efforts by the French had in fact increased the spread and the harm of the pollution. Like the damages claims themselves, this provision would have to be argued during the second trial over which he would be presiding, the one that would add up the bill of *Cadiz*'s pollution and determine how much Amoco would have to pay.

Second, and potentially much more important to Amoco, was McGarr's decision to hold Astilleros Espanoles responsible to Amoco for damages, to the degree that the builder's negligence and fault contributed to the disaster. Like the claims against France for negligent cleanup, though, this would have to be argued later. And whatever portion of the blame McGarr might assign to Astilleros, it was inevitable that Amoco would have to sue the builder in Spain in order to collect—but only after having first paid the punitive damages assessed in the second trial, which determined the damages owed. This concession of a guilt shared with Astilleros Espanoles offered Amoco the hope of cutting its losses to a certain extent. But that would depend on the kind of imponderable that a calculating businessman hates to take: that a Spanish court would show itself to be as serene in rendering justice as Frank J. McGarr had been, while making a decision that could cost dozens or even hundreds of millions of dollars to a company that was not only Spanish, but government-controlled as well. There were many long faces around 200 East Randolph Drive as the preparations for the trial on damages began to get under way.

16.

The Legacy

The human animal's notorious penchant for learning things the hard way—and most especially where his presumption about the magnificence of his creations is concerned—was quite nicely exemplified by the entire saga of Amoco *Cadiz*. What she taught about steering gears and contradictory lines of authority may not have been as dramatic as the lessons learned about metal fatigue when the English Comet jets and the American Electra turboprops began falling out of the sky, or those concerning the inaptitude of hydrogen as a lifting force when the *Hindenburg* made its last mooring in Lakehurst, New Jersey, or the inadvisability of racing through ice packs before the invention of radar, which *Titanic* demonstrated once and for all, but, everything considered, Pasquale Bardari's VLCC did a first-rate job of providing future generations with food for reflection. In the field of pollution and the jurisprudence proceeding therefrom, it was more like a banquet.

"A quelque chose malheur est bon," says an old French proverb, the rough equivalent of the ill wind that blows English-speakers no good. This was indubitably true for the hordes of scientists of all description who swooped down upon the Breton coast, making this, the worst peacetime oil spill and ecological disaster in history, also the one most thoroughly studied. On the other hand, the region's ordinary folk were less inclined to any perception of positive benefits, even many years after the fact. More than five years had passed since the grounding when I returned to Portsall, and the contrast

with March of 1978 was vivid, indeed. The little circular port was clean, sprinkled here and there with wooden fishing boats reposing on the mud, and the place smelled like low tide rather than a furnace repair shop. The main road, where you had to watch your step five and a half years earlier—many a journalist had gone ass over teakettle by rushing too recklessly over the oil-slicked pavement— was as tidy as a Swiss sidewalk, and the environing beaches and rocks bore no trace whatsoever of Arabian Light or Iranian Light. On the surface, then, everything was copacetic, but inside Les Brisants (The Breakers), the portside cafe owned by Jean-Laurent Jule, the boys were telling a somewhat less optimistic story that morning.

"It took two years before it got back to looking normal," said one of the fishermen, who was breaking his fast with a glass of *blanc sec*. "It looks fine now, but things aren't really the same. The lieu [the whiting that were traditionally associated with Portsall] are gone now, the lobsters are much rarer, and you can only find sea spiders by going much farther out than before. The crabs [étrilles] and abalone [ormeaux] are finished, and in some places the seaweed still smells of petrol. The gravettes, the little worms we use for fishing, are there under the beaches, but they're all soft now, and when we dig them up they don't stay alive as long as they used to. It's not like before."

Ironically, of all the ecological studies carried out in the aftermath of the grounding, the greatest single source of funding was none other than Amoco. Through a $2 million grant to the National Oceanographic and Atmospheric Administration (NOAA, a branch of the U.S. Department of Commerce), Amoco significantly contributed to advancing the scientific world's understanding of how oil spills act on the environment. The Amoco grant was a major factor in a vast, multidisciplined Franco-American scholarly effort that was coordinated through France's Centre Océanologique de Bretagne (COB), a division of the Centre National Pour l'Exploitation des Océans (CNEXO), and comprised thirty major scientific programs by thirteen laboratories and organizations. Up to a thousand persons were involved when the operation was at its high point. Lasting five years in all, the NOAA-CNEXO program was of a scope and a quality that destined it to become a model for future studies of oil spills, and a crucial point of reference for Judge McGarr's second trial in Chicago.

A presentation of even the preliminary conclusions of these many study programs would require a book many times the length of this one, and a corps of specialists for translating the Latin nomenclature (*Mytilus edulis* = mussels, if you really want to know). But whether they were written in Latin, French, or English, the results that began appearing in various scholarly publications spelled unanimously gloomy news for Amoco. However the oil spill was viewed, it was going to cost someone a whole lot of money—much, much more than the famous 77 million Poincaré francs of the CLC.

How much? That was the single capital question, the one to which the lawyers, scientists, politicians, and various technical experts who had been involved in the first half of Judge McGarr's trial—and those who came onstage for Act II as well—pointed their most passionate energies. This was the grail, the bottom line, the reason why they had started the frustrating, exhausting, and ruinous procedure in the first place. After McGarr's ruling on who was responsible for the mess, the time came to determine how much the culprits should be made to pay. To this question would be devoted the second half of the bifurcated trial: the damages phase. Barring an out-of-court settlement (à la ABS, but infinitely bigger), this phase promised to be just as horrendously complicated as the first one had been—if not even more so. Why? Because new ground was being broken. Jurisprudence was in the making.

Shippers have been spilling oil into the water ever since the nineteenth century, when they carried the stuff in barrels stashed in the holds of freighters, but it was only with the galloping industrialization of the post–World War II period that pollution began to become a concern, and only with the advent of the supertankers that the pollution from a single accident had the potential for causing damages on a scale unimaginable before. Add to that the Western world's suddenly urgent concern for ecology, and you have the stuff of which great lawsuits are made. Until Amoco *Cadiz* came along, no oilpot had polluted so widely and horribly, but even for smaller spills there existed no hard and fast rules for compensating victims.

In Brittany as elsewhere, it was a fiendishly difficult undertaking to determine who had suffered what, and how much the reparations should come to. For the central government, it was relatively simple: 400 to 500 million francs, the direct cost it claimed for the cleanup and cash advances to fishermen and oystermen, plus the outlay for the trial. So was it for PIL, Shell's captive insurance company: $22.9 million, the market value of its oil at the time of the wreck. The oyster farmers of the abers and in the bay of Morlaix were able to present black and white documentation on tons of stock dug up from beds and ploughed into the ground. But for the others? How can you prove with mathematical certainty that the hotels and restaurants had forty percent (or whatever other figure you choose) fewer clients? How do you show that the fish swam away from the area—and even if they did, how do you calculate the extra cost involved in taking a fishing boat farther out to sea, or to another part of the coast? And what is the cost to the shoreside population in anger, anxiety, and disgust, and to Brittany as a whole for a sullied reputation? And what about the ecological detail: What is the price of a sandworm or a seagull? What yardstick do you use to evaluate the monetary worth of a befouled littoral? Is it the same for an isolated, unpeopled tidal swamp gorged with animal life and, say, the beautifully manicured shoreline of a country club's golf course? What counts? Where do a country's sensibilities lie? Is it more criminal to rob a bank than kill a brood of trumpeter swans, sperm whales, or pandas? Or, for that matter, sandworms?

The United States, as the world's number-one consumer of oil, offered several precedents and points of reference for McGarr to consider in his deliberations. The relatively new phenomenon of ecological awareness had engendered some significant legislation on the national level, such as the Federal Water Pollution Control Act, the Trans-Alaskan Pipeline Act, and the Deepwater Port Act, which included stringent measures against hydrocarbon pollution and affirmed the principle of indemnification for damage to the environment. At the local level, several states had also made their own codes for punishment of polluters. Washington, Florida, and Virginia, for instance, had fixed tables of prices for destroyed fish, based on various criteria: the purchase cost of each type at a hatchery; estimates by the American Fisheries Society; or price scales established by the local Department of Natural Resources. California went even further into detail after a heavy pollution from an oil rig off Santa Barbara in 1969, fixing the price of each species according to the rates charged in the catalogs of supply houses specializing in selling marine animals to laboratories, and by consulting the commodity quotations of the *Los Angeles Times*. The state of Alaska opted for a straight system of fines, calculated according to the volume of pollutants and the place of the spill: $10 per gallon in a river or other freshwater milieu; $2.50 per gallon in estuaries or confined or intertidal zones; and $1 in open seawater, on open public ground, or into freshwater areas without notable aquatic life. The dollar value of the fines are regularly updated, to stay in line with inflation.

No one could tell beforehand, of course, to which of these precedents, if any, Judge McGarr would refer when it came to assessing damages. He was not bound by any, and was free to interpret as he liked. The one to which the lawyers, scientists, and academics—especially those identified with the suit of the Côtes-du-Nord parties—referred the most often was the case of *Zoe Colocotroni,* a small Greek tanker that in the early morning hours of March 18, 1973, went aground on a coral reef three miles off the southern coast of Puerto Rico. In order to free his ship, the captain dumped 5,000 tons of crude oil directly into the drink, after which the winds and tides carried the slick deeply into a virgin mangrove swamp at Bahia Sucia. The U.S. government, the government of the Commonwealth of Puerto Rico, and a group of private citizens brought action against the owner for damages to the environment. Predictably enough, lawyers for *Zoe*'s owners argued that their liability should be judged according to the traditional yardstick of the market value of the commodity that had been damaged: that is to say, a swamp, whose market value was about nil. This time, however, the courts stepped into new grounds of jurisprudence, ignored the old market-value argument, and ruled that the plaintiffs were entitled to redress for ecological damages. From appeal to appeal, the case knocked interminably around the U.S. court system—the Puerto Ricans had to learn patience long before the Bretons—but the fundamental premise of the first judgment remained: The concept of market value no longer held; the environment itself has a value.

Hundreds of scientists, academics, students, and investigators of all sorts were involved in the business of trying to put a figure on that value for Brittany, but the one who stood above all the others was Professor Claude Chassé, resident star of oceanography and marine biology at the Université de Bretagne Occidentale in Brest. His colleagues, assistants, students, and volunteer helpers studied one hundred and sixty sites along the coast, fanning out to their posts as soon as the news of the wreck was known, measuring and sampling and then awaiting the pollution to do the same again, thereby laying the foundation for a comparative study of the oil's effect. Chassé was the man who put the pieces of the puzzle together, and his work was the rock on which the Côtes-du-Nord parties built their damages case.

He was an imposing presence, Chassé. Charged with energy and mirth in spite of the weight of his responsibilities and his multiple diplomas, he was only forty-six when I met him in the sympathetic chaos of his university office, but his appearance was ageless, neither old nor young: out of time. With his long white beard, brilliant eyes, and florid countenance he looked like a refugee from the North Pole—Santa Claus!—and as he spoke of his work he leaped back and forth from subject to subject, from year to year, and from site to site, all the while flinging my way a barrage of booklets, reports, and reprints of scholarly meetings, all of them terrifyingly scientific and laden with Latin polysyllables. Read this, read this, read this, it's all there. Indeed it was, especially as concerned his masterpiece, Project Bighorn.

Chassé's interests were so wide-ranging, his joy in discovery and invention so great—he was a true synthesizer, a big-picture man who directed others, digested their mass of detail, and made it coherent, a *kapellmeister* of marine biology—that he could not resist the temptation to indulge in a triple-pronged play on words with the name of his master study. As his jump-off point for comparing the mortality rates of the coastline's intertidal and subtidal zones, he chose a common and abundant critter that was neither too delicate nor too oil-resistant, but of average survival capacity: the herbivorous gastropod known in English as periwinkle and French as bigorneau. In French, "bighorn" and "bigorneau" are pronounced exactly alike, with the sole addition of an "oh" at the end of the latter. With that, the reference to General Custer's disaster at the Battle of the Little Bighorn in 1876 was too good to miss, so he took the catalog of creatures that were available to him, rearranged them according to his fancy, and came up with a nifty acronym for the official name of his study: *"BIomasse brute des Gastropodes Herbivores Opercules des milieux Rocheux Normalisés"* (Gross Biomass of Herbivorous Operculate Gastropods in Standard Rocky Milieu), or BIGHORN. In this case, however, the Seventh Cavalry was the coastline's periwinkle population, and Sitting Bull was either Pasquale Bardari or Lord Amoco, depending on how you like to look at it.

What this investigation produced was a scale of crude-oil aggressiveness, based on the survival rate of periwinkles but including the other populations of rock and sand along the coast. Chassé discovered that survival was lowest where the pollution was the most severe, which was only logical, but also that the mortality rates dropped in relation to the length of time that the oil had been floating on the water. In other words, old oil was less toxic than new oil. Comparing the survival rates of the different species with those of the periwinkles and then taking into account the scale of crude-oil aggressiveness, he was able to calculate the losses of each species and of the totality of the biomass along the 350-odd kilometers of shoreline visited by *Cadiz*'s oil. This was the capital, "the live-stock," as he explained it to me. But there was also the interest to consider, the offspring never born because of the progenitors that were wiped out.

Predictably, he found the toll heavy. Although no species was entirely erased by the pollution, many were significantly diminished and others affected in odd ways, like the sickly, malformed sand-worms and the fish with pustulant skin surfaces and damaged ovaries, possibly unable to reproduce. Extrapolating from his con-trol sites, Chassé calculated that the "capital" of animals immedi-ately destroyed and the "interest" of offspring that would never be born on these polluted shores came to approximately 400,000 tons of biomass wiped out by the *Cadiz* pollution.

Because the natural balance of the ecosystem had been dis-turbed, several anomalies appeared in the wake of the grounding, certain of which were readily apparent, even to the nonscientific eye. There was a surprising proliferation of prawns, for example, which were attracted to the most heavily polluted fields of algae, because tiny crustaceans had found their happiness there, reproducing in great numbers. The prawns in turn ate the crustaceans and thrived as never before. So it was with the seaweed, which in the first few months after the grounding appeared to have suffered terrible dam-age. It soon became apparent that it was precisely the opposite that had occurred: The seaweed was still flourishing richly when I re-turned in 1983, and the little wooden boats with the hand-cranked cranes and the L-shaped picking arms bobbed contentedly among the shoals near Portsall, winching in fine harvests. There were two theories to explain this unexpected bounty: stimulation of the algae's growth hormones by some mysterious chemistry of crude oil; and the death of many seaweed-eating predators. Windfalls of this sort were depressingly rare, however. In general, the plot of the story ran in the other direction.

"Bacteria recover in a few hours," said Chassé. "Plankton in a month, and small animals in a year. But for the 'noble' animals, like lobsters and the large crabs, one generation means twenty or twenty-five years. So we will have to wait until the year two thou-sand to have a complete recovery here."

So where do you put the price tag, and what do you set it at?

For *Zoe Colocotroni,* the courts made a stab at it by estimating the cost of replacing the mangrove swamp's fauna at six cents per animal. California, as we have seen, now has an official price list: so much for a sandworm and so much for a seagull. For NOAA, which in July of 1983 issued its much awaited report on the Amoco *Cadiz* disaster, there were "no credible methods for making monetary estimates of the estimated physical losses of noncommercial marine biomass and seabirds," but Chassé did not agree. He was prepared to make the plunge and put a figure, in dollars, on the cost of making the Breton coast well again. In fact, he reasoned, it was absolutely necessary both for present Brittany and other littorals in the future, to put it in terms of dollars and cents, as ecological signposts that even the most myopic of corporations would be able to read.

"We are in a merchant society," he had written in one of the papers that he flung my way that afternoon in Brest, "where everything without a price tag is scorned, considered as worthless, where interests in conflict have nothing but their financial weight. This is why all the aspects of a catastrophe must be expressed in monetary terms, even if mere monetary award cannot take the measure of the contemptuous insult felt by the shoreline dwellers, the esthetic injuries, the loss of beauty, the feelings of disgust and moral disarray or the disturbance to the ecosystem. For want of a better way, we must put a value on everything, in order to dissuade and prevent.

"It must become more expensive to pollute, even if reparations are paid, than to take adequate measures of safety and prevention."

Dissuade and prevent. Chassé's words recalled the vengeful cries that so many journalists had heard around Brittany after the disaster, like the politician who had sworn that Standard Oil would be made to "pay in blood." Even Mayor Legendre of Portsall, who appeared to be the least vindictive of men, had urged that Amoco be "punished" for the pollution, because only through such draconian measures could the big companies be made to understand that safety was the best investment. When I spoke with him, Chassé pulled in his horns somewhat, and used more of the language of the diplomat.

"We are not seeking punitive damages," he insisted, "but only justice. We don't want to break Standard Oil of Indiana, and we don't expect to. But international law is silent on this matter, and jurisprudence is still in the making. The law is not something that is pickled or frozen—it is made every day. The final decision will depend on the wisdom of the judge, but for us the principle of the extinction of the debt must be based on the entire recovery of the life that was damaged. There are several ways to calculate this, but no matter which one you use, it adds up to a terrible bill."

Using the California system of assigning commercial value to animals destroyed, Chassé rated the bill at a minimum five 1978 francs per kilo. Applied to his figure of an estimated biomass loss of 400,000 tons, this made two billion 1978 francs. With the wild fluctuations of exchange rates over the years, it was difficult to translate this into an immutable figure for dollars. At four francs to the dollar (the approximate 1978 value), this made $500 million; at eight francs to the dollar (approximate 1983 figure), $250 million; at ten francs to the dollar, $200 million.

Chassé's sum covered only damage to the littoral. Cleanup costs, losses to tourism and business, and the value of the cargo itself would be added on top of it. NOAA's experts released their final report in 1983, and it proved to be considerably less alarming, estimating a total cost of the disaster (including the ship, its cargo, the cleanup, business and tourism losses, and ecological damages) at about one billion 1978 francs, plus or minus an error range of twenty percent, for a dollar figure of "only" $190 to $290 million, all in. In spite of the fact that this was well below the total that Chassé's figures would have given, it completely dominated the estimated costs of any of the other great "historical" oil spills: *Torrey Canyon,* $73.8 million; Santa Barbara, $28.8 million; *Zoe Colocotroni,* $21.2 million.

Naturally, the figures were contestable, as diligently and sincerely as all the experts had worked in the five years of their study—and Amoco could be counted upon to contest them to the bitter end. Just as Chassé said, jurisprudence was amaking, and Frank J. McGarr was in a position to be one of the most important artisans of change and precedent. But how would he determine the price tags? Henri Smets of OECD summed up the damages dilemma with a little conundrum worthy of Gertrude Stein: "What is a seagull worth? The same price per kilo as a chicken? I don't know the answer."

Beyond the matter of the direct responsibility for the accident, the whodunnit that Judge McGarr's liability ruling sought to unravel, the wreck of the Amoco *Cadiz* left the world at large with a legacy that was twofold: the harvest of scientific information from Chassé and the dozens of other scholars who came to the Breton coast; and, on the legal side, the chance to push a bit further into the jungle of inchoate jurisprudence, and contribute to modern theory of compensation for damage to the ecology. McGarr was perhaps not prepared to name the price of a seagull or a sandworm, but he had, in his Chicago courtroom, more information on this subject, and more able lawyers to interpret it, than any other magistrate in history—which, of course, explains why the trial dragged on for so many years.

In the domain of shipping, Captain Bardari's misfortune resulted in an amended set of IMO requirements for steering gear being written into the Safety of Life At Sea (SOLAS) Convention, most notably one section that called for a switching system capable of automatically shutting down a damaged side of a hydraulic servomotor and activating the other side in its place. If Amoco *Cadiz* had been built with such a device, the chances are good that the Manises would not have bled three-quarters of the way to death before the engineers could arrive on the run and begin shutting down valves, and the tanker probably could have made it safely to Lyme Bay.

Significantly, IMO also called for tankers to be better equipped for emergency towing and, in 1979, adopted a resolution recommending that participating governments take steps to safeguard the authority of ships' masters, protect them from the threat of unwarranted dismissal, and insure that their decisions regarding the safety of their ships and the protection of the environment not be impugned by owners, charterers, or any other persons. IMO is far too diplomatic an organization to name any names, but the hint this time seemed as big as a barn.

For the Brittany shoreline, Amoco *Cadiz* provided the shock that prodded the French government to take actions that had already been planned, to be sure, but that should have been taken earlier: the stationing of powerful salvage tugs fulltime at Brest (and at Toulon and Cherbourg at the same time, to cover the Mediterranean and northern sectors); the institution of a new traffic separation scheme, developed in consultation with IMO, for moving tankers and other vessels carrying dangerous cargo farther out to sea, away from Ouessant; increasing the navy's budget to improve its patrolling capacities, especially in the mouth of the Channel; and, probably the most important of all, the building of an entirely new, ultramodern Centre Régional Opérationel de Surveillance et de Sauvetage (Regional Operations Center for Surveillance and Rescue, known in French by the initials CROSS) at Corsen Point, the westernmost tip of land in France, some 10 kilometers north of Le Conquet, where Chaput, Leborgne, and their friends at the radio station had exchanged messages with the tanker and the tug years before. The spanking new CROSS installation acts exactly like an air-traffic control center, identifying and following every ship that passes out in the Channel. With this efficient instrument at its disposal, it is unlikely that France will ever again "loose" a VLCC in the cracks between administrations, as it did with the Amoco *Cadiz*.

The safety will never be total, though. With or without navigational aids, the eighty-five nautical miles that separate Ouessant from Lizard Point on England's southwest shore are the densest maritime crossroads anywhere in the world. Such is the result of geography, history, and the great wealth that commerce has brought to Western Europe since the Industrial Revolution. Into and out of the approaches to the Channel pass something like a billion tons of merchandise a year, or a quarter of the world's circulation of goods. Nowhere else in the world is there such a concentration of maritime freight. More than a million tons of crude oil pass off Ouessant every day for an average of 750 tons a minute. Up and down, back and forth, the interminable commerce goes on, and more than three hundred boats take the route in one direction or another between Ouessant and Lizard, day in and day out. The figures are an awesome reflection of the power of trade, but they are also sobering and a bit frightening: This is equivalent to the entire world's population of boats squeezing through these eighty-five nautical miles twice a year. There's only so much room out there, and the boats always seem to be in a hurry. When they are costing their owners two or three thousand dollars a day—or more—just to keep them crewed and in condition to navigate, the constraints, slowdowns, and queuing-up demanded by a traffic lane system tend to be interpreted with considerable poetic license by skippers who have reports to fill out and deadlines to meet and vice presidents looking over their shoulders from distant boardrooms. As a result, the skippers are tempted to take chances. A few years ago, two laden VLCCs nearly collided in the Channel because they were racing to be the first to catch the pilot into Rotterdam.

No, that kind of lunacy doesn't happen every day, thank God, but there is some dangerous chemistry in the air when you have so many big ships with such expensive cargoes in such a small space. Boats are fallible, men are ambitious, and men make mistakes. The fact that Amoco *Cadiz* demonstrated a quite unusual degree of fallibility, mistakes, and misguided ambition does not mean that the magic formula of corporate expedience will never again influence events in the world's shipping lanes. Quite obviously, it will. Given the numbers of vessels on the world's commercial waters, and given the nature of the human beast, this is a mathematical certainty. The next escalation in the record book of ecological horrors might be in Japan or the United States or South Africa or Indonesia. There are plenty of possibilities, plenty of choice spots where the atoms of commerce can link up with those of bad luck and bad judgment to form the critical mass of potential tragedy. When it happens, the world at large will briefly read about the poisonous pall inflicted upon some place equally obscure as the Breton coastline, then turn the page and forget about it. More dead birds.

Every other place outside of your own immediate area, it seems, is obscure and, finally, unimportant. The delegation of Breton mayors discovered this fundamental but still distressing truth when they flew into America ready to answer questions, and found that no one had any. Brittany didn't count. Hardly anyone knew where Brittany was. And, then, all of that was so long ago . . . You never miss the water till the well runs dry, and you never realize how bad it can be unless it happens to you. That's how it is with another fundamental truth: that oil spills represent only about three or four percent of the pollution of the earth's waters. The rest is the perpetual drip, drip, drip of the industrial, productivist society: industry, municipalities, small businesses, garages, and simply private citizens, all of them dumping their wastes down the drain and forgetting about them.

No one is to blame and everyone is to blame. It just happened that fate descended and plucked up Pasquale Bardari as a symbol for the rest of us to gaze at for a moment, a mirror for a fleeting glimpse of ourselves. And to bring the wheel full circle and settle firmly into place the ironies that govern human existence, let us recall that only a few years before the wreck of the Amoco *Cadiz,* the progressive citizens of Brest had been lobbying to have their magnificent roadstead selected as a site for a petroleum refinery that was then in the planning stage. There was much bitter disappointment when they lost and the refinery was built elsewhere.

Index